Modernism and Negritude

Modernism and Negritude

The Poetry and Poetics of Aimé Césaire

A. James Arnold

Harvard University Press
Cambridge, Massachusetts
London, England   1981

Publication of this book has been aided by a grant from the
Andrew W. Mellon Foundation.

Library of Congress Cataloging in Publication Data

Arnold, Albert James.
    Modernism and negritude.
    Includes bibliographical references and index.
    1. Césaire, Aimé—Criticism and interpretation.
2. Blacks—Race identity.   I. Title.
PQ3949.C44Z53   841   80–29007
ISBN 0–674–58057–5

For Jo

Contents

Acknowledgments

I am grateful to the colleagues who read my final draft and offered many useful suggestions for revision: Roger Shattuck and Alfred MacAdam of the University of Virginia and Thomas A. Hale of Pennsylvania State University. The flaws remaining are my responsibility; their generous assistance has helped me to avoid others.

The American Council of Learned Societies made it possible for me to undertake this project as a Fellow in 1975–1976, and the University of Virginia assigned me to its Center for Advanced Studies as an Associate during that year. The National Endowment for the Humanities provided a Summer Stipend in 1977 to explore new directions and resolve problems encountered along the way. The University of Virginia made available a stipend for research in the summer of 1978, which ensured the completion of the book. To all these sources of financial support I express my sincere thanks.

I am happy to acknowledge the sources of the poetry quoted in this book and to thank the following publishers for granting their permission:

Editions Gallimard, Paris, for selected passages from *Les Armes miraculeuses* by Aimé Césaire, copyright © 1946 by Librairie Gallimard, copyright © 1970 by Editions Gallimard, reprinted 1976 by Editions Désormeaux, Fort-de-France, Martinique; for "Zone" and "La Jolie Rousse" from *Oeuvres poétiques* by Guillaume Apollinaire, copyright © 1965 by Editions Gallimard; for "L'Immaculée Conception" by André Breton and Paul Eluard from *Oeuvres complètes*, vol. 1, by Paul Eluard, copyright © 1968 by Editions Gallimard; for "Pour fêter une enfance" by Saint-John Perse from *Eloges and Other Poems*, copyright © 1953 by Librairie Gallimard, copyright © 1960 by Editions Gallimard; for "Le Cimetière marin" from *Oeuvres*, vol. 1, by Paul Valéry, copyright © 1957 by Editions Gallimard.

Société Nouvelle Présence Africaine, Paris, for parts of *Cahier d'un retour au pays natal* by Aimé Césaire, copyright © 1956, 1971 by Editions Présence Africaine; for *Notebook of a Return to the Native Land*, translated by Clayton Eshleman and Annette Smith, which first appeared in *Montemora*, 1979; for "Réponse à Depestre" by Aimé Césaire from *Présence Africaine*, April–July 1955, reprinted by Editions Désormeaux as "Le Verbe marronner" in *Oeuvres complètes*, vol. 1, by Aimé Césaire.

Editions du Seuil, Paris, for selected passages from *Cadastre* by Aimé Césaire, copyright © 1961 by Editions du Seuil, reprinted 1976 by Editions Désormeaux in *Oeuvres complètes*, vol. 1, by Aimé Césaire; for passages from *Cadastre* translated by Emile Snyder and Sanford Upson, copyright © 1973 by The Third Press, Joseph Okpaku Publishing Co.; for passages from *Soleil Coucoupé* by Aimé Césaire, copyright © 1948 by K Editeur, reprinted 1970 by Kraus Reprint; for selected passages of *Ferrements* by Aimé Césaire, copyright © 1960 by Editions du Seuil, reprinted 1976 by Editions Désormeaux in *Oeuvres complètes*, vol. 1, by Aimé Césaire.

Editeurs Français Réunis, Paris, for "Sales Nègres" from *La Montagne ensorcelée* by Jacques Roumain, copyright © 1972 by Les Editeurs Français Réunis.

Société Nouvelle des Editions Pauvert, Paris, for "La Providence tourne" by André Breton and an untitled poem by André Masson from *Martinique charmeuse de serpents* by André Breton, copyright © 1972 by Jean-Jacques Pauvert.

Edinburgh University Press, for Graham Dunstan Martin's translation of "The Graveyard by the Sea" by Paul Valéry, copyright © 1971 by Graham Dunstan Martin.

Editions Seghers, Paris, for permission to translate a passage of *L'Immaculée Conception* by André Breton and Paul Eluard from *Oeuvres complètes*, vol. 1, by Paul Eluard, copyright © 1968 by Editions Gallimard.

Princeton University Press, for the Louise Varèse translation of "To Celebrate a Childhood" by Saint-John Perse, from *Eloges and Other Poems*, Bollingen Series LV, copyright © 1956 by Princeton University Press; and for permission to cite in English "Le Cimetière marin" by Paul Valéry, *The Collected Works in English*, Bollingen Series XLV, vol. 1, *Poems*, trans. David Paul, copyright © 1971 by Princeton University Press.

My translation of "Zone" and "The Pretty Redhead" by Guillaume Apollinaire is published by permission of New Directions, New York, publishers of Guillaume Apollinaire's *Selected Writings*, translated by Roger Shattuck, copyright © 1950 by New Directions.

Modernism and Negritude

Prologue: Being Black and Being French

MANY CONNOISSEURS have placed Aimé Césaire in the first rank of mid-twentieth century French poets. He is also a writer of great prestige in Third World nations, where he has been read primarily for his ideological message. The decolonization of culture has been the principal theme of Césaire's popular influence, whereas in Europe and North America he is appreciated by a public who consider him the heir to the poetics of surrealism. These two readerships share so few common assumptions that when they approach Césaire's work, each draws from it something bearing a minimal resemblance to what most concerns the other. This situation is by no means unique, but it deserves careful attention because it is symptomatic of two quite different views of the role of literature in contemporary life. In one view Aimé Césaire represents the late flowering of a French brand of modernism; he is read therefore as a poet in the belletristic tradition that culminates in a posture of revolt and in the practice of metaphor as ambiguity. In the other view, this same writer is considered to be one of the principal ideologists of negritude, which some readers interpret as a progressive movement of liberation, while others see it as an obfuscation of sociopolitical realities. Who is this Janus?

Aimé Césaire was born on 26 June 1913 in the small town of Basse-Pointe in the north of Martinique, where his mother was a dressmaker and his father held a minor bureaucratic post as a tax inspector. Aimé was the second of six children. His family's way of life was close to that of the rural poor, but the level of education of both his father and his paternal grandfather, as well as the father's status as a functionary, set them apart and provided the children with a nurturing environment in which being black and being French were not perceived as conflicting aspects of existence.

Fernand Césaire, Aimé's grandfather, although born only twenty
years after the abolition of slavery by the French, managed to
acquire sufficient education to become a schoolteacher and to be
promoted into the secondary school system before his early
death at age twenty-eight in 1896. The extent of his accomplishment can be measured against an official statistic: in 1880 there
were considered to be no more than one hundred fifty children in
Martinique who could benefit from a secondary school education.
Fernand Césaire was then twelve years old and may be presumed
to have been one of that elite group.

Fernand Césaire's widow, Eugénie, was by all accounts a remarkable woman who exercised considerable moral authority
and was a kind of spiritual adviser to the people around her.
Grandmother Eugénie assumed the important role of first teacher
of the Césaire children. Under her tutelage Aimé learned to read
and write by age four, two years before entering primary school.
His close daily contact with this grandmother, who he recalls as
having been pronouncedly African in physical type, left a permanent impression on the young boy. The terms in which he described her to M. a M. Ngal in 1967 suggest that Césaire's strong
affective bond to the "African" grandmother may have had a part
in his special appreciation of Mother Africa as a young man.[1]

Aimé Césaire has accredited the existence of a heroic ancestor,
who is presumed to have founded the paternal line (a pious belief
for which there is no solid evidence): a slave or freedman named
Césaire who was involved in an uprising in December 1833 in the
locality of Grand'Anse. The lawyer for the ninety-three code-
fendants, who were tried, condemned to death, and subsequently
pardoned by the king of France, presented Césaire as a timid,
simple young man, scarcely capable of leading a slave rebellion,
but who had the misfortune of being in the vicinity at the time of
the burning and looting. This rather undistinguished figure came
to represent in Aimé Césaire's mind the prototype of the noble
African who led a just revolt against intolerable conditions of
servitude: "I have never known from what part of Africa my ancestor came. He had been freed and had taken part in an insurrection in the north of Martinique and had been condemned to
death under Louis-Philippe. I know that Benjamin Constant spoke
on the Césaire affair in the Chamber. There is in my family a
tradition of political struggle for the freedom of blacks. I believe

that influenced me a great deal" (quoted in Ngal, p. 257, note 10). Benjamin Constant may have been eloquent, and his literary reputation certainly adds luster to this version of the events, but the suggestion that he participated in this scenario testifies to its literary nature: at the time of the trial Constant had been dead for over three years. Ngal has built a good case for Aimé Césaire's having made an imaginary identification with a heroic progenitor who, as it happens, bears a compelling resemblance to his first dramatic hero, the Rebel of *And the Dogs Were Silent (Et les chiens se taisaient)*. Whether or not the Césaire of 1833 was in fact his ancestor, the stature of culture hero that Aimé Césaire has ascribed to him is a fact of another order. It testifies to the kind of support he received from his family, in terms both real and intangible, and to their importance in his eventual affirmation of the values of Africanness, or negritude. In the timid young man condemned to death in 1833 Aimé Césaire had found his Kunta Kinte.

The long poem *Notebook of a Return to the Native Land (Cahier d'un retour au pays natal)* evokes the grim living conditions of the speaker's family in such a way as to convey a poetical rather than an autobiographical truth. The reader of Montaigne's *Essais* could conclude that he was an only child, whereas he had five brothers. Through a similar rearrangement of the facts, Césaire's speaker is given six brothers and sisters instead of his own five. The mother is presented as endlessly pedaling her Singer to make ends meet, without ever really succeeding, and the father is a worried breadwinner, both given to fantasy and consumed by a gnawing poverty, alternating between tender melancholy and flaming anger. The poverty of the Césaire family was like that of other black Martinicans of their status. They were different not so much in the degree of their poverty as in their will to rise out of it. Four of the six children managed, through merit and perseverance, to join the ranks of the functionaries whose task it was to administer the French Empire. Of the two sisters, Mireille became an English teacher in the lycée of Fort-de-France, while Denise became a magistrate in Dakar, the capital of Senegal. The third son, Georges, completed a doctorate in pharmacology and taught in the University of Dakar. The eldest and youngest sons, Omer and Arsène, remained permanently in Martinique, the one in business, the other working as a typographer. This is an extraordinary success story for a black family in Martinique in the 1930s.

The combined influence of the paternal grandmother and the father, also named Fernand, had the determining role in turning the children toward success within the educational and administrative system provided by France. Primary education was free and universal. Secondary education, leading to the possibility of university training in France, required that families outside Fort-de-France make considerable sacrifices to send a child to the Lycée Schoelcher, the only secondary school for Guadeloupe, Guiana, and Martinique until after the Second World War. The Césaire family not only made this sacrifice, eventually moving to Fort-de-France; they also arranged for several of their children, including Aimé, to receive a basic musical education and to study piano. Aimé Césaire's later political evolution naturally owes something to the particular conditions of his early upbringing. Although black and poor, he did not belong to the class of agricultural laborers as did the vast majority of black Martinicans in a society where the principal industry had always been the cultivation of sugar cane and, later, of bananas. The Césaire family had already been for two generations a part of that tiny fraction of the black population that was struggling to rise into the middle class. This was of course anything but a privileged environment, but it did offer to Aimé Césaire and his brothers and sisters the minimal conditions necessary to succeed within the existing system.

Acquiring the French language and its culture was the paramount social goal for black children born into these circumstances. Creole is the first language of all black Martinicans; but it has always been the servile language in the scheme of social, economic, and political power obtaining in French-dominated societies in the Caribbean. To be exclusively a Creole speaker is to be a nigger. In order to eventually affirm blackness as a positive value, Martinicans of Césaire's generation had first to master the language of the colonial authority. Aimé Césaire did this through the schools, of course, but the function of language and culture in his home environment had special importance. There was for Césaire a symbolic value in his being given the keys to French language and culture by the grandmother he identified with the Senegalese physical type of Casamance, as he has described her. Grandmother Eugénie could as well have communicated with Aimé exclusively in Creole, the ordinary household idiom. She did not, and the rest of the family did not, as far as we know.[2]

The family's conscious effort to inculcate French cultural norms is indicative of their middle-class aspirations. The program was remarkably successful, to judge by the results. Fernand Césaire's classical education was put to practical use in the rearing of his children, to whom he would read the French prose classics and the poetry of Victor Hugo. The Frenchness of the family circle marked the Césaires as different from other poor blacks and made it much easier for their children to acclimate themselves in the somewhat alien surroundings of the lycée.

It is important for the reader who is unfamiliar with Creole society to realize that, though French language and ways may come to be second nature to educated blacks, they are not first nature. They have been acquired at the cost of repressing their Creoleness, and these repressed affective relations are likely to return in unexpected and disguised forms. Frantz Fanon wrote eloquently and with the passion of personal experience on this subject in *Black Skin, White Masks*. Because of his family's concerted effort in this direction, Aimé Césaire repressed Creole in favor of French quite completely and at a very early age. He was consequently even less able than other writers of his generation to envisage Creole as a vehicle for Martinican cultural expression. Creole was never a real choice for him precisely because of the dynamics of culture and power to which he was introduced as a young child. As a writer and a poet, Césaire would be faced much later with the painful task of cutting through those knots he had tied in the process of becoming assimilated into the French world. The North American reader may find it useful to consider the analogy or the immigrant experience in the United States. To become Americans, immigrants had to identify themselves with an alien language, culture, and history. This process took place largely in the schools, as it has for black Martinicans. Black Americans will understand better than most others the extent to which the question of color complicates and subsumes all other questions. Bearing in mind the various elements of the analogy, one can best sense the nature of Césaire's predicament as a future artist by describing him as an immigrant within his own very small, insular society.

Class and caste have historically been inseparable in the French West Indies. While there exists no parallel to the legalized racial segregation that followed upon the abolition of slavery in the

United States, blacks have been very effectively held at the bottom of a rigid tripartite social arrangement. V. S. Naipaul, who knows intimately the British version of West Indian colonialism, commented on the significant difference of the French West Indies in *The Middle Passage:* "If the French have exported their civilization to Martinique they have also exported their social structure. The hard social prejudices of the metropolitan bourgeoisie have coalesced with the racial distinctions derived from slavery to produce the most organized society in the West Indies."[3]

Until the middle of the nineteenth century, or as long as the Martinican plantation economy used the slave labor of imported Africans, it was common for the mulatto offspring of white masters and black slave women to be given their freedom and often a parcel of land. At the end of the eighteenth century this rapidly developing ethnic caste of some twelve thousand individuals in Martinique already held one-third of the titles to property and owned a quarter of the slaves.[4] At the time of the abolition of slavery in 1848 this numerous and relatively comfortable caste was in a position to become a true middle class, dominating the professions and that part of commerce not already controlled by the large landowners. Today the planters, or *békés* as they are called in Creole, represent scarcely more than a hundred families and about one percent of the population. Their effective control of the island's economy, however, has made them redoubtable adversaries of any broad social reform. Neither does the mulatto middle class have anything to gain from a shift of power into the hands of the numerically superior poor blacks. The rigidity of this social scheme has changed only in degree in the last hundred years. When Aimé Césaire was a student, 208 proprietors, or 3 percent of all landowners in Martinique, held 61 percent of the cultivable soil.[5] Under these conditions the university, and the promise it offered for social advancement, was the only positive alternative to wretched poverty and very real social domination.

The French colonial system in the West Indies used a network of recruitment to attract the most promising young minds, form them in a proper Cartesian mold, and offer them careers as administrators in its overseas empire. Martinicans had for some time been prominent in this field, since the principal recruiting point for the Caribbean was the Lycée Schoelcher in Fort-de-France. At age eleven Aimé Césaire entered the system of which he would ultimately become one of the most paradoxical products. At the Lycée Schoelcher he met Léon-Gontran Damas from Guiana, who would later join him in formulating the ideology of negritude. Damas and Césaire together organized two soccer teams at their school, Light-Foot and Good Hope. Between the ages of twelve and fifteen Césaire demonstrated considerable enthusiasm for team sports and already showed signs of leadership. Soccer and reading were his great passions, and according to his sister Mireille, he would react very physically to interruptions of his reading. By age fifteen the rigors of the intellectual competition in which he was seriously engaged obliged Césaire to give up soccer and sport entirely. From then on he was to be an intellectual.

He was described by Gilbert Gratiant, one of his teachers of this period, as being "extremely nice. No difficulties. He did everything very well. Gentleness itself. The most gentle of children. Césaire was so perfect that it seemed abnormal. A very gracious little boy. I wasn't astonished to see him succeed" (quoted by Ngal, p. 29). This testimony concurs with that of many others who have dealt with Césaire as a private person. His impeccable and genuine politeness nonetheless coexisted with a tumultuous, seething spirit that eventually expressed itself in equally genuine, if literary, violence. Much later Césaire came to see himself as a volcanic personality, making the comparison with Mt. Pelé, which dominates the Martinican landscape and in 1902 erupted unexpectedly, wiping out St. Pierre, the old capital of the colony.

One teacher stands out for the special encouragement he gave to a worthy but clearly underprivileged young scholar at the lycée. Eugène Revert was a geographer of considerable note who undertook to interest his students in their physical environment, an otherwise ordinary thing for a teacher to do, except that the centralization of the French educational system meant that Martinicans would receive the same examination questions as their peers in Lyons or Quimper. The result of this system, when applied to the French colonies, was that blacks learned about their ancestors the Gauls and about viticulture rather than sugar-cane culture. As Ngal has pointed out, Dr. Revert certainly contributed to awakening Aimé Césaire to the capital importance, for a society beneath the tropics, of the unique fauna and flora and to the peculiar geographical characteristics of Martinique. All of these aspects of Martinican life would later be incorporated into Césaire's poetry in such a way as to set off its un-French character. It was Eugène Revert who identified Aimé Césaire as a candidate for the premier institution of the French intellectual meritocracy, the Ecole Normale Supérieure in Paris; and it was Revert who recommended him to the Parisian Lycée Louis-le-Grand, in which Césaire was to prep for entrance to "Normale." On his graduation from the Lycée Schoelcher in 1931 Césaire took prizes in French, Latin, English, and history and was designated the best student overall.

When Césaire left Fort-de-France and Martinique behind, he did so with a light heart. He is quoted by Ngal as saying, "Whereas the thought of exile saddened most of my classmates, it brought joy to me: Paris, a promise of fulfillment; in fact, I was not at ease in the Antillean world" (p. 33). In 1931 there was no thought of an eventual heroic return to his native land. That phase of Césaire's life, and the spiritual revolution it presupposed, were to come about in Paris, during an eight-year stay that brought both unhoped-for stimulation and growing awareness of the social and psychological realities of colonialism. In September of 1931 began the long, arduous process of competitive examinations for places in the Ecole Normale Supérieure. Four more years of intellectual cramming were the necessary prerequisite. At the Lycée Louis-le-Grand he met two African students who were to have an important personal influence on his sense of values as a black: Ousmane Socé and Léopold Senghor, both from Senegal. Senghor was to become the first president of the independent Republic of Senegal, and Ousmane Socé his first ambassador to the United States. Senghor joined Césaire and Damas in 1934–1935 in a collective venture intended to bring together on the common ground of blackness the students from Africa and those from the West Indies. The future colonial administrators from the Caribbean had tended as a group to look down on the Africans as uncivilized savages, considering themselves to be European in culture if not in pigmentation. The Martinicans in particular were more aggressive politically, but their sociopolitical models were as European as their literary culture. Even their frontal attack on the administration of the West Indian colonies in 1932 had taken its title from a surrealist predecessor: *Légitime Défense*. As Césaire said to the Haitian poet

René Depestre in 1967, the protesters of *Légitime Défense* "were Communists, and therefore we supported them. But very soon I had to reproach them—and perhaps I owe this to Senghor—for being French Communists. There was nothing to distinguish them either from the French surrealists or from the French Communists."[6]

Aimé Césaire did not participate in *Légitime Défense*, and one must assume on the available evidence that he did not share its Marxist conviction that culture renewal must be preceded by political revolution. He and his fellow students writing for *L'Etudiant noir*, which published five or six issues before succumbing in 1936 to poor sales and political pressure, were divided on this central point. Only the issue for March 1935 appears to have survived; in it Césaire took a firm stand against the cultural assimilation of blacks. It was in this context that he coined the neologism *négritude*, calling for a resurrection of black values. Both Senghor and Damas attributed paternity of the term to Césaire's writing in their student newspaper. His African friends certainly were a decisive influence on his new sense of belonging to an ethnic community. Their experience of being rooted in black history through African language and tribal customs was surely communicated to him as an ideal relation to life, one of which West Indians had been deprived by reason of the combined effects of colonialism and slavery. Given these differences in background, it was inevitable that the concept of negritude should ultimately come to mean something quite different for the African statesman and poet, who used it as the cornerstone of a political position, and for the Martinican parliamentarian and writer.[7]

Numerous personal reminiscences by fellow students at the Ecole Normale Supérieure offer a composite picture of a young man who was cordial but reserved, sometimes merry but more given to intellectual wit. An anecdote from 1933–1934, related to M. a M. Ngal by J.-B. Barrère, who had known Césaire slightly at Louis-le-Grand before joining his study group at Normale, revealed a first-rate student who had the nerve to needle the professor and regale the class while giving a letter-perfect answer to a question on Roman history. Professor Roubaud's course was not particularly entertaining and Césaire's behavior in this instance points to a will to challenge authority as well as to be favorably noticed by his peers.

Among the students who remember him best from those days, Césaire also stood out for his lack of religion. He appears not to have experienced any religious crisis in the usual sense during childhood or adolescence, possibly owing to his father's pronounced views as a freethinker. The Catholic church, into which Martinicans are customarily born, came to represent for Césaire at an early age the spiritual arm of French colonialism. There was never any question in his mind of reconciling Catholic belief with the values of the black world, a project that was to become a permanent feature of Senghor's version of negritude. During the early years of Césaire's apprenticeship as a future professor—for that was his goal at the time—he was primarily engaged in absorbing the masterpieces of French and European culture. The original contradiction in the concept of negritude can be found in Césaire's biography: he articulated the necessity of a refusal of cultural assimilation at the very moment when he was most involved in that process of assimilation, while preparing for the entrance examinations to the Ecole Normale Supérieure.

Those examinations in the summer of 1935 took a great toll on Aimé Césaire's health. He had not in fact been expected to pass, a situation that surely heightened the stress surrounding them. J.-B. Barrère has recounted to Ngal how he learned the happy but unexpected news that he and Césaire were to be admitted to Normale. Césaire visited Yugoslavia during the summer vacation with his friend and classmate Petar Guberina. During their stay on the Adriatic coast Césaire's memories of Martinique were stirred, quite possibly by the linguistic proximity of the name of the Yugoslavian island of Martinska to the name of his own island home. It was at that time that he began the first notes that resulted some four years later in the prewar version of *Notebook of a Return to the Native Land*.[8] Césaire spent the next summer vacation in Martinique after an absence of nearly five years. This new contact with his own milieu proved deeply disturbing. He found himself in 1936 quite removed from the conditions of spiritual and material impoverishment of his homeland. The shock of this encounter with an old experience served to stimulate his writing. During the academic year 1937–38 Césaire continued to work on the poem while completing a Diplôme d'Etudes Supérieures on the theme of the South in black American literature. Like other documents from his early years, including youthful, imitative poetry and the draft of a novel, this thesis survives only as a reminiscence. If one draws on the evidence in the magazine *Tropiques*, one may infer at this period a considerable admiration for the poetry of James Weldon Johnson, Jean Toomer, and Claude McKay.

The Harlem Renaissance was known to black students in Paris, in part through the literary and artistic salon of the four Nardal sisters, Martinicans, and the *Revue du monde noir* (1931–1932), which Paulette Nardal organized in collaboration with a Haitian, Dr. Sajous. Césaire read the *Revue du monde noir* during his first year in Paris and through it became acquainted with the writings of Langston Hughes and Alain Locke, as well as the poets just mentioned. René Maran, the author of the novel *Batouala,* which had received the Goncourt Prize in 1921 and received the further honor of being banned in the French colonies in Africa, had his own open house on Fridays, which attracted black Americans in Paris. Although Senghor frequented them, Aimé Césaire had little contact with these salons, for reasons that are indicative of his own social orgins and his future evolution. He considered them too bourgeois, too *mulatto*—a term that described quite perfectly the Martinican middle class at the time—and too Catholic. Despite the revelation of important black American writers, the *Revue du monde noir* was seen by Césaire as "superficial," as he said to Ngal in 1967. In Césaire's eyes, the positive benefits of the Nardal group's dissemination of information about Africa was overshadowed by the social orientation of the *Revue du monde noir,* which served to preserve the status quo while exhibiting the relative prestige and the advantages of a colored elite. This group prided itself on what it thought to be its perfect assimilation into French society—the very attitude Césaire would soon be compelled to reject and oppose. The real sources of Césaire's concept of negritude were in his extensive reading and in the personal inspiration of Senghor's Africa. Césaire seems to have accepted with good grace and perhaps a little pride the Ethiopian title *ras*, bestowed on him by one of his white peers in the study group, or *turne*, at the Ecole Normale Supérieure.[9] It may well have fed the imaginary identification with noble Africans that he was beginning to cultivate in the mid-thirties; he would later express that identification in his poetry as a unique heroic persona.

By 1939, when Césaire returned to Martinique for the longest uninterrupted stay of his adult life, he had acquired the mental set that would nourish his literary and political activity for the next decade. He had constructed a personal version of literary modernism that was to ally him as a poet with the European surrealists led by André Breton. The exigencies of his negritude, the search for universal black values, had taken him in a complementary direction. His principal source of information on black Africa, Leo Frobenius, was an irrationalist and a late Romantic. Both the current of modernism that Césaire cultivated and the ethnography of Frobenius led to a pervasive antirealist attitude that was to influence his evolution as a poet. The complications that could not fail to arise for him in the political arena were still well in the future, but the elements were already in place.

On 10 July 1937 Aimé Césaire had married Suzanne Roussy, a Martinican student whom he had met during their collaborative journalistic effort on *L'Etudiant noir*. She shared his passionate interest in the African origins of the black peoples of the diaspora and would later participate as a full partner in the definition of negritude in their magazine of Martinican culture, *Tropiques* (1941–1945). The first of several children was born in 1938. (The marriage would be terminated by a long separation, and Suzanne died relatively young. Aimé Césaire has never remarried.)

In 1939 Aimé and Suzanne Césaire expected an uneventful return to Fort-de-France and the beginning of a teaching career. Within months the French possessions in the West Indies felt the impact of the European war. After the fall of France to the Germans, Martinique, Guadeloupe, and Guiana found themselves governed from Vichy. From 1941 to 1943 elements of the French fleet that had made their way to the Antilles were bottled up by the United States Navy. This concatenation of events had a decisive impact on the development of Césaire's concept of negritude. The presence of thousands of French sailors in Fort-de-France on more or less permanent shore leave put to a serious test the official attitude of racial tolerance and assimilation. The racism of the sailors made itself felt on a daily basis and threatened the long-cherished notion that black Frenchmen were, first of all, French. The insensitivity of this military regime also made it difficult for Martinicans to ignore the fact that they were a colony like any other, a conclusion that the official policy of assimilation had masked somewhat. These conditions contributed to radicalizing Césaire and his friends, preparing them for a more anticolonialist posture at the end of the war.

The curious position of Martinique during the war years created something of a hothouse effect on the insular society. The serious contradictions between the colonial economy and administration on the one hand and the republican ideology in which Martinicans of all classes and groups were raised suddenly became glaringly apparent. On the positive side Aimé Césaire, unlike most other writers of his generation in Europe, sat out the war at home, writing a great deal and perfecting a style. He edited the literary magazine *Tropiques* from 1941 through 1945, in which he and his closest collaborators spelled out very clearly the ideological connections between the evolving Martinican version of negritude and the culture of European modernism. Both biographically and in terms of cultural history *Tropiques* was a synthesis of the previous decade's accomplishments for Césaire.

In 1944 Césaire spent seven months in Haiti, from May to December. He was invited to read a paper entitled "Poetry and Cognition" at the international philosophical conference devoted to epistomology and held in Port-au-Prince in late September. Césaire's treatment of the subject provides the most valuable and detailed information we have on his relationship to the culture of modernism in Europe and its place in the rise of the negritude movement. This first visit to Haiti had very important implications for Césaire's writing as well. Two figures from the Haitian revolution have played important roles in Césaire's creative life. Toussaint Louverture, who had been instrumental in defeating the French in the course of the first successful black slave revolt in history, had already figured prominently in the early version of Césaire's long poem *Notebook of a Return to the Native Land* in 1939. Much later Césaire devoted a volume to Haiti's emergence as the first black republic in the Americas. His *Toussaint Louverture* (1960) is a serious historical work that organizes the Haitian revolution around the political commitments of the island's three color castes: the insurrection of the white planters, the mulatto revolt, and the black revolution. The Haitian example demonstrated to Césaire that blacks could hope to realize their own legitimate aspirations only by opposing the resistance of the entrenched interests of a white elite and a colored middle class.

Henri Christophe, the cook turned king of Haiti (1811–1820), provided an example of another type. His stone citadel, jutting out over Cape Haïtien in the north of the island, stands as haunting testimony to the memory of a black leader whose destiny was to repeat the errors of the whites he had helped to defeat. Césaire worked from 1961 to 1963 on *The Tragedy of King Christophe* (*La Tragédie du roi Christophe*), which many consider to be his best play. Henri Christophe became for Césaire a dramatic symbol of the risks that awaited the newly free states of black Africa in the decade of the sixties.

It has been said that Césaire's visit to Haiti had such a profoundly positive impact on him that it cured a persistent stammer. Ngal seems to have received this information from an enthusiastic Haitian who was intent on emphasizing the very real importance of Césaire's visit. Although there is no evidence that Césaire was in need of any such cure, since the stammer has not been confirmed by friends or relatives, Haiti did take on a kind of exemplary value for him. Despite the vicissitudes of its long history as a republic, Haiti represented for the colonized Martinican the possibility of cultural autonomy for blacks in the Caribbean, a central feature of his own concept of negritude.

In 1945 Césaire found himself quite unexpectedly called on to become a public man. The first elections of the postwar period created an odd situation that has thoroughly conditioned the remainder of Aimé Césaire's life. He was elected mayor of Fort-de-France and deputy from central Martinique on the Communist ticket. The surrealist poet committed to black particularism soon found himself representing a colonial branch of a Stalinist political party. The contradictions occasioned by this turn of events were to have serious repercussions upon his poetics. They place Césaire among those writers of the first rank who have had a serious commitment to the ideals of Marxism only to be disappointed sooner or later by the realities of the party. In Césaire's case the break came in 1956, simultaneously with but not caused by the Soviet invasion of Hungary. A period of confusion followed, but in 1958 Césaire became the undisputed leader of the independent socialist Martinican Progressive party (PPM).

It is Césaire's charismatic presence and his great personal dignity that have kept the PPM intact for over twenty years and insured Césaire's return to the French legislature in every subsequent election. His politics have appeared contradictory to some over a period of years. In 1946 he cosponsored the bill that transformed the Caribbean colonies into overseas departments of metropolitan France. In 1958 he gave last-minute support to De Gaulle's constitutional referendum on the Fifth Republic, apparently as a result of André Malraux's visit to Martinique as De Gaulle's emissary and because of his conversation with Césaire. Since the founding of the PPM Césaire has favored a qualified autonomy for Martinique along the lines of the Italian federalist model, which would give to Martinique a status similar to Sicily's within Italy. Careful analysis of Césaire's concept of negritude shows that it bears no necessary relationship to any given political position, that it is, in short, a sociocultural ideology without a firm theoretical base. As such Césairean negritude has been at the mercy of shifting political conditions.

Because of the European war Césaire came to be known as a poet in the Americas before his work received any attention in Europe. The *Notebook,* his epic of Martinican negritude, was twice published in translation before it appeared as a separate volume in Paris. A Spanish-language edition translated by Lydia Cabrera and illustrated by Wifredo Lam, with a preface by Benjamin Péret, was published in Havana toward the beginning of 1943.[10] Péret was a French surrealist who spent the war years in Latin America steeping himself in Amerindian folklore. Cabrera was a second-generation representative of the Afro-Cuban movement and a writer of short stories. Lam was a surrealist painter of Afro-Chinese ancestry whose style had taken shape in Europe. Their collaboration on this project testifies to the type of interest Césaire's early poetry stimulated in that part of the Caribbean which had already developed an ethnic cultural consciousness.

New York was, however, the focal point of Césaire's initial impact as a poet, owing to the presence there of André Breton and an important group of French writers and artists. Breton had met Césaire in Martinique in April 1941 and had been tremendously impressed by the young black poet. His subsequent support of Césaire was the decisive factor in establishing the Martinican as a poet of international stature. Breton had a number of Césaire's shorter surrealist poems published in *VVV* in 1942–1944 and in *Hémisphères* in 1943–1944. Among the European exiles in New York was the cosmopolitan poet Ivan Goll, who teamed with Lionel Abel to produce the first bilingual edition of *Cahier d'un retour au pays natal,* which they translated as *Memorandum on My Martinique.* Brentano's, the publishing house and bookseller that did so much for French writers in exile during the war, published the volume in January 1947. It included Breton's dithyrambic introduction to Césaire, "A Great Negro Poet." André Breton, who is remembered more for his idiosyncrasies and his noisy excommunications from surrealist orthodoxy than for his service to poetry, deserves much credit for having given Césaire to the larger world of letters. At the same time, he began the legend of Césaire's otherness, of his exoticism:

> I recollect my first elementary reaction on discovering him to be such a pure black, all the more mask-like on first view as he smiled . . . he was able to stand alone in an epoch when many anticipated a general abdication of the spirit, when nothing seemed created any longer except for the purpose of perfecting the triumph of death, when art threatened to be frozen in old accomplishments: the first new revivifying breath, able to recreate total confidence is the contribution of a negro. And it is a negro who today governs the French language as there is no white man able to govern it.[11]

For Breton, whose judgment in poetic matters was quite uncanny, Césaire was the embodiment of the prophetic speaker of the *Notebook.* It is not uncommon for major literary figures to become swallowed up by a legend or by a larger-than-life version of one characteristic or one work, and Césaire has not escaped this fate. For most of the world, the Third World in particular, he remains the visionary of the *Notebook.* During the early postwar period Césaire managed to combine his political activity as a communist deputy with continued association with the surrealists. He was published in the surrealist magazine *Labyrinthe* in 1946 and the following year contributed to *Le Surréalisme en 1947,* the exhibit catalog edited by Breton and Marcel Duchamp. His next collection of poetry, *Beheaded Sun (Soleil cou coupé),*

was put out in 1948 by the K publishing house, which was identified with Breton's movement and which also published Artaud.

In 1947 L.-G. Damas, Césaire's former classmate, produced the
first anthology of poetry from the French Empire. He included in
it one of Césaire's longer poems from his first collection, *Miraculous Weapons (Les Armes miraculeuses),* which Breton's connection with the Gallimard publishing house had helped to have
published the previous year. But the next major event in Césaire's
poetic career came in 1948 with the publication of a second and
far more influential anthology, this one devoted exclusively to
black and Malagasy poetry. The third member of the original
triumvirate of negritude, Senghor, edited it for the Presses Universitaires de France on the occasion of the centenary of the
abolition of slavery in the French Empire. The anthology, which
is still in print over thirty years later, owes much of its celebrity
to the preface by Jean-Paul Sartre entitled "Black Orpheus"
("Orphée noir"). In it Sartre employed his virtuosity to present
to white Europe the image of its ultimate salvation through the
black world. His interpretation of the negritude movement rapidly
became the dominant one and it is still the most widespread today. Sartre's essay contributed directly to the way in which
Césaire has been read:

> A Jew, white among whites, can deny that he is a Jew,
> can declare himself a man among men. The Negro cannot
> deny that he is a Negro nor claim for himself that abstract
> colorless humanity: he is black. Therefore he is driven
> toward authenticity: insulted, enslaved, he stands up, he
> picks up the word "nigger" that they had thrown at him
> like a stone, he asserts his rights as black, facing the white
> man, with pride. The final unity that will draw all op-
> pressed people together in the same combat must be pre-
> ceded by what I call the moment of separation or of nega-
> tivity: this antiracist racism is the only road that can lead
> to the abolition of racial differences.[12]

This endorsement of negritude was accompanied by the founding of a new magazine and publishing house devoted to the dissemination of literature and contemporary thought of interest to
the black world. In 1947 Césaire joined the foremost black intel-

lectuals and writers in French, as well as such white supporters as Sartre, Albert Camus, and André Gide, in founding *Présence africaine,* edited by Alioune Diop, which has regularly published his principal statements on culture and politics, as well as many of his poems. Through *Présence africaine* Césaire has been read throughout the French Empire and, since 1960, in the new states of black Africa formerly colonized by France.

Césaire may have met Pablo Picasso at one or another of the postwar Communist meetings to promote world peace and solidarity that both men attended. Their cultural-political sympathies produced in 1950 a collaborative effort of great interest. Césaire published a small, tightly organized collection of poems entitled *Lost Body (Corps perdu),* which Picasso illustrated in a bold, stark style.

The period 1946–1950 is the moment of Césaire's greatest optimism both as a poet and as a public man. As the cold war became a protracted economic battle, and as the promise of the French Fourth Republic faded, Césaire entered a more reflective stage that produced the beautiful poetry of *Shackles (Ferrements)* but that also led to his eventually abandoning lyrical expression in favor of writing for the theater. During the sixties Césaire wrote and produced three plays dealing with colonialism, liberation, and the problems of political power, two of which, *The Tragedy of King Christophe* (1963) and *A Season in the Congo* (1967), are known to readers of English in the fine translations of Ralph Manheim, published by Grove Press. The third play, entitled *A Tempest* (1969), is a very original adaptation of Shakespeare's *Tempest* that places the questions of power, racism, and colonialism in a Caribbean setting.

Césaire's activity as a major poet spans two decades, from the end of the thirties to the end of the fifties. The curve of his poetic evolution can be traced in the principal events of his public life: an abrupt and violent departure from the dominant French tradition in search of his African past, with a syncretic mythology replacing European cultural norms; a heroic moment in which the end of colonialism seemed about to usher in a rebirth of the black world; and a reflective, elegiac mood corresponding to the gap between aspiration and realization in politics.

Part I
NEGRITUDE
AND MODERNISM

1

Césaire's Negritude in Perspective

Tepid dawn of ancestral virtue
Blood! Blood! all our blood moved by the male heart of the sun
those who know about the femininity of the moon's oily body
the reconciled exultation of antelope and star
those whose survival travels in the germination of grass!

Eia perfect circle of the world, enclosed concordance!
                Césaire, *Notebook of a Return to the Native Land*

Tiède petit matin de vertus ancestrales
Sang! Sang! tout notre sang ému par le coeur mâle du soleil
ceux qui savent la féminité de la lune au corps d'huile
l'exaltation réconciliée de l'antilope et de l'étoile
ceux dont la survie chemine en la germination de l'herbe!

Eia parfait cercle du monde et close concordance!
                Cahier d'un retour au pays natal (1939)

NEITHER CÉSAIRE nor the Martinicans can be credited with initiating the black consciousness movement in the Caribbean islands, although they did bring to it a unique flavor. Caribbean literature of the twenties and thirties was in a state of general ferment. Several literary movements shared one or more features with the Martinican version of negritude that would eventually eclipse them. G. R. Coulthard traces the beginnings of the Afro-Caribbean movement to the Puerto Rican writer Luis Palés Matos, who in 1927 published in the magazine *Paliedro* an article with strong Spenglerian overtones. Palés Matos predicted of "The Art of the White Race":

> The aesthetic sense of the white race has reached a dangerous cerebralisation, cutting itself off from its cosmic

roots. I do not believe in a monumental art of purely cerebral representation; I only believe in an art which identifies itself with the thing and fuses with the essence of the thing. An art which is as little art as possible, that is, where the aptitude for creation is subjected to the urge of the blood and instinct, which is always the right urge, because it carries with it the thousands of years of experience of the species.[1]

In the most Spenglerian strophe of the *Notebook* Césaire a decade later treated the imminent collapse of European culture in similar but more expressive terms:

> Hear the white world
> horribly weary from its immense effort
> its stiff joints crack under the hard stars
> hear its blue steel rigidity pierce the mystic flesh
> its deceptive victories tout its defeats
> hear the grandiose alibis of its pitiful stumblings
>
> Pity for our omniscient and naive conquerors!

> Ecoutez le monde blanc
> horriblement las de son effort immense
> ses articulations rebelles craquer sous les étoiles dures
> ses raideurs d'acier bleu transperçant la chair mystique
> écoute ses victoires proditoires trompeter ses défaites
> écoute aux alibis grandioses son piètre trébuchement
>
> Pitié pour nos vainqueurs omniscients et naïfs![2]

This is doubtless more than a fortuitous coincidence in the work of two significant Caribbean writers. Both Palés Matos and Césaire appear to have seen in Spengler a cause for optimism; the inevitable fall of the West would, in their view, occasion the renaissance of cultures oppressed by the West. Through Césaire, Spengler's *Decline of the West* unexpectedly heralds the future glory of the Third World. But there is no question of an influence of Palés Matos on Césaire. Neither the articles nor the Afro-Caribbean poetry of Palés Matos would seem to have been available to Césaire before 1945, and there is no evidence that he ever read them. We witness here instead the not unusual phenomenon of parallel development from a common source.

An examination of literary developments in Cuba produces similar results. The *Revista de Estudios Afrocubanos,* edited in Havana between 1937 and 1940, drew on Frobenius' version of African civilization at a time when Césaire had already incorporated aspects of it in his *Notebook.* Moreover, the Afro-Cuban poets were seldom of African ancestry, and their poems are strikingly dissimilar to Césaire's in that they view the black experience from outside, as a source of new poetic material. Nicolás Guillén, the only nonwhite among the early Afro-Cuban poets, is a special case. As Coulthard points out, citing Cintio Vitier, "The great difference is that he writes 'from within,' and the Negro theme is not just a fashion, a subject for literature, but the living heart of his creative activity."[3] But his view of Afro-Cuban culture does not systematically develop the aggressive appeal to blackness characteristic of Césaire. One might search in vain among the black and mulatto poets of French expression for a poem like Guillén's "Ballad of My Two Grandfathers," which accepts lovingly the combined heritage of white and black.[4] It is a poem in the tradition of the "América mestiza" propounded by José Martí and echoed today by Roberto Fernández Retamar in his *Caliban.* In the French-speaking areas of the Caribbean, when mulatto poets such as L.-G. Damas (*Pigments,* 1937) did react against white society, they were apt to do so with violence. Their situation had in many ways been more equivocal than that of blacks. Witness the title of the autobiographical narrative by Mayotte Capécia, *The White Negress* (*La Négresse blanche,* 1950), which situates the mulatto uncomfortably on the horns of a dilemma. In Cuba the mixed nature of the culture has received official sanction. In the French territories and in Haiti the mulatto has been obliged to choose between the white and the black worlds and their attendant values. Not until the Second World War did a serious schism occur between the more radical mulattos such as René Ménil, who put Marxist orthodoxy ahead of ethnic consciousness, and blacks like Césaire, who concluded in 1956 that orthodox Marxism did not speak to or for Caribbean blacks. But this development was still in the future and quite unforeseen in 1939, when Césaire published the first version of the *Notebook.* Furthermore, Césaire seems to have remained un-

aware of contemporary movements in the Spanish-speaking areas
of the Caribbean until 1941 at the earliest.

Wifredo Lam, a Cuban surrealist painter in whom both Picasso
and André Breton had begun to show considerable interest, returned to Cuba in 1941 via Martinique. Since he had been resident
in Europe for fifteen years, first in Madrid and then in Paris, he
had not participated directly in the Afro-Cuban movement centered in Havana. Like Guillén, Lam was of mixed parentage:
his mother was a mulatto and his maternal grandmother was
Congolese; but his father was an aged Chinese steeped in his own
culture. Thus, Lam's Africanism in painting was, like that of so
many poets, a nostalgic search for his past. Perhaps it was he
who called Césaire's attention to the Negro-Cuban tales related
by Lydia Cabrera. Or perhaps it was André Breton, through his
contact with Benjamin Péret. Or Césaire may have read three of
her "Black Stories from Cuba" ("Contes nègres de Cuba") in the
translation of Francis de Miomandre when they appeared in the
Cahiers du Sud in 1934.[5] Césaire's admiration for Cabrera's art
was certainly returned in kind, since she prepared a Spanish-
language edition of his *Notebook*, which was published in Havana
in 1943 with illustrations by Lam and an introduction by Benjamin Péret.

Wifredo Lam was highly praised by Césaire in the second issue
of *Tropiques* (July 1941), and his biography and artistic development were treated at some length by Pierre Mabille in Césaire's
magazine toward the end of the war. The issue of *Tropiques* for
January 1945 (no. 12) reprinted from the *Cahiers d'Haïti* an
article by Alejo Carpentier on the cultural evolution of Latin
America. The treatment of the subject was very broad, however,
and nowhere did it mention the recent experiments in negritude
in Cuba. The documented reports of contact between Césaire
and the Afro-Cuban movement end there. On balance it would
seem that up to the end of the war Césaire had received relatively
little from Cuba and given rather more. This was also the opinion
of Fernández Retamar in a conversation in Ottawa in August
1973. Césaire himself stated explicitly to René Depestre in an
interview that he did not know the Afro-Cuban movement as
such at all during his formative years.[6]

By 1944 Haiti was to assume a special place in Césaire's view
of black culture. The 1939 printing of the *Notebook* contained a
now celebrated passage on Toussaint Louverture that develops

blackness as a positive value against the cold, lifeless, and deadly whiteness of European civilization. At that early date, however, Césaire was quite ignorant of the black revival under way in Haiti. He told Depestre that he discovered the Haitian movement and Jean Price-Mars's *Ainsi parla l'oncle* very late (presumably in 1944). *Ainsi parla l'oncle* was a popular essay on ethnography issued in 1928 by a Paris publisher for the Bibliothèque Haïtienne. The magazine *Les Griots* began publication in Port-au-Prince in 1938, when Césaire's initial formulation of the concept of negritude was already well advanced. Jacques Roumain was to create the Bureau d'Etudes Ethnographiques in 1941, at a time when Haiti was largely cut off from Martinique by the war. As for the *Revue indigène*, founded by Jacques Roumain in 1927, it antedates the militant phase of the negritude movement. In the words of Ghislain Gouraige: "The *Revue Indigène* did not offer a model. The poems of Jacques Roumain, Emile Roumer, Philippe Marcelin, Carl Brouard, André Liautaud, Antonio Vieux, and Daniel Heurtelou bore the stamp of Marinetti, Cendrars, and Apollinaire and took the form of a mirthful and noisy protest against the literary tradition. It was a revolt; but it was also the charm of the machine age, the taste for naked goddesses dear to Paul Morand . . . The *indigénistes* gave their blessing to modern conformism in Haiti."[7] In short, the *Revue indigène* represented the introduction of modernism without negritude into Haitian culture. Césaire's contribution would be to reveal the dialectical relationship between the two currents.

Roumain contributed as well to the Parisian *Revue du monde noir* (1931–1932), which Césaire considered too much concerned with middle-class values. But some of Roumain's poems announced the birth of a new attitude. His hard-hitting poem "Dirty Niggers" ("Sales Nègres") is all the more impressive since Roumain belonged to the privileged mulatto elite in Haiti. Several details in Césaire's *Notebook* recall images and devices in Roumain's poem. In 1947 Césaire added a passage on the theme of the pariah at the beginning of the second movement:

> As there are hyena-men and panther-men, I would be a
>   jew-man
> a Kaffir-man
> a Hindu-man-from-Calcutta
> a Harlem-man-who-doesn't-vote

Comme il y a des hommes-hyènes et
des hommes-panthères, je serais un
homme-juif
un homme-cafre
un homme-hindou-de-Calcutta
un homme-de-Harlem-qui-ne-vote-pas[8]

Roumain's poem contains a very similar, and rather well known, statement of solidarity with the world's pariahs, using the same terms—*Jew, Hindu, nigger*—in inverted order:

for we will have chosen our day
the day of dirty niggers . . .
of dirty Hindus . . .
of dirty Jews . . .

car nous aurons choisi notre jour
le jour des sales nègres . . .
des sales hindous . . .
des sales juifs . . .[9]

The context, and consequently the meaning, are different in the two poems, however. Whereas Roumain was calling the proletarians of the world to the banner of communism, Césaire's poem remains one of ethnic revolt and heightened consciousness. The motif of the downtrodden rising up is anything but unexpected here, and the poets introduce it in strikingly similar ways. Césaire opens the final movement of the *Notebook* with, "And we are standing now, my country and I" ("Et nous sommes debout maintenant, mon pays et moi"). Roumain related this uprising directly to the "Internationale" in "Dirty Niggers"; And here we are now standing / All the wretched of the earth" ("Et nous voici debout / Tous les damnés de la terre"). The notion that the renewal of the black world will come on the heels of the ruin of Euro-American civilization is expressed analogously by Roumain and by Césaire. Roumain: "To have done / once / and / for / all / with this world" ("Pour en finir / une / fois / pour / toutes / avec ce monde"). And Césaire: "One must begin somewhere. / Begin what? / The only thing in the world worth beginning: / The End of the world of course" ("Il faut bien commencer. /

Commencer quoi? / La seule chose au monde qui vaille / la peine de commencer: / La Fin du monde parbleu").

We may choose to see in these textual similarities either a parallel but independent evolution of two writers with like concerns who are drawn to the same molders of contemporary sensibility (Oswald Spengler, for example) or a direct influence of the one on the other. In view of the number of textual echoes between Roumain's poem and Césaire's, one is tempted to leap to the second conclusion. Yet the complexity of the issue is such that both hypotheses may be posited simultaneously. It is very probable that Césaire read Spengler enthusiastically at an early date.[10] And it is entirely in keeping with Césaire's generous nature that he should have paid belated tribute to a respected colleague by incorporating some well-digested elements of a renowned poem into his own. This type of intertextuality becomes a kind of creative cannibalism, a trait Césaire was to praise in his *Discourse on Colonialism*.

Harlem Renaissance

In the thirties the Harlem Renaissance poets as a group had more influence on Césaire than did either the Haitians or the Afro-Cubans. Langston Hughes, Claude McKay, Jean Toomer, Countee Cullen enjoyed a heroic status among black intellectuals when Césaire arrived in Paris in 1931. Socialist magazines (*Nouvel Age, Europe, Minutes*) had published their poems, and some were represented in the anthology of new American poetry edited by Eugène Jolas. McKay's novel *Banjo* had been published in French in 1928. In crossing the Atlantic the Harlem Renaissance movement took on political colors more familiar to French readers. When in 1932 the Martinicans who published *Légitime Défense* set out to attack the conformist poetry of the French Antilles, they did so using Langston Hughes and Claude McKay as models. The communist-surrealist editors of *Légitime Défense* adopted the Americans (and for my purposes here the Jamaican McKay may be enrolled among them) with youthful enthusiasm. Etienne Léro claimed that "these two revolutionary black poets have brought to us the African love of life, the African joy in love, the African dream of death."[11] In order to set this judgment in perspective, the reader should consider that the contemporary

Antillean poetry to which *Légitime Défense* objected was a pale reflection of French Parnassianism, an assiduous copy of Victor Hugo's technical virtuosity, or an emulation of the saccharine symbolism of Albert Samain. The different cultural climate in which the Martinicans found themselves (in the *Légitime Défense* group all but Léro were mulattos, that is, not only light skinned but middle class) of necessity contributed to their version of the importance of the Harlem Renaissance.

The significance of Claude McKay for the Caribbean originators of negritude can be usefully contrasted with the critical reserve expressed toward him by one of the most recent American historians of black letters. In his *From the Dark Tower* Arthur P. Davis finds no redeeming feature in McKay's "decided bias against light-skinned Negroes," and although he does not side with W. E. B. Du Bois's disgusted reaction to *Home to Harlem,* Davis expresses opprobrium for the mix of color consciousness and sympathy for social revolution in *Banjo:* "The work, of course, contains all of McKay's pet themes: the hypocrisy of the Negro middle class, color prejudice among Negroes themselves, the superiority of African primitives to American and West Indian blacks. It is also highly anti-religious. As a substitute for the existing survival movements among Negroes, he seems to be urging them to study the Irish revolution, the Russian revolution, and the Indian people's movement under Gandhi. There is a certain falseness to *Banjo.*"[12] Yet the most conservative of the negritude poets, L. S. Senghor, has seen McKay as the spiritual father of negritude: "Claude McKay can rightfully be considered the true inventor of Negritude. I speak not of the word, but of the values of Negritude . . . Far from seeing in one's blackness an inferiority, one accepts it, one lays claim to it with pride, one cultivates it lovingly."[13]

To do justice to both McKay and black American critics such as Davis, one must remember that McKay—like Marcus Garvey a Jamaican—has more in common with the Martinicans' acute consciousness of the links between color and caste than with Du Bois or the other arbiters of black culture in America during the twenties and thirties. This is an important key to understanding the persistent confusion surrounding the concept of negritude in North America. The problem arose in sometimes bitter terms in the exchange between Césaire and American representatives at the First International Congress of Negro Writers and Artists in 1956. In this context one of the ironies of Césaire's position in social thought is that negritude—or rather its dominant theme, the affirmation of blackness—should derive indirectly from Garveyism. Neither Césaire nor any of the other non-African proponents of negritude ever espoused a back-to-Africa movement, although Césaire manifestly began his literary career by opting for an Africa of the heart. In this respect too, Césaire's *Notebook* shares with McKay's *Banjo* a sympathy for primitivism, a feature Davis and others view with concern. Did Césaire know Garvey's injunction to the black world: "Negroes, teach your children that they are direct descendents of the greatest and proudest race who ever peopled the earth"? Césaire probably had only a vague notion of Garvey before his student days in Paris. He related to René Depestre that he had heard of Marcus Garvey as a young boy in Martinique. Despite these obvious parallels, Césaire's negritude developed along different lines from the utopian scheme of Garveyism.

There can be no doubt, however, that the Harlem Renaissance writers, who flourished in the same atmosphere that provided the mass appeal of Garveyism, were an important factor in Aimé Césaire's formulation of negritude. Before examining in detail what Césaire has had to say about the Harlem Renaissance, it will be instructive to draw a parallel between Garvey's affirmation of his blackness and Césaire's attitude in the *Notebook of a Return to the Native Land*. In 1923 W. E. B. Du Bois wrote disparagingly of Garvey, stressing his Negroid features much as a caricaturist might do; he depicted Garvey as "a little, fat black man, ugly, but with intelligent eyes and a big head."[14] In *The Black Vanguard* R. H. Brisbane comments that "Garvey used this description of himself time after time to demonstrate that the greatest enemy of the blacks in America was not the white people but the mulattos or light-skinned Negroes such as Du Bois" (p. 85). Garvey used the intended insult strategically. By identifying himself with the characteristics of blackness, he refused to acknowledge the pretensions of the American mulatto bourgeoisie, whose fundamental interests, according to Brisbane, were those of maintaining their own superiority within a caste system while simultaneously denying the importance of the color issue among blacks themselves. In short, Garvey's affirmation of negritude is not at all dissimilar to Césaire's in the *Notebook*. In the poem Césaire's speaker at first joins in the chorus of laughter at the appearance of a great, sprawling "nigger" in a trolley car. The speaker's ultimate identification with his own negritude opens the way for a transformation of blackness as it is perceived by other blacks.

A concise appreciation of American black poetry was published in Césaire's cultural magazine, *Tropiques,* in July 1941. These half-dozen pages may have been taken directly from Césaire's recent university thesis; they surely reflect the spirit in which he read and responded to the poets of the Harlem Renaissance. His declared intention was to introduce the Martinican reader to three poems by James Weldon Johnson, Jean Toomer, and Claude McKay: "The dominant feeling of the black poet is one of malaise, better still of intolerance. Intolerance of reality because it is sordid, of the world because it is a cage, of life because it has been stolen on the high road of the sun."[15] This posture of revolt, which the *Notebook* reveals as more thoroughly exclusive in Césaire's early work than in that of the American poets, calls for a new existential attitude. Black poetry must be transformed from within to articulate adequately the lived experience of black people. Césaire is writing in opposition to the stifling cultural vacuum that had earlier incensed the authors of *Légitime Défense* when he says that the black poet "by no means intends to be a painter, an evoker of images, but rather committed to the same adventure as his least respectable heroes" (p. 38). Césaire envisages the black writer henceforth as embracing the struggle and the concerns of the most lowly of his comrades.

He professes admiration for the special religious sentiment he finds flowing through the work of the Harlem Renaissance poets, something he attempted to translate in Martinican terms in the section of the *Notebook* that deals with the painful mixture of forced gaiety and gnawing fear in the celebration of Christmas. It is surely a commentary on the Europeanization of Martinican sensibility that Césaire felt he had to differentiate this religious sentiment from the ascetic mysticism of a Meister Eckhart, whom he quotes at some length. Part of his description of the blacks' experience of the sacred follows: "Here, too, a God speaks directly to his creatures. But it is a humbler manner of companionship with God, of familiarity not on the divine plane like that of the mystic but on the terrestrial plane. In other words, whereas thought dehumanizes man . . . here it is God who submits to the limitations of space and time, who initiates himself into the life of the body, who takes his place in the world and truly enrolls himself in the midst of our humility" (p. 39). This appreciation of black religion is notable in that it corresponds rather closely to the shift from a transcendental notion of the sacred as being essentially outside human experience to a notion of the immanence of the divine. Césaire was to draw on just such a view of the world in his *Miraculous Weapons (Les Armes miraculeuses)*, which he wrote during the war.

On the basis of Césaire's scathing attack on attempts to essentialize the African's world view in his *Discourse on Colonialism*, several commentators have depicted Césaire as being fundamentally antireligious. This is far from the truth. In the 1939 version of the *Notebook* Césaire included numerous specifically Christian references and at one point presented his speaker as a martyr. All such references were eliminated from the text before publication of the two 1947 editions. But neither the *Notebook* in its earliest form nor *Miraculous Weapons* was conceived as being incompatible with a mode of experience that can be considered religious.

There is just as great a danger in interpreting Césaire as a true neo-African poet whose poetic word is the African equivalent of word magic. This was essentially the thesis of Jahnheinz Jahn in *Muntu.* Since for him *Notebook of a Return to the Native Land* "inaugurated neo-African poetry," it could not for that very reason bear any positive relation to European poetry and to surrealism in particular.[16] Jahn's desire to prove the systematic unity of neo-African culture led him to overstate his case. At this early stage in Césaire's evolution as a poet it was in part his hope to reestablish contact with his African heritage. What Jahn and those who have followed him overlook is that Césaire's quest was prompted precisely by the absence of a living African tradition in his culture. Thus the truly remarkable work Jahn did on Haitian voodoo, for example, cannot be generalized so as to include Césaire. What may hold for an oral tradition alive among Haitian blacks cut off by their illiteracy from European contact is beside the point when one considers the art of the highly cultivated Césaire. Césaire's desire for an efficacious spiritual principle in the thirties and early forties is a manifestation of nostalgia. Witness his reference to European mysticism in a sympathetic exposition of black Christianity in North America. Césaire's assumption—and it was the right one—was that his Martinican readers were more likely to relate to European mysticism than to the African "universe of forces."[17]

To return to the July 1941 issue of *Tropiques,* Césaire claimed that the black epiphany is attained in a manner fundamentally different from European mysticism. He quite properly stressed the element of frenzied rhythm as its identifying characteristic: "As this people does in all things they seize upon their God voraciously. They know that he will come one day and in the expectation of the 'coming of the Lord' there is the most astonishing divine quest imaginable" (p. 39). Black American poetry, or at least those aspects of it he was describing in the 1941 article, is an expression of the same basic attitude: "And finally, here is a poetry that does not offer the ear or the eye an unexpected and undubitable body of vibrations. Neither the brillance of colors nor sonorous magic. At most rhythm, but primitive, of jazz or tom-tom, beating down man's resistance at that point of most basic humanity, the nervous system" (p. 41). Césaire's appreciation of the Harlem Renaissance is partial and open to question. Certainly historians like Davis will not agree with its emphasis. What matters most, however, is not that Césaire was right or wrong in his literary judgment but that through his quite personal, ideological, and sometimes political reading of their work, poets such as Johnson, Toomer, and McKay contributed significantly to the formulation of a version of negritude that would return to the United States three decades later in a highly political form as the Black Power movement.

Césaire chose to accentuate the features of contemporary black poetry in America that were compatible with his own conviction that the elemental, the primitive—that which is inherent to black experience before its contact with European culture—is to be prized above the most refined achievements of the West. Granting that this is a one-sided version of the Harlem Renaissance, one cannot but be impressed by the fact that in 1962 Langston Hughes found in Césaire's work a reasonable likeness of the earlier movement. Speaking at the Conference of African Writers of English Expression at Makerere University in Kampala, Uganda, in June 1962, Hughes is reported to have found "nothing mysterious about the notion [of negritude] . . . Césaire had done exactly what the writers of the Harlem Renaissance did before [him], back in the nineteen-twenties; only the Harlemites had not given it a name."[18] Three years earlier, in the best American essay on "Négritude and its Relevance to the American Negro Writer," Samuel W. Allen (the poet Paul Vesey) had drawn a similar conclusion. Going beyond the concern of the negritude poets with the African past—which he too related to the Harlem Renaissance—he called attention to "that aspect of négritude which . . . is simply an affirmation of self, of that dwarfed self, denied realization because of the root of its identity . . . It would appear that the American Negro, like the African, has an imposing interest in the development of his image in the universe, in the correction of the distorted image of himself in this society . . ."[19]

An Africa of the Heart

The Harlem Renaissance offered Césaire an exemplary literary attitude for contemporary blacks. But in the thirties he had a thirst for knowledge of his African origins that required real documentation. This he found during his student years, both in the form of intellectual currents of the moment and in the personal testimony of his friend Léopold Senghor. Senghor was Césaire's senior by seven years, a difference in age that would in itself suffice to account for the great personal influence he exercised over Césaire during the period leading up to the *Notebook*. The native land to which Césaire would return was only in part the physically and spiritually impoverished island of Martinique. It was also a postulation of the spirit. What he would return with, by a supreme act of poetic imagination, were the resources for regenerating in Martinicans a sense of personal and collective identity as blacks.

Since the fifties Senghor has put his notion of negritude to a narrowly political use, in effect creating a quasipolitical, quasireligious amalgam for the emerging nation of Senegal, of which he became the first president. One must therefore take the greatest care to differentiate between the meanings *négritude* would assume in the later careers of its two principal artisans. Nonetheless, at the time he is reputed to have coined the term, Césaire was very much impressed by Senghor's notions of African spirituality.

His principal readings in African history and civilization were to confirm him in this view.

Maurice Delafosse was, in the twenties, the most influential scientific popularizer of Africa in France. His four books on the subject published in that decade, the last posthumously, are notable for their marked sympathy toward black Africa.[20] Among his contributions to a better understanding of African mores and institutions was his refutation of the notion, disseminated by colonial administrators and missionaries alike, that black Africans are fetishists with no true sense of religion. According to Delafosse, African animism is a profoundly religious world view that links mysticism to a sense of collective belonging. Césaire's idea of the religion of the blacks in America, quoted above, is basically an extension of the thesis of Delafosse that "the divinity is not, for the Negroes, something far-off, extraordinary or difficult of approach, but on the contrary, it is in a way, an integral part of society itself or of the environment in which the society lived. Their gods are familiar beings whose presence is revealed at every instance, apart from whom it is materially impossible to exist, and whose immediate and constant influence is exercised over all their daily acts and directs the orientation of all their concepts."[21]

Before 1945 Césaire was to write of the collective unconscious of black peoples in terms that raise the thorniest philosophical problems. At first glance one would be inclined to think that in certain pages of *Tropiques* Césaire was borrowing from Carl Jung, whose theory of the collective unconscious has proved so fascinating to many literary minds. Publication dates indicate, however, that Césaire could not have read Jung, at least not in French, at the time when he was beginning to refer to an atavistic memory. It is probable that he picked up this notion as well from scientific writers such as Delafosse, who had claimed in *Les Nègres* (1927): "We may imagine the combat that takes place unconsciously in the depths of the Negro who is caught between his individual instincts and the obedience that he owes to the collective will, when this obedience demands the suppression of these instincts."[22] This faith in an irrational power greater than the self was also in keeping with the major tenets of Leo Frobenius, who oriented Césaire's reflections toward their possible literary applications. The fact that such terms as *instinct* and *collective will* in Delafosse are susceptible of a variety of interpretations only reinforces the probability that Césaire adapted them to his own purposes.

The influence on Césaire of the German ethnographer Frobenius, although it was destined to have an importance greater that that of Delafosse, was marginal until 1936, when his late work *Kulturgeschichte Afrikas* was translated into French.[23] Delafosse, particularly in the chapters of *Les Nègres* devoted to the arts in Africa, had prepared Césaire for headier stuff. The real merit of Delafosse was that he put the stamp of scientific approval on the vogue that *l'art nègre* had enjoyed in Paris for a decade. This was not his specific intention; Delafosse had the gravest reservations concerning jazz and its supposed African identity. Notwithstanding this reluctance he performed a service in calling attention to the literary traditions of black Africa, popular and oral as well as scholarly and encyclopedic. He was deeply sensitive to the high degree of achievement attained by African cultures in the decorative arts, and his appreciation of the Benin bronzes was such that he easily disposed of the specious claim of their Portuguese origin. In *Les Nègres* Delafosse offered a rapid overview of African musical instruments and modes, an outline that Césaire doubtless completed in his conversations with Senghor. But he dismissed African architecture in one paragraph, whereas Frobenius was to make of it a major proof of his theory of two complementary principles of civilization in Africa.

In short, the work of Delafosse—Honorary Governor of the Colonies, professor at the Ecole Coloniale and at the Oriental language school of the University of Paris—represented to the young black student from Martinique an official *nihil obstat* to affirming one's blackness as a cultural value. He may even have contributed inadvertently to the coining of the neologism *négritude*. In an interview Césaire implied that he had not read Delafosse in the thirties, that Frobenius' *Histoire de la civilisation africaine* was his sole ethnographic source on Africa; but this seems doubtful.[24] I do not know that anyone has observed previously the significance of the title of Delafosse's last book, *Les Nègres*. Earlier in the decade Delafosse had conformed to contemporary usage with regard to colonized blacks by entitling his monograph of 1922 *Les Noirs de l'Afrique*. Before 1927 he had used the term *nègre* only as an adjective, as in his title *L'Ame nègre* (1922). During the same period this usage is confirmed by the titles of H. Clouzot and A. Level's *L'Art nègre et l'art océanien* (1920) and Stephen-Chauvet's *La Musique nègre* (1929). The title *Les Nègres* gave a new respectability to a noun that in the French West Indies had had the intentionally offensive connotation of "nigger."

When Césaire was a student in Paris in the early thirties, no black Martinican intellectual considered himself to be a *nègre*. As Frantz Fanon put it a generation later in his book *Pour la révolution africaine:* "The African was, over in Africa, the real representative of the black race [*race nègre*]. Moreover, when a boss tried to get an extra work effort out of a Martinican he could expect to be told: 'If you want a nigger, go find one in Africa,' meaning that slaves and forced labor were recruited elsewhere. Over there, in the home of the niggers . . . The Antillean was a Negro [*noir*], but the nigger [*nègre*] was in Africa. In 1939 no Antillean in the French West Indies considered himself to be black, claimed to be black."[25] Whereas for French society at large, *nègre* and *noir* as nouns may have been considered interchangeable at that time, Martinican sensibilities were much touchier on the subject of ethnic identification. Césaire must be credited with being the first black intellectual outside Africa to have taken the humiliating term *nigger* and boldly transformed it into the proud term *black*. The transformation was all the more difficult because, unlike the analogous situation in English, the one French noun *nègre* had to be made to serve in both antithetical capacities. *Negro (noir)* had been appropriated by those who wished to pass for European and for that reason had to be avoided.

Not until *Tropiques* was reissued in 1978 did Césaire comment directly on the nature of his interest in Frobenius. Since the first critical studies on Césaire did not pursue this lead, the general impression, until publication of M. a M. Ngal's thesis in 1975, had been that Frobenius was just another author read by Césaire, perhaps less important than Delafosse in the formation of the concept of negritude. Whereas Delafosse rendered African studies intellectually respectable, it was Frobenius and the French translation of his *Histoire de la civilisation africaine* that provided the spark and fired the creative impulse in Césaire.

Normally one would not choose Senghor as a reliable authority on Césaire because of their ultimate divergence on the meaning of negritude; but on the question of their joint reading of Frobenius in 1936 there can be no more reliable source. When asked to write a foreword to an anthology of Frobenius' writings, Senghor began by describing the capital importance of the *Histoire de la civilisation africaine* for Aimé Césaire, Léon Damas, and himself: "I still have before me, in my possession, the copy of the *History of African Civilization* on the third page of which Césaire wrote: "décembre 1936" . . . We knew by heart Chapter II of the first book of the *History,* entitled "What Does Africa Mean to Us?", a chapter adorned with lapidary phrases such as this: 'The idea of the "barbarous Negro" is a European invention, which in turn dominated Europe until the beginning of this century.' "[26] These are the very pages of Frobenius' praise for traditional African cultures that Césaire chose to print in *Tropiques* for April 1942.

The eight pages on "What Does Africa Mean to Us?" reprinted in *Tropiques* were preceded by a long editorial paragraph that situates Césaire's understanding of negritude at that date much closer to Senghor's than has been thought. Senghor has consistently maintained the position that negritude is biologically grounded and that the specifically negroid characteristics, as he sees them, of emotion and intuitive reason, art and poetry, image and myth ("Lessons of Leo Frobenius," p. x), are both essential to black cultures and predetermined. In recent decades Senghor has shored up the notions he found initially in Frobenius (no longer a respectable reference in scientific circles, if indeed he ever was) with frequent mentions of the "scientific" Catholicism of Teilhard de Chardin, of Jacques Maritain, or of the partially Senegalese ancestry of French philosopher Gaston Berger. In the case of Senghor, critics of negritude have been quick to denounce the racist implications of his frequent references to blood ties. Césaire has been at pains to dissociate himself from the possibility of a racist interpretation of his own version of negritude. He has insisted that it is not a biological but a historical concept: "I do not in the slightest believe in biological permanence, but I believe in culture. My negritude has a ground. It is a fact that there is a black culture: it is historical, there is nothing biological about it."[27] While this was surely Césaire's position in 1969 when he gave this interview, it is incorrect to assume that this statement reflects his position between 1936 and 1942, dates for which we possess solid documentation. Indeed there is in the editorial introduction to Frobenius in *Tropiques* no. 5 for April 1942 presumptive evidence for a biological reading of Frobenius: "There flows in our veins a *blood* that requires of us a unique attitude toward life . . . we must respond . . . to the special dynamics of our complex *biological reality*" (italics mine).

I would not want to link Césaire irrevocably to a racist concept of negritude. The point that must be made without ambiguity, however, is that this attitude toward blackness profoundly marked Césaire's intellectual, creative, and even spiritual beginnings in the thirties. It is entirely to Césaire's credit that he eventually worked through the problems of Frobenian ethnography—as Senghor has not done—to arrive at a more reasoned understanding of the relationship of black peoples to their culture.

Fortunately there exists an excellent compendium of those aspects of the work of Frobenius that had the greatest impact on Aimé Césaire and his closest associates. The first issue of *Tropiques* (April 1941) included an article by his wife, Suzanne Césaire, entitled "Leo Frobenius and the Problem of Civilizations." The article is a condensation of the central theses of Frobenius as the Césaires understood them. The term *vital force* or *life force* recurs frequently as an approximation of Frobenius' *Païdeuma,* the prehistorical, prehuman power that in his view shapes civilizations independently of mankind. The resulting morphology of civilization that Frobenius proposes is not a historical process in any usual sense. The païdeuma itself is presented as a biological given. Although it is precultural, it gives rise to forms of civilization that are polar opposites: the Hamitic form identifies itself with animal symbolism, whereas the Ethiopian is plantlike, vegetative. Suzanne Césaire observes that according to Frobenius these two opposite principles could still be seen in their pure state among certain African tribal groups at the turn of the century. It is evident from her enthusiastic tone that for Suzanne Césaire—and doubtless for Aimé as well—this is not merely a topic for objective study; an option has been chosen, and a profound emotional investment has already been committed. Black Martinicans are to see themselves as the biological heirs of the Ethiopian world view, to identify with it, and to draw their pride from it. In her conclusion Suzanne Césaire suggests that a world brought to its present catastrophe by the Hamitic characteristics of Euro-American civilization can only be redirected through the renewal of the Ethiopian strain: whence the special mission of negritude.

The peculiar tension in Césaire's early poetry has to do in part with the fact that the Martinican cannot simply, naturally give himself over to these qualities, however real and important they may seem. Unlike Senghor, whose expansive, fluid verse would convince us of the unimpeded natural nobility of negritude, Césaire even at this early date was convinced of his cultural dualism. The editorial paragraph introducing Frobenius, which includes the references to blood cited above, also made this important point: "It is obvious that our conscious reactions are determined by European culture: its arts, science and technology. And we are determined to use these weapons of precision, with their latest refinements . . . Is it not our task to realize our total humanity? We cannot attain it . . . except by the expression—thanks to precious European technology—of all the exigencies of our negritude."

The ethnography of Frobenius was quite irrationalistic in its fundamental presuppositions. In this respect it proved to be a vital link to the currents of European modernism, literary and intellectual, that Césaire was to cultivate in the thirties and forties. Senghor in "The Lessons of Leo Frobenius" reminds us of the extent to which he, as well as Césaire and Damas, were attracted to German irrationalism, in part because of one of the most novel theses of Frobenius:

> We had to wait for Leo Frobenius before the affinities between the "Ethiopian," that is the Negro African, and the German soul could be made manifest and before certain stubborn preconceptions of the 17th and 18th centuries could be removed. One of these preconceptions is that the development of every ethnic group, and of humanity itself, is linear, univocal, passing from the Stone Age to the age of steam and electricity and to the atomic age of today. . . Frobenius tells us that, like individuals, ethnic groups are diverse, even opposed, like the Hamites and the Ethiopians, in their feelings and their ideas, their myths and their ideologies, their customs and their institutions; that each ethnic group, having its own *paideuma*—once again, its *soul*—reacts in its own peculiar way to the environment and de-

velops autonomously; that though they may be at different stages of development, Germans and "Ethiopians" belong to the same spiritual family. And he concludes: "The West created English realism and French rationalism. The East created German mysticism . . . the agreement with the corresponding civilizations in Africa is complete. *The sense of the fact in the French, English and Hamitic civilizations —the sense of the real in the German and Ethiopian civilizations!*" (p. xi)

Leo Frobenius not only triggered in the founders of negritude a wave of enthusiasm for an Africa that was, in Césaire's case, an affair of the heart; he also legitimized the violent revolt against the French rationalism of their formal education.

The Ambiguities of Art Nègre

In the same vein as the works of the ethnographers, Césaire may be supposed to have appreciated the 1927 essay *L'Art Nègre* by Georges Hardy, then director of the Ecole Coloniale de Paris. This enlightened representative of colonialism argued for a means of permitting the indigenous arts of Africa to recover from the disastrous effects of contact with Europe. His review of the contemporary decadence of the arts in colonized Africa, which he contrasted with their former splendor, is both an implied condemnation of the violence inherent in colonization and a tribute to the spiritual strength of black Africa, which had to a surprising degree, given the circumstances, avoided being overwhelmed by alien cultural imports.

The line to be drawn between negritude as a cultural affirmation and as a racist posture is a fine one indeed. Nowhere is it more difficult to draw that line than in the case of Count J.-A. de Gobineau, who, besides being a notable nineteenth-century practitioner of the short story and the novel, laid the groundwork for the racism of Houston Stewart Chamberlain and Alfred Rosenberg. Césaire spoke frankly of Gobineau in an interview with M. a M. Ngal in 1967: "Yes, we read Gobineau, Senghor and I. It was essentially to refute him, since he was the great French theoretician of racism. But at the same time, I must admit, Senghor liked him a great deal. His liking is understandable; he was grateful to [Gobineau] for saying: 'Art is black.' The Black is an artist. If there are artists in Western civilization, it is because there are nonetheless a few drops of Negro blood in them. Consequently the attitude toward Gobineau was very ambivalent."[28] I take it that Césaire meant to include himself in the ambivalent judgment of Gobineau. Certainly this reference to blood and to a biological negritude goes part way toward explaining the presence of a troubling reference to blood in his presentation of Frobenius in *Tropiques*. In Césaire's case the ambivalence toward Gobineau extended to *art nègre* as well.

There is a widespread assumption that the vogue of *art nègre* in Parisian cultural circles had a special meaning for the young black students, few in number still, drawn to the French capital from all corners of the colonial empire in the early thirties. But Césaire was aware that black entertainers in particular were first and foremost exotic creatures, an imported thrill for a tired civilization. In his *Notebook* Césaire reacted with disgust to the popular image of himself as an alienated object:

> Or else quite simply as they like to think of us!
> Cheerfully obscene, completely nuts about jazz to cover their extreme boredom.
> I can boogie-woogie, do the Lindy-hop and tap-dance.
> And for a special treat the muting of our cries muffled with wah-wah. Wait . . .
> Everything is as it should be. My good angel grazes the neon. I swallow batons. My dignity wallows in puke . . .

> Ou bien tout simplement comme on nous aime!
> Obscènes gaiement, très doudous de jazz sur leur excès d'ennui.
> Je sais le tracking, le Lindy-hop et les claquettes.
> Pour les bonnes bouches la sourdine de nos plaintes enrobées de oua-oua. Attendez . . .
> Tout est dans l'ordre. Mon bon ange broute du néon. J'avale des baguettes. Ma dignité se vautre dans les dégobillements . . .[29]

It would surely be wrong to conclude that *art nègre* as a recreational product, the latest discovery of the leisure class, could contribute directly to the formulation of negritude. Césaire was of course also aware of the positive, creative force that *art nègre* represented for some whites as well as for blacks. Picasso was among those artists whom he respected, and who came to respect him. Years later Picasso contributed engravings to the original, de luxe edition of *Lost Body (Corps perdu)*, and he contributed financially to the troubled Paris production of *The Tragedy of King Christophe*. Guillaume Apollinaire too is frequently mentioned in this context. No one doubts that Césaire borrowed the title of his second collection of poems, *Beheaded Sun (Soleil cou coupé)*, from the final line of Apollinaire's "Zone." And one occasionally encounters in writings on Césaire an allusion to the lines that lead up to this striking poetic closure by decapitation:

> You walk toward Auteuil you want to go home on foot
> To sleep among your fetishes from the South Seas and
>   Guinea
> They are Christs of another form and another belief . . .

> Tu marches vers Auteuil tu veux aller chez toi à pied
> Dormir parmi tes fétiches d'Océanie et de Guinée
> Ils sont des Christ d'une autre forme et d'une autre croy-
>   ance...[30]

But there has been total silence concerning the next line: "These are the inferior Christs of obscure hopes" ("Ce sont les Christ inférieurs des obscures espérances"). Despite the manifest second-class status Apollinaire ascribes to non-European religious experience, Césaire recognized the poet of "Zone" as one of his literary ancestors.

Arthur Rimbaud occupies an especially privileged position among European antecedents of negritude for this declaration of revolt against his heritage of domination and colonialism: "Yes, I have my eyes closed to your light. I am a beast, a nigger . . . I am entering the true realm of the children of Ham" ("Oui, j'ai les yeux fermés à votre lumière. Je suis une bête, un nègre . . . J'entre au vrai royaume des enfants de Cham."[31] Rimbaud went so far as to imagine himself colonized by Europeans (p. 149): "The whites are disembarking. The cannon! One must submit to baptism, wear clothes and work" ("Les blancs débarquent. Le canon! Il faut se soumettre au baptême, s'habiller, travailler"). This passage is echoed in the text of Césaire's dramatic poem "And the Dogs Were Silent" ("Et les chiens se taisaient") in 1946:

Chorus
The whites are disembarking, the whites are disembarking.

The Rebel
The Whites are disembarking. They are killing our daughters, comrades.

Chorus (*terrified*)
The Whites are disembarking. The Whites are disembarking.

Chorus
Les blancs débarquent, les blancs débarquent.

Le Rebelle
Les Blancs débarquent. Ils nous tuent nos filles camarades.

Le Choeur (*terrifié*)
Les Blancs débarquent. Les Blancs débarquent.[32]

Quite naturally Césaire prized this imaginary projection of negritude by a white poet—so long, that is, as he did not know or admit to himself that Rimbaud subsequently expressed a desire to purchase slaves. Enid Starkie's *Rimbaud en Abyssinie* was published in Paris in 1938 by Payot. The literary press took sides on the issue of Rimbaud's trafficking in slaves, and it is doubtful that the book could have escaped Césaire's attention. Whatever Césaire may have concluded concerning Starkie's revelation (she succeeded in documenting only the intention to buy slaves) Césaire has never qualified his admiration for Rimbaud the poet. Most probably Césaire's surrealist orientation at this date was such that he could overlook or deny the more disturbing aspects of Rimbaud's Abyssinian adventure. In any event ambiguity was central to Césaire's relationship with Rimbaud, as J. Ngaté suggests.[33]

In his interview with René Depestre, Césaire mentioned as well the names of Maurice de Vlaminck and Georges Braque and the *Anthologie nègre* of Blaise Cendrars. With the ambiguous Europeanization of *art nègre*, this examination of the origins of Césairean negritude touches on the point, both historically and conceptually, where his negritude supposes an adaptation of literary modernism.

Negritude and Marxism

The concept of negritude has known mixed fortunes in its forty-five-year history. It has been successively a cultural rallying cry, a modish literary label, and an ideology. The problematical nature of Césaire's grasp of the term he himself coined can be rendered schematically by statements he made to interviewers over a ten-year interval. "I am an African poet!" claimed Césaire in the magazine *Afrique* in October 1961. This assertion, which has been widely disseminated by his commentators and frequently taken at face value, has oversimplified the problem to the point of absurdity. In December 1971 Césaire told Lilyan Kesteloot: "All of us blacks have our own countries, and I am an Antillean now." In the same interview, which has been published in Kesteloot and Kotchy's *Aimé Césaire, l'homme et l'oeuvre,* he added, concerning his initial awareness of Africa: "Of course my knowledge of Africa was bookish; I and my whole generation were dependent on what whites wrote about it.[34] In his 1971 interview with Kesteloot, Césaire repudiated Senghor's political-cultural position without mentioning him by name: "I am for negritude from a literary point of view and as a personal ethic, but I am against an ideology founded on negritude" (p. 235). A year earlier Césaire had expressed some exasperation at the repeated attempts to lock him into a closed system of negritude. On that occasion he articulated his differences with Senghor in detail, after noting the unity of their position in the mid-thirties: "Later on things changed somewhat and there is one point on which I no longer agreed at all with Senghor . . . : it seemed to me that Senghor made a kind of metaphysics out of negritude; there we parted company. He tended rather to construct negritude into an essentialism as though there were a black essence, a black soul, . . . but I never accepted this point of view."[35]

In squaring this denial with the evidence to the contrary in *Tropiques* that was cited earlier, one must bear in mind that Césaire is sensitive to the fact that the Marxist left in Africa and the Caribbean, as well as in Europe, has denounced the ideology of negritude as an essentially conservative and culturally separatist movement that serves as a brake on the presumably inevitable socialist revolution. Sometimes these critics, like Maryse Condé, make an effort to differentiate between Senghor's and Césaire's versions of negritude.[36] The most extensive of these attacks, a book-length essay by Stanislas S. K. Adotevi, frequently lumps the Césaire of the *Notebook* together with Senghor in an effort to discredit all statements made in the name of negritude. Adotevi, who at times is a good political satirist, claims to find no merit in the term *negritude* itself, preferring *melanism* as a more accurate rendering of its denotation: "What does socialism have to do with 'negrity' or, more precisely, with melanity? If socialism is the negation of capitalist exploitation, is the otherness postulated by the reduction of the capitalist threat black or white? If exploitation in the colonies assumes particular forms, does it differ fundamentally from capitalist exploitation in Europe or in China?"[37] Adotevi's Marxist logic must ultimately refuse the claims of negritude based on ethnic particularism. Maryse Condé, in "Négritude césairienne, négritude senghorienne," sees the essential differences between Senghor's and Césaire's versions of negritude as an outgrowth of their class origins. This difference exists "not simply, as has been claimed, because the latter is an Antillean, a direct descendent of a transplanted slave, and the former an African, not severed from his roots. It is especially because one is a child of laborers whereas the other is the son of wealthy landowners (he takes pleasure in pointing this out), and he therefore belongs to that part of African society that saw its privileges relatively respected by the colonizers" (pp. 414–415). An Antillean herself, Condé demonstrates greater sensitivity to Césairean negritude than does Adotevi, who is primarily concerned with the political options of black Africa. She is right to insist on Césaire's class origins, although she has overdone it somewhat. Condé is incorrect, however, and for the same reasons as Adotevi, in relegating Césairean negritude to the recent past: "In the case of Césaire [negritude] sees itself as preliminary, temporary, but indispensable to the awakening of consciousness that leads to the struggle for liberation" (p. 418). In terms of Condé's logic Césairean negritude is not an error in itself; it is merely outdated in a new historical perspective that has surpassed the objective conditions that brought it into being. Have conditions really changed so crucially in France's Antillean dependencies? Adotevi's argument is that black Africa—colonized for a relatively short period by the English, French, and Belgians, not to mention the short-lived German and Italian colonization, and now politically if not economically free—has no use at present for an ideology of blackness. Sociologically he is on firmer ground.

In general, current Marxist thought on this question is afflicted with a voluntary color blindness. Jose Martí worked out the approach to the problem of ethnic identity and cultural-political consciousness in the Caribbean that has been adopted officially by Castro's Cuba. Roberto Fernández Retamar articulated the Cuban Marxist version in his polemical essay *Caliban* (1971).[38] It stands in marked contrast to Césaire's negritude. A common Caribbean experience nonetheless serves as a societal model that we can reduce to its fundamental elements. Three conditions must be present: (1) a colonial economy based on de facto slave labor, enduring over a sufficiently long period to permit (2) the evolution of a distinct caste system characterized by mixed blood in which (3) the mulattos occupy a position of relative privilege and social superiority over blacks. Given this situation—which is basically different from the situation in Senghor's Senegal—two different attitudes toward class and race have evolved: the Césairean solution of negritude (blacks proclaim their blackness as constitutive of their relation to the world around them); and the current Cuban solution of an *América mestiza* (the entire culture proclaims its mixture—biological and cultural—as its identifying trait). The Cubans subsume the particularity of blacks, who are relatively less numerous than mulattos in Cuban society, within a larger whole, which is then declared to be compatible with the Marxist dialectic of the class struggle. But the model outlined above points to a double determination: the most economically disadvantaged members of society are also the blackest. They are identifiable by their melanism, to give a real content to the term Adotevi uses derisively.

There are some few Latin American Marxists who have felt

that Fernández Retamar was too quick to pass over the particular situation of blacks as a social class, rather than merely a biological element, in his account of the class struggle in Latin America. Marta E. Sanchez, whose position was basically sympathetic to his, nonetheless objected: "By stressing *mestizaje,* Fernández Retamar not only shies away from confronting the question of race but also ignores the question of class . . . By losing himself in the midst of *mestizaje,* Fernández Retamar refuses to confront the problem dialectically. His emphasis overspills too much in one direction. The relationship and interdependencies between cultural roots and economic roots should be an ongoing polemic and dialectic in Latin-American thinking."[39] Although she manifestly does not wish to raise the question of negritude directly, Sanchez concludes her article in a manner quite consonant with Césaire's attitude: "But just as the Black militant movement in this country ten years ago repudiated the terms 'Negro' and 'colored' for their denotations and connotations of 'inferior,' 'other,' 'undesirable,' all terms employed by the white ruling element to designate the black man, and emphasize *Black,* in turn, as the symbol of self-affirmation, self-dignity, and self-pride, so likewise to assent to Caliban's struggle is to live his dialectic: to adopt with honor what is originally meant as an insult" (p. 61). I see in this argument ostensible evidence that the central theses of Césairean negritude are being appropriated even by some Marxists who have become convinced of the necessity of stressing cultural particularity. The special value of Caliban as a symbol— albeit a shifting, problematical one—was to emerge in Césaire's play *A Tempest (Une Tempête).*

Césaire has argued in recent years that in a society such as that of Martinique, whose only industry of any importance is agriculture, it would have been fruitless to attempt to stimulate the class consciousness of blacks by appealing to the Marxist scenario based on the situation of urban, industrial Europe. It is easy for us to point to Mao's China or even to Nyerere's Tanzania as situations analogous to that of Martinique, with its rural economy; but who besides Mao would have had such a bold thought in the thirties, when Césaire was working out his notions of negritude? Furthermore Césaire's more recent discussions of negritude represent a significant departure from views he held during the thirties and early forties.

A few preliminary conclusions can be drawn thus far. First of all, if similar societal models can produce either the Césairean version of negritude or the Cuban ideology of a mixed culture, then surely there is no rigid determinism at work. Moreover, both these solutions are politically mutable, depending on the relative dominance of other socioeconomic conditions. Limiting ourselves to a few obvious examples, we can see that the Cuban and the Martinican experiences do not exhaust the possibilities. François ("Papa Doc") Duvalier used his version of negritude to support a benighted and thuggish tyranny in Haiti. Brazil has long vaunted its racial harmony based on ethnic intermixing. Even if one grants that this situation may represent more than a self-congratulatory patriotic exercise, nothing in this cultural mix appears to prevent Brazil's periodic reliance on military strongmen. In short, nothing in the claims of negritude as a cultural-political posture ensures a given political or ideological result.

Is this to say that Adotevi is right in arguing that negritude, based as it is on ethnicity, is irrelevant to the crucial decisions facing the newly independent African nations? To answer in the affirmative is to ignore the social dynamics of two of the newest African republics, Mozambique and Angola. Unlike most black African states they resemble the Caribbean island nations in having been colonized for several centuries by a European power, during which time an important mulatto caste established itself in a buffer position between the Europeans and the blacks. In 1977 Angola suffered a bloodletting in which political oppositions were drawn along ethnic lines. On one side were the followers of President Agostinho Neto, a Marxist, an accomplished poet in Portuguese, and a mulatto, whose government was bolstered militarily by several thousand Cuban troops. On the other side were the rebels, followers of former Interior Minister Nito Alves, who hoped to install a radical black socialism in Angola. The Soviets and Cubans had shifted their support from Alves to the Neto camp, which embraced a more orthodox Marxism. The two parties in conflict bore a remarkable similarity to Césairean negritude and Cuban *mestizaje*, respectively. The armed conflict itself, while fought under political banners, had the unmistakable markings of a race war. Doubtless the term *negritude* is unimportant in the case of the recent civil war in Angola, but the social dynamics that originally gave rise to the negritude movement are all in place there. The Angolan pattern will almost certainly be re-peated elsewhere.[40]

In the Caribbean region the coals of a similar social conflict smoulder in Jamaica. In the seventies the People's National party under the leadership of Michael Manley attempted to hold in check the potential for violence among the black lumpenproletar-iat while aligning itself with Castro's Cuba. The Jamaican ex-ample presents a valuable analogue to Césaire's version of negri-tude. The Rastafarians, cultural leaders of many dispossessed Jamaican blacks, have pieced together a syncretic pseudomythol-ogy justifying themselves as displaced Africans. Popular reggae songs of the type known as "roots" reggae are used as hymns in some of the Abyssinian or Ethiopian churches and are frequently taken as allegorical references to the revolution to come. In cer-tain Marxist circles the Rastas are seen as a truly popular revolu-tionary movement, untouched by the taint of bourgeois culture. The values of the Rastafarians, however, are more religious than political, and their stated goal is a return to the mystical home-land. Their influence has now extended to the U.S. Virgin Islands, where in 1978 a flyer was circulated to this effect: "The planters were paid at the abolition of slavery. We have yet to be paid. We are the sons and daughters of slaves. We have come to the end of this service. We desire return back to Africa. Transportation to and finance of such a venture is a responsibility of Babylon U.S.A. and her allies."[41] There is an ambiguity in Rastafarian thought that similarly affected Césaire's early formulation of negritude. The current social scheme is perceived as unacceptable, but the tensions between the desire to modify the society itself and the desire to escape from it spiritually admit of no simple solution. Cultural manifestions resulting from this state of affairs are un-avoidably self-contradictory.

The numerous political ramifications of negritude demonstrate that it is far from being an ideological dead letter. For this reason too it is unwise to consider negritude passé as a literary move-ment. The problems posed by Aimé Césaire from the mid-thirties on are still very much alive in several parts of the world. In this respect Césaire's work speaks, through the indirection typical of modernist literature, to the sociologist and the political theorist, as well as to those concerned with literature in the belletristic tradition.

2

Césaire
and Modernism

Poets have always known. All the legends of antiquity attest
to it. But in modern times it is only in the nineteenth century, as
the Apollinian era draws to a close, that poets dared to claim
that they knew.

Césaire, "Poetry and Cognition"

De tout temps les poètes ont su. Toute la légende antique
l'atteste. Mais dans les temps modernes, ce n'est qu'au XIXe
siècle, au moment où commence à se fermer l'ère apollinienne,
que les poètes ont osé prétendre qu'ils savaient.

"Poésie et Connaissance"

FOR THE FOUNDERS of negritude, their relation to
history and myth was to prove the decisive intellectual problem.
In Frobenius they discovered an apparent legitimization of their
blackness, even though the Caribbean writers could experience
the black soul, or paideuma, only in distorted, fragmented or
residual manifestations. But for Césaire and many others of his
generation, the survival of remnants of an African culture in the
midst of a modern technological civilization suggested a quest for
origins. Thus the first phase of negritude, which for Césaire runs
from his earliest, no longer extant writings to his collections of
poems *Beheaded Sun (Soleil cou coupé)* and *Lost Body (Corps
perdu),* involved an increasing reliance on various approaches to
myth and a concomitant refusal of the claims of rationalist and
empiricist historical writing.

The importance of Frobenius for the negritude writers situates
them in the company of some important European and American
modernists, among whom Ezra Pound, W. B. Yeats, and André
Malraux are particularly noteworthy. Pound's deep interest in

Frobenius has been documented since the first attempts at exegesis of *The Cantos*. Guy Davenport traced Pound's reading of Frobenius to the mid-twenties. A few years later *Erlebte Erdteile* (1929) contributed significantly to the theory of cultural history Pound would incorporate in *The Cantos*. It was not Africanism per se but rather the belief in the paideuma that attracted Pound's attention. An interesting letter from Yeats to T. Sturge Moore in 1929 gives some indication of Pound's enthusiasm and of the version of Frobenius he promulgated among some of the most influential modernists:

> Ezra Pound has just been in. He says, "Spengler is a Wells who has founded himself on German scholarship instead of English journalism." He is sunk in Frobenius, Spengler's German source, and finds him a most interesting person. Frobenius suggested the idea that cultures (including arts and sciences) arise out of races, express those races as if they were fruit and leaves in a pre-ordained order and perish with them . . . He proved from his logic—some German told Ezra—that a certain civilization must have existed at a certain point in Africa and then went and dug it up. He proved his case all through by African research.[1]

This personal version of Frobenian ethnography is not so very different in tone from the enthusiasm Césaire's magazine *Tropiques* was to lavish on his *Kulturgeschichte Afrikas*.

The Yeats letter is significant in another respect as well. It pairs Frobenius with Spengler, who did in fact draw on the author of *Das unbekannte Afrika* (1923) in *The Decline of the West*. In Frobenian terms the *Abendland* of Spengler's title pairs quite neatly with his own outline of Hamitic civilization. Spengler shared with Frobenius a cyclical view of universal history that could only signal the end of the dominion of colonial oppression of blacks in both Africa and the Caribbean (in the eyes of the negritude writers, at least). Thus, albeit for quite different reasons, Césaire and an important group of European modernists were attracted to a similar historical imagination. Frobenius, particularly when paired with Spengler, provided a much-desired sense of an ending of the present order of things.

André Malraux too, in his early years especially, found Spengler attractive as a philosopher of history. It is less well known that he actually used Frobenius as the type for the scholarly character Möllberg in *The Walnut Trees of Altenburg*. In that novel Malraux attempted an intellectual synthesis of a generation that had known Nietzsche (he goes so far as to have his narrator's uncle accompany the mad Nietzsche home from Turin) and had seen an epoch end in the 1914–1918 war. The Möllberg of the novel had frequently been mistaken for "a fictional projection of Oswald Spengler" until Armand Hoog thought to question Malraux about him. Malraux replied that "ideologically [Möllberg is] Frobenius (insofar as the characters of a novel are ever anyone)."[2]

It is very important, I believe, for us to become more aware of the extent to which the negritude writers paralleled and prolonged a mental set that existed, sometimes diffusely but occasionally with a remarkably similar focus (as the examples of Spenglerian and Frobenian thought demonstrate quite clearly), in the work of the foremost modernist writers of their own and the preceding generation. There is probably no direct connection to be made between Césaire and Pound, Yeats, or Malraux. Yet Césaire had at his disposal the same European intellectual traditions as these writers when he set out to become the poet of negritude. He did not dredge up Mother Africa from some atavistic racial memory, despite some early claims to the contrary, nor did he in his surrealist phase gratuitously distort reality through automatic writing. (The automatism effect in Césaire is a poetic style that pairs associative metaphors with intertextuality.) A degree of demystification is in order on this subject. Some further probing of Césaire's points of contact with modernism will help us to place his work in a much broader context as well as to assess its contributions to world literature.

I alluded in the preceding chapter to Césaire's reading of Spengler. The foregoing examples of the parallelism between Spengler and Frobenius are certainly suggestive of the import for Césaire of Spengler's *The Decline of the West*. For Césaire what mattered most was the poetic grasp of history and culture in terms of birth, death, and rebirth—essentially an optimistic version of the eschatological imagination that occurs so prominently in modernist thought from Yeats to Toynbee and from Spengler to Sandburg, as Lemuel Johnson has suggested.[3] The concept of the cycle of culture is present in Spengler as well as in Frobenius, but the notion of rebirth as Césaire imagined it is closer to the heart of a thinker whose shadow falls across them both.

The name of Friedrich Nietzsche occurs prominently several times in *Tropiques* during the first year of its publication. And in the issue for January 1945 Césaire placed the beginnings of modern literature under the aegis of Nietzsche's mythological pair, Dionysus and Apollo. Césaire's grasp of Nietzsche was complex and his appreciation selective. The aspect of Nietzschean thought that stands in the closest relation to this theory of history, the eternal return of the same, can scarcely have held a great appeal for Césaire. Negritude after all was concerned in its early stages with the heroic affirmation of blacks and their culture as other than the dominant Euro-American values that had enslaved and degraded them. It was the inebriating effect of Nietzsche's theory of the will, freed from the constraints of a stultifying reason, that induced Césaire to exploit this source of new poetic myths. In this respect Césaire was merely repeating and extending, quite independently I am sure, a process of adapting Nietzsche to a French cultural climate that the symbolists had begun around the turn of the century and that the existentialists were themselves carrying forward simultaneously with Césaire. The historical cycle of culture, which could be taken to promise a rebirth of negritude, was for Césaire a mystical, Dionysian experience. The Césairean hero, lyric and dramatic, is a black Overman. Since there is still a distorted image of the Overman present in the culture at large, prudence cautions me to point out that Césaire, like Nietzsche himself, took the Overman to be the exemplary sufferer through whose sacrifice the community is reborn. The Nietzschean will to power also occurs in Césaire's writing at an early date. On the condition that we follow Nietzsche, as I am sure Césaire has done, in specifying that the highest manifestation of the will to power is poetically creative, we can also begin to understand Césaire's frequently cited admiration for Paul Claudel, whose play *Tête d'or* he has consistently listed among those works most important to him in his student years. In his article on "Upholding Poetry" ("Maintenir la poésie") in the October 1943 issue of *Tropiques*, Césaire made quite clear that what he most appreciated in Claudel were his Nietzschean qualities: "Claudel, never so fulgurating as when he ceases to be Catholic to become earth, planet, matter, sound, and fury, super-

ego, *superman* whether he exalts the *will to power* ('Tête d'or')
or opens the homicidal floodgates of a humor à la Jarry ('Soulier
de satin')."[4]

Césaire's insistence on the importance of Claudel and his admission that he had read Nietzsche at an early date have received
very little attention. By considering both Claudel and Nietzsche
intertextually, in the context of Césaire's relation to European
modernism, one gains insight into particular aspects (themes,
symbols, and attitudes) of Césaire's early poetry, especially some
of its more elusive qualities. It has often been noted, for instance,
that Césaire elaborated a solar myth beginning with his first collection of poetry, *Miraculous Weapons,* in 1946. An important
symbol in this myth is the wheel, which, in its revolution, is always ending but simultaneously always beginning anew. The
wheel and related figures occur prominently throughout Césaire's
writing as metaphors of the circular nature of history. They
manifestly connect his poetry to European modernism in its
preference for an undifferentiated mythic experience.

Aesthetic Primitivism

The mythic mode is a well-charted area of modernist writing.
The legend of the otherness of negritude, which stems in part
from Sartre's "Black Orpheus" essay of 1948, has had the paradoxical effect of inhibiting scholars from exploring the renaissance of black writers in French in relation to their European
and American contemporaries. Rarely has such discussion proceeded beyond a summary notation of points of contact with
surrealism as a movement, whereas the truly important issue is
the broad area of common assumptions about poetry, indeed
about mind, that negritude has shared with surrealism. The work
of Aimé Césaire is a most fruitful ground for this exploration because he has excelled in both the lyric and the drama; in the early
years of his career he wrote incisively on the intellectual tradition
from which both movements spring. He gave a detailed outline
of his aesthetics in September 1944; the text was printed in the
twelfth issue of *Tropiques* (January 1945). It is the most important single document we possess for situating Césaire's early
version of negritude with respect to literary modernism. "Poetry
and Cognition" is very explicit on the function of myth within

culture: "Only myth satisfies man completely; his heart, his reason, his taste for detail and wholeness, his taste for the false and for the true, since myth is all that at once. A misty and emotional apprehension, rather than a means of poetic expression . . ."[5] Two propositions dominate Césaire's exposition of the case for the superiority of myth: it promises wholeness to the human person, and it gives access to a fundamental understanding of the world. In short Césaire embraces a position that has always existed in Western thought in the form of a subversive or subterranean undercurrent hostile to the dominant culture. Césaire's position is at bottom similar to that of Herbert Marcuse in *Eros and Civilization*. To paraphrase Marcuse, who drew on the same intellectual and poetic tradition as Césaire, the mythic values of Orpheus and Dionysus must be rehabilitated even at the expense of Prometheus, the divinity of technological society. In Césaire's words:

> Poetic cognition is born in the great silence of scientific knowledge.
> Through reflection, observation, experiment, man bewildered by the data confronting him, finally dominated them. Henceforth he knows how to guide himself through the forest of phenomena. He knows how to utilize the world . . .
> In short, scientific knowledge enumerates, measures, classifies and kills . . .
> To acquire it man has sacrificed everything: his desires, fears, feelings and psychological complexes. (p. 112)

To keep his paper within the boundaries imposed by a meeting of professional philosophers Césaire chose to challenge two well-established arguments. The first is a cornerstone of Western thought and generally enjoys the status of a basic postulate or axiom: the law of noncontradiction along with the logical principle of the excluded middle serves to channel reason and to orient all discourse. But the role of the poetic image is to open our eyes anew to a world in which A *can* be A'. The thrust of the challenge is that, whereas the rules of Aristotelian logic are in fact indispensable to the organization of a modern society, there is nothing inevitable about them. They are the conventions upon which a certain type of rational social order has been founded, but they are not immutable. Worse, according to Césaire, they have impoverished mankind by crippling the imaginative faculty, without the free functioning of which we are incomplete beings.

Césaire also sought to counter the academic neo-Kantián philosophy that had dominated the Sorbonne in the person and the writings of Léon Brunschvicg from about 1909 onwards: "However much effort one may expend to reduce analytical judgment to synthetic judgment; to say that judgment supposes the bringing together of two different concepts; to insist upon the idea that there is no judgment without X; that all judgment is transcendence, it is nonetheless true that in all valid judgment the margin of transcendence is limited" (p. 122). He saw this modern metaphysical tradition as the great impediment to the exercise of creative mind because the dominant Kantian position gave preeminence to the constructive faculty of synthetic intelligence. In symbolic terms it represented for Césaire the contemporary perfecting of the Promethean value system.

Only one professional philosopher is spared in Césaire's general condemnation of accepted modes of reasoning (rarely does his text function as philosophical argument per se). Henri Bergson is the unmistakable guarantor of this enthusiastically proclaimed truth: "Surrender to the vital movement, to the creative élan. Joyous surrender" (p. 118). In this direction, according to Césaire, mankind may rediscover the original creative capacity of the species: "Surrounding the poem about to be made, the precious vortex: ego, id, world. And the most unlikely familiar contacts, all the pasts, all the futures (the anticyclone builds its plateaux, the amoeba loses its pseudopods, lost vegetations encounter one another). . . The body is no longer deaf or blind . . . The whole individual stirred anew by poetic inspiration. And, in a more disturbing manner, the cosmic whole as well" (p. 118). Taking into account the reference to ego and id, which indicates the presence of a parallel movement in contemporary thought, and discounting the total lack of restraint, which the more circumspect Bergson would have carefully avoided, we find here some significant points of contact with the only irrationalist thought the French have officially countenanced in recent times.

Bergson's central intuition of duration as the experiential dimension of human time stands in close relation to that poetic conflation of temporal modes that Césaire was to practice rather frequently. It is a bridge for Césaire between Western thought and an approach to time that Jahn and others have claimed to be peculiarly African. Jahn has cited Césaire's poem "To Africa" as exemplary of African *Hantu*, "time and place in one."[6] And it may well be. But might not Césaire have arrived at this effect through a meditation on Bergson's *Essai sur les données immédiates de la conscience?* Surely this hypothesis is both simpler and more probable than the one entertained by Jahn, for whom Césaire's status as a neo-African poet presupposes precisely that which was lacking in his Martinican experience, namely the traditional transmission of significant elements of African culture.

One other point of contact between Césaire and Bergson, between poetry and philosophy, deserves mention. Césaire constructed his paper "Poetry and Cognition" on a binary opposition: *poetry*—intuitive, creative, synthetic, tending toward wholeness—is opposed to *science*—deductive, classifying, analytic, tending toward the division of mankind into discrete functions. This is of course a very crude representation of modern science and as such it is so distorted as to be false. But it does bear a recognizable likeness to the spirit of nineteenth-century science, which Bergsonian philosophy set out to combat. In fact one has only to substitute *philosophy* for *poetry* in order to recognize in one of Césaire's conclusions a basic premise of Bergsonian thought: "In other words, poetry is an opening outward [*épanouissement*]. Opening outward of mankind to the dimension of the world; a vertiginous expansion [*dilatation*]. And it may be said that all great poetry, without ever renouncing its humanness, at some very mysterious moment ceases to be strictly human so as to begin to be truly cosmic" (p. 119). Bergson for his part had written in *La Science française* (1915) that philosophy "will aim as well—and this is where it distinguishes itself from science —to progressively enlarge the framework of understanding . . . and to expand [*dilater*] human thought indefinitely."[7] Both the philosopher and the poet addressing philosophers accentuated the mind-expanding tendency of thought. They perceived not limits but an opening outward of human faculties to an undetermined point of mystical embrace with the cosmic whole. *Elan vital, Païdeuma, Wille zur Macht:* complementary notions of the creative spirit that moves the world. Césaire's aesthetics in the

forties originates at the point of convergence of these three versions of metaphysical vitalism.

Of the three irrationalist thinkers it is still Frobenius rather than
Bergson or Nietzsche who dominates the type of primitivism that
characterizes Césaire's aesthetics of negritude. In "Poetry and
Cognition" he reveals the Ariadne's thread that in his view connects the "primitive discoverer" to modern man: "And here we
see that which takes us back to the first days of humanity. It is
an error to believe that knowledge, to be born, had to await
the methodical exercise of thought or the scruples of experimentation. I even believe that man has never been closer to certain
truths than in the first days of the species. At the time when man
discovered with emotion the first sun, the first rain, the first
breath, the first moon. At the time when man discovered in fear
and rapture the throbbing newness of the world" (pp. 113–114).
Much of Césaire's early poetry in *Miraculous Weapons* and
Beheaded Sun represents a lyrical effort to recreate a primitive
cosmogony. *Primitive* has a metaphysical rather than a sociological significance as applied to Césaire's poetry. In the same paper
he sketched the poetic lineage with which he associated himself:

> Poets have always known. All the legends of antiquity
> attest to it. But in modern times it is only in the nineteenth
> century, as the Apollinian era draws to a close, that poets
> dared to claim that they knew.
> 1850—The revenge of Dionysus upon Apollo.
> 1850—The great leap into the poetic void.   (p. 114)

Modernism begins, Césaire tells us, with Baudelaire, whom he
cites at length, revealing just how sophisticated his primitivism
is. Indeed his encapsulated history of the modern movement could
borrow the title of Marcel Raymond's celebrated essay *From
Baudelaire to Surrealism*. The more one examines it, the richer
the texture of Césaire's aesthetic heritage becomes.

The Precious Vortex

It is a paradox of the negritude movement that it simultaneously
cultivated a rhetoric of protest and an intensely subjective poetics:
the one, discursive and polemical, turned toward the world; the

other, lyrical and looking inward to a personal renewal, turned toward a form of spiritual salvation or revelation. This second direction, which became the dominant mode in Césaire's early poetry, suggests a psychology compatible with surrealism.

An odd allusion to "the German philosopher Jung" in "Poetry and Cognition" indicates that Césaire was aware of Carl Jung in 1944 but in all probability had not yet read him. Jung, says Césaire, "discovers the idea of energy and its conservation in Heraclitus' metaphor of the eternally living fire, in medieval legends about the halos of the saints, in theories of metempsychosis" (p. 123). Readers of Jung's *Psychology and Alchemy* will recognize the central idea, which Césaire seems to have picked up from a curious figure, self-taught, whose writings are an amalgam of hermetic notions with recent social science. Pierre Mabille's *Miroir du merveilleux* (1940) was considered by *Tropiques* to be an important contribution to the understanding of the imagination. Mabille himself wrote an occasional piece for *Tropiques* and was obviously in close touch with Césaire during the war years. Pierre Mabille, as the new Gaullist governor of the French West Indies, made the official arrangements for Césaire's visit to Haiti in 1944. In a short essay published in Mexico City in 1945 he quoted at length Césaire's 1942 "Literary Manifesto," calling Césaire "the most recent of the great French poets."[8] In 1938 Mabille had published an obscure essay on the life of civilizations, the title of which—*Egrégores*—he borrowed from the occult tradition. According to Mabille's theory an *égrégore*, or human group possessing a personality different from that of its members taken individually, can arise only when an intense emotional shock has, so to speak, galvanized the collectivity. In "Poetry and Cognition" Césaire quotes Mabille in the paragraph that mentions Jung: "And for his part, Pierre Mabille regrets that the biologist should believe it 'dishonorable to describe the evolution of blood corpuscles in terms of the story of the phoenix, or the functions of the spleen through the myth of Saturn engendering children only to devour them'" (p. 123). It is a reasonable hypothesis that at the time he wrote *Miraculous Weapons* (1941–1945) Césaire entertained the hope that such a collective shock might regenerate black Martinique.

The symbolism of the phoenix occurs sporadically throughout Césaire's poetry, as Lilyan Kesteloot has noted.[9] Pierre Mabille, moreover, represents another link in the chain of thinkers great and small who led Césaire to the conviction of a fundamental unity in primitive thought implying the interpenetration of symbolic systems. Thus the lyrical expression of death and resurrection can generate a metaphoric association with the phoenix, with Dionysus, or with Osiris quite indifferently, as the examination of Césaire's poetry will show.

Aimé Césaire was very straightforward in "Poetry and Cognition" concerning his belief in a fundamental unconscious unity in nature. He recalled to the attention of the philosophers "that this unconscious that all true poetry calls upon is the receptacle of the original relationships that unite us to nature . . . In us [resides] the mankind of the ages. In us, all men. In us, the animal, the vegetable, the mineral. Man is not merely man. He is *universe*. Everything takes place as if, prior to the secondary separation of life, there had been a tight primitive unity by which the poets have continued to be dazzled" (p. 118). Césaire's poetics of primitivism involves an idea of the psyche that connects him in a complex fashion to the heritage of Jung. Because the irrationalists who mattered to him were as one in positing a monistic energy in the universe, because in this view the individual psyche is the repository of the wisdom of the age, Césaire also came to Freud with a strong personal sense of what psychoanalysis ought to mean, rather like a latter-day William Blake reading *The Interpretation of Dreams*.

When Césaire mentions in "Poetry and Cognition" the precious vortex comprising ego, id, and world, we must take care not to interpret him too narrowly. Exercising all due caution, I nonetheless find in Césaire's exposition of the poet's relation to the psyche something akin to Freud's theory of racial memory in his late essay *Moses and Monotheism*. This is doubtless the point at which Freudian theory comes closest to the archetypes that, in the Jungian scheme, express a universal symbolism. Much later, in June 1959, Césaire outlined for Lilyan Kesteloot a concept of the image with marked Jungian overtones. The letter in question maintains that "all or almost all images are reducible to some *primordial images*, which—encrusted in the collective unconscious—are universal, as the language of dreams proves, identical for all people above and beyond the diversity of languages and modes of existence."[10]

The promise of Freudian and Jungian psychologism for Césaire was then very great indeed. If the poetic exploration of the psyche could unlock the treasure of symbolic knowledge, then perhaps the disinherited sons and daughters of colonialism and slavery could travel a short route to their ancestral past. Césaire summarized his paper "Poetry and Cognition" in seven propositions. The fourth mentions the presumed role of Freud in this quest: "If affective energy can be endowed with causal power as Freud indicated, it is paradoxical to refuse it power and penetration. It is conceivable that nothing can resist the unheard-of mobilization of force that poetry necessitates, or the multiplied élan of those forces" (p. 126). There is no doubt whatsoever that in these currents of European modernism Césaire thought he had found the instruments, the notions, even the techniques for constructing negritude. His own historical past and that of his people having been obliterated, Césaire in the early forties wagered heavily on the power of poetry to find a subterranean passage to his origins. On the one hand the practice of poetry remains intensely personal: "What emerges is the individual foundation. The intimate conflicts, the obsessions, the phobias, the fixations. All the codes of the personal message" (p. 123). But is not the public or collective message that the poem conveys simultaneously the element of interest to negritude? "And what emerges as well is the old ancestral foundation. Hereditary images that only the poetic atmosphere can bring to light for ultimate decoding. The buried knowledge of the ages. In this sense all the mythologies that the poet tumbles about, all the symbols he collects and regilds are true. And poetry alone takes them seriously. Which goes to make poetry a serious business" (p. 123).

It was doubtless in this dual operation of poetry as a liberation of the unconscious that Césaire initially thought he could legitimately claim both the special black view of the world and a symbolism that would ultimately transcend race. I believe Césaire has been entirely sincere in denying the charges of anti-racist racism that have been periodically leveled at negritude since Sartre coined the unfortunate term *racisme anti-raciste* in "Black Orpheus." Presumably the black poet practicing a poetics of psychic liberation would, in untying his own personal psychic knots, produce a poetry of negritude. But at the same time the interpenetration of the personal by the archaic or collective unconscious would put at the disposition of the poet a fund of universal archetypes communicable to mankind generally. This conclusion, which Césaire did not specifically draw but which follows from his claims in "Poetry and Cognition," would present the poetics of negritude as an enrichment of the world's cultural heritage. If we consider Césaire's early poetics from this angle we find that the content of the term *negritude* approaches the minimal definition: the right to be black and to affirm one's blackness. But to function as Césaire manifestly intended, a poetics of negritude so conceived would necessarily involve three levels of communication:

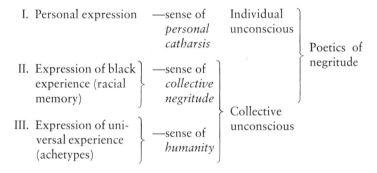

There are serious conceptual difficulties that arise from this theory. The idea of negritude in its psychological dimension involves both the personal and the collective unconscious. It does not correspond specifically to either aspect of presumed psychic function, yet both are assumed to express or reveal a part of it. If category I corresponds roughly to the usual Freudian approach to artistic creation as sublimation, category III is recognizably the domain of archetypal criticism, which knows neither racial nor cultural distinctions as such. Furthermore, by schematizing the concepts associated with a poetics of negritude as Césaire has outlined it, we have revealed in category II a thesis that all reputable social science rejects unequivocally: the transmission of black cultural traits through a racial (ethnic) memory. The postulate of a racial memory in the Freudian sense—common to mankind generally—is already sufficiently controversial. The postulate of an archaic ethnic memory is patently absurd, since it can operate only in conjunction with an ideal ethnic purity. Shall we attribute a part of the symbolism of *Ulysses* to the archaic Gaelic memory of Joyce? Do the Yemenite Jews and the Sephardic Jews have the same ethnic memory? And whose ethnic memory is inherited by mulattos?

The underpinnings of this version of negritude, which Césaire was subsequently to alter and even repudiate, begin to look surprisingly like some of the fuzzier notions of D. H. Lawrence. In Césaire, as in Lawrence, access to a cosmic unity is frequently expressed in terms of a communion of blood, a phallic marriage, in Lawrence's terminology. This is the usual function of eroticism in Césaire's poetry. In the poem "Lost Body," for instance, one of the privileged metaphors of access to the earth mother involves carnal knowledge of Omphale in which the "I" is an implicit Hercules: "And I weigh and I force and I arcane / I omphale" ("Et je pèse et je force et j'arcane / j'omphale").[11] Lawrence's *Fantasia of the Unconscious* systematizes this phallic consciousness, whereas in Césaire it remains metaphoric, never discursive. Yet there is more than momentary coincidence of imagery between Césaire's personal mythology and Lawrence's: "Woman is really polarized downwards toward the center of the earth. Her deep positivity is in the downward flow, the moon-pull. And man is polarized upwards, toward the sun and the day's activity."[12] Both writers give a special place to the symbolism of blood, which provides a biological guarantee of contact with a past that rushes toward the future.

Black Humor

Another of the paradoxes of Césairean negritude is its relation to humor. Aimé Césaire's understanding of *l'humour noir* can be usefully contrasted to the *humour nègre* of which Senghor has said that "the Black, rather than protesting in the name of reason, or affirming with a smile the primacy of intelligence, the Black affirms in a burst of laughter the primacy of life."[13] Senghor cites as an example of *humour nègre* the booming laughter of Langston Hughes, contrasting it with the extreme intellectuality of French humor. Aimé Césaire in "Poetry and Cognition" and elsewhere has elaborated on the theory of *humour noir,* which André Breton put in circulation in his *Anthologie de l'humour noir* (1940). We are offered an especially clear view of Césaire's reliance on modernism in his approach to humor. One would think that if negritude were indeed the naturally transmitted sum of the values of the black world—to paraphrase Senghor's favorite definition—then Césaire's laughter would be closer to Langston Hughes's than to André Breton's. In fact Césaire's earliest attempt to define humor relies heavily on Freud's theory as he outlined it in the 1928 paper "Humour," which has generally been read in France as an appendix to *Wit and its Relation to the Unconscious.*

"In a masterful page," Césaire wrote in 1943, "Freud distinguishes Ego from Superego: Superego, core of the Ego, heir to the parental function that holds the Ego under its strict tutelage."[14] The standard English translation of the text Césaire quoted directly is as follows (less the bracketed adjectives added by Césaire): "We obtain a dynamic explanation of the humorous attitude, therefore, if we conclude that it consists in the subject's removing the accent from his own ego and transferring it on to his super-ego. To the super-ego, thus inflated, the ego can appear tiny and all its interests trivial, and with this distribution of energy it may be an easy matter for it to suppress the [infantile and passionate] reactions of the ego."[15] Since André Breton had used the same text and part of the same passage as the groundwork for his *Anthologie de l'humour noir,* one might have suspected Césaire of borrowing from the more literary, surrealist account. But Césaire's citation is more extensive than Breton's and indicates that he went directly to Freud's *Wit* for a theory of humor. This is all the more interesting in that discussions of Césaire's important readings have never included significant mention of Freud. The central role Césaire ascribed to Lautréamont, both in the 1943 article and in "Poetry and Cognition," situates him in relation to surrealism but already as an independent prospector of the same rich vein.

Césaire's Freudian sense of humor is both European and modernist. It assumes the dominance of intellect over sensibility and imagination in the normal functioning of the ego. In "Poetry and Cognition" he wrote: "Humor alone assures me that the most prodigious reversals are legitimate. Humor alone alerts me to the other side of things" (p. 121). It sets up that special kind of tension that Eliot found to be peculiar to modern poetry. Césaire's surrealist version of Freud draws the father of psychoanalysis

willy-nilly into the orbit of modernist poetics. Freud offered Césaire an unambiguous haven for the ego battered by real ad-
verstiy:

> Humour is not resigned; it is rebellious. It signifies the tri-
> umph not only of the ego, but also of the pleasure principle,
> which is strong enough to assert itself here in the face of
> the adverse real circumstances . . . the denial of the claim
> of reality and the triumph of the pleasure principle, cause
> humour to approximate to the regressive or reactionary
> processes which engage our attention so largely in psycho-
> pathology. By its repudiation of the possibility of suffering,
> it takes its place in the great series of methods devised by
> the mind of man for evading the compulsion to suffer.
> (*Collected Papers*, V, 217)

In short, humor, or *humour noir* as Césaire conceived it in the
forties, was yet another strategem—borrowed from the oppressor
to be sure—devised to outwit and otherwise thwart the claim of
an unacceptable reality, social and psychic. Césaire's negritude
in the forties involved an antirealist aesthetics that shared many
features with other modernist artists and movements but that
enjoyed for a time a very special relationship with surrealism.

Literary Forebears

In "Poetry and Cognition" Aimé Césaire gave a brief analysis
of the modern movement in poetry as he saw it. All the references
are French and none are unexpected. Only the particular accent
Césaire placed on the importance of modernism serves to distinguish his map of modern poetry from that of Marcel Raymond
or Maurice Bowra. He saw Baudelaire as the ancestor of Rimbaud,
citing "Elévation," "Obsession" and "Bohémiens en voyage" as
evidence of the arcane knowledge to which the poet has access.
Baudelaire then becomes the herald, the John the Baptist, of the
new spirit in poetry: "The prosiest nation, in its most eminent
representatives—by the most mountainous routes, the hardest,
haughtiest, and most breathtaking, by the only routes I am willing
to call sacred and royal—with all weapons and equipment went
over to the enemy. I mean to the death's-head army of freedom

and imagination" (p. 114). The anarchism of this judgment is flagrant and indisputable. The modern spirit is a postulation of the absolute. The poetry it inspires, while not an end in itself, does not answer to any other law, since there is none higher. Césaire in 1944 situated himself alongside André Breton as the heir to Rimbaud, whose "lettre du voyant" he called "the incredible seismic tremor" that continues to rock the world.

> And the result is known to you: strange cities, extraordinary countrysides, worlds twisted, crushed, torn apart, the cosmos given back to disorder, being given over to becoming, everywhere the absurd, everywhere the incoherent, the demential. And at the end of all that! What is there? Failure! No, the flashing vision of his own destiny. And the most authentic vision of the world if, as I stubbornly continue to believe, Rimbaud is the first man to have experienced as feeling, as anguish, the modern idea of energetic forces in matter that cunningly wait to ambush our quietude. (p. 125)

Whereas at a distance Césaire's commentary on Rimbaud appears to add little to the ambient surrealist view, his interpretation of Mallarmé was quite original for the time. He took seriously Mallarmé's statement to Verlaine that the "Orphic explication of the Earth is the sole duty of the poet" (p. 116) and concluded that the author of *A Roll of the Dice (Un Coup de dés)* was an "engineer of the spirit of very special importance" (p. 115). In his earlier "Views on Mallarmé," printed in the fifth issue of *Tropiques* (April 1942), Césaire had applied to a number of Mallarmé's poems categories of analysis taken from Freud for their hermeneutic potential: impotence and transfer of affect in "Hérodiade," a psychic parthenogenesis in "Gift of the Poem" ("Don du poëme"), return to the womb in "Renewal" ("Renouveau"), or a vain attempt at normalization of the ego in the prelude to "The Afternoon of a Faun" ("L'Après-midi d'un faune"). None of these suggestions is really developed; a short quotation is offered to illustrate each idea. Césaire's overriding notion is that of the "power of the Libido [at] the very heart of the most audacious metaphysics" (p. 55). What is worth retaining is Césaire's conviction of the creative thrust of the pleasure principle, even and especially in so austere a poet as Mallarmé. This brief glimpse is, however, adequate to demonstrate that Césaire's orientation to psychoanalytic thought was not the typically reductive one that has plagued literary criticism. He clearly anticipates the psychocriticism that Charles Mauron would elaborate some years later.

Apollinaire is represented by a lengthy quotation from the middle of "The Pretty Redhead" ("La Jolie Rousse"), beginning at "You whose mouths are made in the image of God's / . . . Pity for us who combat always at the frontiers / Of the limitless and of the future" ("Vous dont la bouche est faite à l'image de celle de Dieu / . . . Pitié pour nous qui combattons toujours aux frontières / De l'illimité et de l'avenir"). No poem expresses better the transitional position of Apollinaire, caught between order and adventure but, according to Césaire, surely the "enthusiastic adventurer." Césaire was also sensitive to the typographical experimentation in *Calligrammes* and borrowed from "Smoke" ("Fumées") in two passages of his own "The Thoroughbreds" ("Les Pur-Sang"). After the original edition of 1946, however, Césaire reverted to a normal horizontal disposition of the words in question. He may have judged that this borrowing was simply too transparent. Apollinaire's "The Pretty Redhead" ends on the supplicating note, "Take pity on me" ("Ayez pitié de moi"). The third poem in *Miraculous Weapons* was entitled in the original edition "Take No Pity on Me" ("N'ayez point pitié de moi"). The personal element, *de moi,* which most readily suggests Apollinaire, was removed from the title in the 1970 and 1976 editions.

Césaire reserved for André Breton the position of preeminence among the modernists. He especially admired the section of the *Second Manifesto of Surrealism* (1930) that vaunts surrealist activity as the hope of determining the point at which all oppositions resolve themselves in synthesis. At this juncture in his 1944 paper Césaire brings literary history and irrationalist metaphysics together to convince us that modernist poetics of the sort he envisages will in fact found a new epistemology: "More and more, the word ventures to appear [to function] like an algebraic notation that renders the world intelligible" (p. 119). It is finally the surrealist image that will make available to us the immemorial wisdom of the species. Césaire admits that this "new science" is still in the shadows, although poetry certainly points the way to it.

"Poetry and Cognition" Assessed

It has been necessary to set forth in detail Césaire's position on the nature of poetry in 1944 because most previous assessments of his work, based as they were on Césaire's attitudes in the fifties, could not accept that he ever took all this seriously. The paper on "Poetry and Cognition," although it has been available for several years, has not previously been brought to bear on Césaire's evolution as a poet. The fact that the author of the *Discourse on Colonialism*, written but six years after "Poetry and Cognition," would reject much of what has been discussed in this and the preceding chapter must not blind us to another, equally important fact: this was the frame of mind in which Aimé Césaire composed the poetry of *Miraculous Weapons, Beheaded Sun,* and *Lost Body.* He arrived at this position gradually over a ten-year period.

In this overview of Aimé Césaire's intellectual and literary coordinates, two important names are omitted: Karl Marx and Victor Hugo. Those who have chosen to stress Césaire's role as the poet of decolonization have often based their arguments on his belonging to and representing the Communist party of France from 1945 to 1956. Many of these suppositions have been wrong because they did not take into account his poetics prior to war's end. Usually the errors concern the *Notebook,* which has often been read in a politically reductive fashion. In point of fact no trace of a Marxian influence is discernible in Césaire's writing before he was elected to the French legislature. Concerning Césaire's political orientation during his student years in Paris we know little more than that he was sympathetic to the left and read *Commune* with some regularity.[16] From 1934 to 1944 Aimé Césaire was so imbued with various forms of irrationalism that he was largely outside the orbit of Marxian thought.

Victor Hugo must be mentioned for quite another reason. Everything in Césaire's poetic development at this period should have drawn him to the titan of nineteenth-century French poetry. In his biographical study Ngal related this confidence supplied by Césaire: "My father, who died not long ago, had a solid classical literary background. I well recall that in the evening he read Victor Hugo aloud . . ."[17] That Césaire has not publicly commented on the author of *La Légende des siècles,* of the "On the Edge of the Infinite" ("Au bord de l'infini") section of the *Con-*

templations, or of *Punishments (Les Châtiments)* is not especially strange. Hugo's importance as a poet was very much in eclipse during Césaire's formative years, as he suffered the purgatory to which all great writers, in France at least, are invariably confined for an indefinite period. Not until Aimé Césaire did French culture again produce a poet with the moral and social influence of Victor Hugo. Since Victor Hugo only Césaire has written poetry in French that combines the voice of righteous indignation with the confidence that the poet is in communication with the truth of the ages. In this respect we can see as well how intimately the strand of modernism to which Césaire belongs is the contemporary prolongation of what was most compelling in the poetry of romanticism.

The undeniable dialectical movement of much of Césaire's poetry raises the question of whose dialectic the poetry embraces. Probably the only valid answer in the final analysis is the internal dialectic of the poem. But Césaire's later affirmation of solidarity with Marxism—he joined the Communist party of France about 1942, according to the dates provided by Ngal—makes this a matter of some intellectual-historical moment. My reading of the longer poems, the *Notebook of a Return to the Native Land* and "The Thoroughbreds" ("Les Pur-Sang") especially, points to an idealist dialectic. A statement Césaire made to Ngal tends to support this interpretation. Commenting on his professors at the Lycée Louis-le-Grand in Paris from 1931 to 1935, Césaire has said: "Then [in 1933–34], I had Le Senne, whom I understood better. He was less haughty. He had a dialectical conception, not that of Marx, which called to mind somewhat that of Hamelin, of French idealism. But it was a dialectic nonetheless. Secondly he was a very eloquent man, very cultivated. He taught courses in German philosophy, which he knew thoroughly. He knew Husserl, Kierkegaard, the first German existentialists. It was avant-garde teaching. He was truly an awakener of ideas, no doubt about that."[18] This is one of the rare cases in which one can affirm that Césaire took away something truly important from his university education.

By the time Césaire entered the Ecole Normale Supérieure in 1935 he found that he could no longer write on literary subjects following the established academic models. The experimental writing he began in 1935–1936 gradually became his first and most famous literary publication, the *Notebook of a Return to the Native Land*.

Beyond any possible doubt, when Césaire began to elaborate his own artistic vision, he did so using the means provided by some of the foremost European writers of the previous generation. His approach to historiography as well as his understanding of depth psychology and the workings of the imagination derived from European models. However, the literary purposes to which Césaire subsequently put these modes of thought were complex with respect to his attitude toward Europe and North America. In attempting to challenge the world view that had engendered colonialism and slavery, Césaire was constrained by his education to forge weapons out of the adversary's own arsenal. The dialectics of negritude gradually took shape as the negation of a negation. Pure positivity was presumed to exist in an idealized African past. Modern Europe represented the negation of that ideal, and its French manifestation in rationalism was held accountable for the spiritual homelessness of the descendants of enslaved Africans. Insofar as modernist culture attacked some of the same traditions as did Césaire, it became the principal source of his inspiration and even of his techniques. As a black Martinican, Césaire stood inside and outside the culture of France and of Europe. His struggle was to prove especially painful and its outcome especially problematical, because in attacking modern Europe he was at the same time attacking a part of himself.

3

Poetry and Cultural Renewal: *Tropiques*

> Mute and silent land. I am speaking of our land. And my hearing measures the frightening silence of Man across the Caribbean.
>
> Terre muette et stérile. C'est de la nôtre que je parle. Et mon ouïe mesure par la Caraïbe l'effrayant silence de l'Homme.
>
> Césaire, Presentation of *Tropiques*, April 1941

THE EARLIEST VERSION of Césaire's first significant work of literature, his "Notebook of a Return to the Native Land," was printed in Paris by the magazine *Volontés* in August 1939, just as its author was preparing his return to Martinique. Its presence in an obscure literary magazine went quite unnoticed. War was imminent, and more local preoccupations were soon to engross Césaire. In late August 1939, with his wife, Suzanne, and their year-old child, Césaire returned from France to Martinique on board the *Bretagne*. The ship was torpedoed by the Germans on its voyage back to France. Within months the French possessions in the West Indies were doubly victims of the European war: governed from 1941 to 1943 by a representative of Vichy France, Admiral Robert, whose fleet was bottled up by the U.S. Navy in 1942–1943. It was in these conditions that Césaire settled into a teaching position in French and classics at the Lycée Schoelcher in Fort-de-France, the school he had left joyfully eight years earlier.

Césaire's efforts to teach the poetry of Lautréamont, Rimbaud, and Mallarmé to young Martinicans of all racial groups met with surprise on the part of his pupils, accustomed to a diet of Parnassianism dressed up as modern poetry. These curricular innovations provoked real consternation in the ultraconservative cultural climate of Fort-de-France.

In addition Aimé Césaire organized a magazine, *Tropiques,* in concert with Suzanne Césaire, René Ménil, and Aristide Maugée, the husband of his sister Mireille. The importance of *Tropiques* (April 1941–September 1945) to the cultural and political awakening of Martinique can scarcely be overestimated. No one today seriously questions the proposition that before *Tropiques* writing in French by black and mulatto Martinicans represented an attempt to demonstrate, by a virtuoso performance in the tongue of the colonial power, that one was culturally white.[1] The profound alienation engendered by such behavior has been analyzed by Frantz Fanon in his *Black Skin, White Masks.* Fanon, who was a pupil at the Lycée Schoelcher during the war years, described Aimé Césaire's effect on the island's blacks: "For the first time one saw a lycée professor, therefore apparently a worthy man, simply say to Antillean society 'that it's beautiful and good to be black.' It was a scandal for sure. At the time rumors circulated that he was mad and his contemporaries outdid one another in providing details of his supposed malady."[2] In the eyes of blacks the sheer weight of two centuries of white "truth" proved Césaire mad. The white mask worn by mulattos required that they reach the same conclusion. The extraordinary complexity of the racial composition of the French West Indies has been a major obstacle to the achievement of a national sense of pride. Michel Leiris addresses the question squarely in *Contacts de civilisations en Martinique et en Guadeloupe.*

The relative status of a colored Antillean being a function of the multiple combinations possible among physical type and skin tone, there has evolved an extensive vocabulary of racial subtleties that is both concrete and hierarchical. In a society so permeated by the awareness of color, to have stated that black is good and beautiful must at first have appeared to be an objectively mad act.

Of the Caribbean islands officially proclaiming a French cultural tradition, only Haiti in 1940 could point to an existing indigenous heritage touching all or nearly all groups in the society.[3] Paradoxically, the original yet highly syncretic Creole culture of Haiti, which evolved in conditions of relative isolation from European influence after 1803, can itself be viewed as a product of the functional illiteracy and crushing poverty of 90 percent of the population. Contrariwise, the Martinican proponents of negritude were educated in the humanist mold of metropolitan France and were effectively cut off from direct participation in what remained of the folkloric tradition, which survived among that part of the rural population whose only working language was Creole. The resulting situation of the Martinican writer is a complex form of alienation in which the colonizer remains present even in the linguistic expression and mode of thought in which the writer conveys his sense of revolt. Césaire's reply to an interviewer's question concerning the absence of Creole in *Tropiques* was uncharacteristically aggressive and somewhat embarrassed.[4] He replied that neither he nor Ménil could have written in Creole, adding that he was not sure that such a project would have been conceivable in view of the primitive state of Martinican Creole; and he actually avoided the question concerning the use of Creole in his parents' house. A few moments later, however, Césaire specified that all black Martinicans, even the most apparently assimilated, are bilingual and that Creole best expresses certain aspects of his sensibility whereas French is the natural mode of expression for others. This point must be taken into consideration in any attempt to assess the peculiar inflection Césaire has given to the French language in his literary writing. Seen in this light and retrospectively, Aimé Césaire's progressive reliance on a surrealist use of language to explode from within the French rationalism inculcated by his education can be considered a personal necessity and a strategy for cultural survival.

Tropiques: Beginnings and Coordinates

The publication of *Tropiques* marked the first serious penetration of surrealism into the French dependencies in the Caribbean. (*Légitime Défense* must be considered a Parisian phenomenon that had little or no impact on Martinique itself.) Most previous discussions of the magazine have been concerned with the degree to which Aimé Césaire and his collaborators were at the outset engaged in an orthodox surrealist project. Some have considered *Tropiques* to be primarily a vehicle for the ideology of negritude. I feel that the two purposes are inseparable. As it happened, André Breton found the first issue of *Tropiques* quite unexpectedly in a store window as he walked through Fort-de-France. In that issue Césaire published an early version of the poem "The

Thoroughbreds," the style of which is markedly surrealist. However, the more significant questions concern not orthodoxy but the function of surrealism in the concrete social (that is, colonial and racist) experience of the Martinican writer.

Nonetheless the historical influence of surrealism on Césaire and his group remains to be firmly established. René Ménil was the principal link between the Paris surrealists and Césaire during the latter's student days in the French capital. Of the group of Martinicans who had published *Légitime Défense* in 1932 he was the only member to join Césaire in creating *Tropiques*. Throughout the war years he regularly contributed articles on aesthetics. In the first of these, entitled "Birth of Our Art," which appeared alongside "The Thoroughbreds" in April 1941, René Ménil placed his essay on the possibility of a Martinican art and culture under the aegis of Nietzsche, not Breton, but concluded with a surprising allusion to Tristan Tzara's *homme approximatif*. The thrust of the essay, like that of Césaire's poem, though using a different mode of discourse, was that no Martinican culture can flower without being rooted in a Martinican experience. This thesis, with its corollary that all cultural imitation is cultural alienation, was developed in advance of the direct, personal influence of André Breton on *Tropiques*. Ménil's essay also contained the germ of the argument Frantz Fanon was to develop in much greater detail and with such brilliance in *Black Skin, White Masks*.

In the presentation of *Tropiques* that opened the April number Aimé Césaire had given this definition of civilization: "that projection of man onto the world, that modeling of the world by man, that striking of the universe in the image of man." He has never retreated from this credo, which is neither exclusive nor racist as his critics have sometimes charged. The term *négritude* did not appear in this statement; it was rarely used as a rallying cry in later numbers of *Tropiques,* doubtless because it might needlessly have attracted the attention of the censor. Its message, however, was there from the start. For Césaire—and for the magazine of which he was editor-in-chief and guiding spirit—surrealism had an importance that is best considered dialectically. The meeting between André Breton and Aimé Césaire in April 1941 did indeed influence the direction of *Tropiques*. The "hour of Charles Péguy" announced by Césaire in the first issue became, in the second, a decidedly surrealist "Orientation of Poetry"—

the title of Ménil's second essay on aesthetics. The contradiction is merely apparent and speaks eloquently of Césaire's own conception of surrealism. In presenting Péguy he had stressed the poet's sense of belonging to a land, to the earth, as well as to a people. On the same page he quoted Nietzsche on the determination of cultural values in terms of greatness and truth. The role of the poet is clear: to communicate authentically with himself he must be in communication with his environment; therein lie truth and value.

Césaire had already begun to write in a recognizably surrealist vein, but the meeting with André Breton manifestly convinced him that here were a man and a movement dedicated to goals similar to his own. The evidence in the first issues of *Tropiques* leaves no doubt: Breton became something more than a literary influence for the little group of young Martinicans. His presence in Fort-de-France was that of a hero, a living exemplar of their own struggle. Consequently Breton displaced both Péguy and Nietzsche in the pages of *Tropiques* while serving much the same function—that of a privileged mediator. When *Tropiques* was reissued in 1978 Césaire provided this account of Breton's effect on the Martinicans' enterprise: "Breton brought us *boldness;* he helped us to take a straightforward position: he shortened our search and our hesitation. I became aware that most of the problems I was pondering had been resolved by Breton and by surrealism . . . I will say that the meeting with Breton confirmed the truth of what I had discovered on my own. That enabled us to make up time; to go much faster, much farther . . . The meeting was *extraordinary.*"[5]

Surrealism primarily afforded Césaire the example of a poetic mode, intensely subjective and rooted in desire, which proclaimed its intention to throw off all those constraints that have brought about the estrangement of man from himself. Aimé Césaire was to interpret this surrealist revolution as inseparably binding together personal and collective liberation. In the same issue of *Tropiques* (no. 2 for July 1941) Suzanne Césaire concluded an article ostensibly devoted to Alain's aesthetics by declaring that surrealist art was the only means available for gaining access to a more humane world. All of these statements, particularly when considered together, direct us toward the type of social and literary commitment that Aimé Césaire was to adopt after the war.

Nor should one lose sight of the fact that *Tropiques* was printed and distributed under tight rules of censorship that rendered direct discussion of the colonial question even more difficult than usual. It is understandable that under these circumstances *Tropiques* should not at first have adopted a political stance. Lilyan Kesteloot has argued that no such opposition was possible under the Vichy regime of Admiral Robert, which is true; but she concluded that *Tropiques* adopted its surrealist posture in large measure as a kind of cryptography, inscrutable and incomprehensible for the white and mulatto bourgeoisie of Fort-de-France. This is scarcely satisfactory as an explanation, since it supposes that the commitment of Césaire to surrealism was due exclusively to the war. Thomas A. Hale has attempted to verify Kesteloot's hypothesis by decoding some of the poems Césaire published originally in *Tropiques*. He finds in "Miraculous Weapons" ("Les Armes miraculeuses"), for example, "numerous carefully disguised attempts to force the barriers of censorship and attack the occupant."[6] I am not entirely convinced by the results, which raise serious questions concerning the status of these texts as poems. That the poems contain a powerful ideological thrust is, however, borne out by my own analysis of "The Thoroughbreds." The evolution of the magazine indicates that surrealism was a necessary steppingstone for Césaire between the first exploratory efforts to define negritude in prewar Paris and the resolute commitment, artistic and political, to destroy the edifice of colonialism after the war. By February 1944 Césaire was openly attacking the colonial capitalism of Martinique in the pages of *Tropiques*. One must bear in mind, however, that the Vichy regime had been brought down in Martinique by July 1943.

From our present vantage point we can see that Césaire set out to reformulate the means as well as the goals of literature: from an introspective, poetic exploration of the imagination (individual and collective) he evolved toward a literature of praxis in which the privileged vehicle was to be the theater. It is the bitterest irony of his career that Césaire's efforts have in fact had so little political success in Martinique, where a de facto colonial economy remains essentially unshaken by the island's having been legally integrated into French society and institutions. That irony is further heightened by the knowledge that, as a newly elected member of the National Assembly, Césaire had sponsored the law that in effect institutionalized Martinique's neocolonial status

after 1946. Césaire has long since come to regret the political naïveté that he shared at war's end with a substantial segment of the
French left. In February 1944 (*Tropiques*, no. 10) Césaire rose up
to "condemn any idea of Antillean independence," preferring a
"willed, calculated, and rational Martinican dependence" that
would exploit to its own benefit the advanced technology of metropolitan France. His attitude at that time was encouraged by
the prevailing policy of the Communist party of France toward
the colonial dependencies of the French Empire.

No one will fail to notice a parallel with the history of Breton's
group in Césaire's adherence to surrealism, then to communism,
and finally to an independent socialism. And yet a basic distinction should be made between the black writer's experience and
that of Breton: it is at bottom as much a question of class as of
race.[7] For Aimé Césaire, or any writer who has known the alienation of colonial oppression, artistic authenticity is inconceivable
outside the struggle for collective liberation. It is true, of course,
that at the outset the writers of the negritude movement felt compelled as blacks to insist on their difference from the French proletariat. Much more recently Césaire has come to view this assertion of collective difference as the necessary first step toward
the awakening of a national consciousness in the French West
Indies.[8]

What was Césaire's literary position before André Breton's
arrival in Martinique? Careful analysis of "The Thoroughbreds"
will point up those aspects of the poem that are most helpful in
situating Césaire with respect to surrealism. Published in the April
1941 issue of *Tropiques* (no. 1) as "Fragments of a Poem," it has
the form of a monologue in which the poetic voice speaks first in
its own name, then for black humanity, and in the conclusion for
the Caribbean islands themselves. The thematic development,
more fully fleshed out than in most surrealist poems, is that of an
individual and collective catharsis. Insofar as the liberating effect
on the collectivity remains to be accomplished, with but a spiritual
direction and an outline for individual liberation drawn here, the
poetic voice is prophetic and fully justifies the epigraph taken from
Rimbaud's "Lettre du voyant": "I declare that one must be a
seer, make oneself clairvoyant."

There are three moments in the poem's development that do
not unfold so much as they spring forth from one another. Thus
the opening strophes (p. 11) are identified as a prelude, "The eye-

lid of the breakers closes—Prelude—" ("La paupière des brisants se referment [sic]—Prélude—"), a passage marked by repeated exclamations and unanswered questions and closing on the isolated word *silence!* (p. 12). A transitional statement of one line suffices to introduce the first movement (p. 12): "The sky yawns from black absence!" ("Le ciel bâille d'absence noire!"). There follows an ample development that leads to awareness of the unacceptable, stifling, disgusting nature of reality. The strophic form is constructed on a succession of rhythmically balanced declarations loosely but effectively held together by the reiteration of the coordinating formula: "And now . . . / And . . . / And . . . / And now . . ." ("Et voici . . . / Et . . . / Et . . . / Et voici . . .").[9] Césaire's introduction in praise of the French poet Charles Péguy seems to apply doubly to his own poem: "Shouts. Oaths. Or praise worse than oaths. The fish-eyed Men did not understand that there passed before them, terrible, accusing, the incarnation of true grandeur" (p. 39).

If one examines the relationship of metaphor to syntax in the poem, the conclusion that emerges is that thematic and metaphoric development combine to form a dialectical movement from initial order (the syntactic norm respected, with a gradual passage from simile to metaphor of the surrealist variety) to creative disorder (slight disruption of the syntactic norm, marked increase in density of metaphor with considerable lexical insistence on unreason, delirium) to a catharsis culminating in a new order (the syntactic norm restored with violence giving way to a peaceful surreality): "The branches were gathering a surreal peace" ("Les branches picoraient une paix surréelle"). Structurally there is a striking isomorphism between this poem and the *Notebook*. The major distinguishing feature is the difference between the epic form (albeit mixed) and the lyric. "The Thoroughbreds" concludes with the poetic voice lulling violence to sleep, and the final lines telescope the aspects of temporality into a characteristically mythic eternal present:

"Sleep, my cruelty," thought I.

My ear pressed to the earth, I heard
Tomorrow pass.

"Dors, ma cruauté," pensai-je.

L'oreille collée au sol, j'entendis
passer Demain.

There is in the prelude and first movement a type of poetic statement that was already present in the 1939 version of the *Notebook*. Postwar versions of the *Notebook* have a much higher frequency of surrealist metaphor, very similar in type and function to those in the second movement of "The Thoroughbreds." They intend to break the shackles of an oppressive order whose agent in the psyche is logic. Already in the prelude this revolt is announced more straightforwardly as theme:

> But how, how could one not bless,
> such as my logics have never dreamed it,
> hard, cross-grain splitting their worthless pile
> and their ruminations, and more pathetic
> than the fructifying flower,
> the lucid cracks of unreason.

> Mais comment, comment ne pas bénir,
> telle que ne l'ont point rêvée mes logiques,
> dure, à contrefil lézardant leur pouac[re] ramas
> et leur saburre, et plus pathétique
> que la fleur fructifiante,
> la gerce lucide des déraisons?

However, in the second movement, the instance of total negation, Césaire's speaker invites his reader through the tortuous and menacing labyrinth of a self-analysis in which the stakes are high indeed:

> Ah!
> I desire the sole, the pure treasure,
> That which makes gifts of all others,
> I want life;
> Be it at the price of Death.

> Ah!
> Je veux le seul, le pur trésor,
> Celui qui fait largesse des autres,

Je veux la vie!
Fût-ce au prix de la Mort!

The prescription is accurate: the prize (as in the ancient myths of the Hero's perilous journey) can be won only at the risk of the ultimate sacrifice. The single line announcing the beginning of the second movement indicates that the salvation of some collectivity is riding on the outcome of the quest:

We are adrift through your sacrifice.

Nous dérivons à travers votre sacrifice.

The first movement has prepared the reader for a voyage downward into the heart of things that are not merely objects:

My eye plummets into the thing
no longer contemplated but contemplating.

Mon oeil coule à pic dans la chose
non plus regardée mais regardante.

A descent into hell, then—a voyage in which Rimbaud once again serves as tutelary divinity. The entrance for the island poet is quite naturally marine and calls up associations of a dive to great depths:

From a nodding of the wave I jump
ancestral onto the branches of my
vegetation.
I lose myself in the fruitful
complications.
I swim to the ships
I plunge into the sluice.
. . . . . .
. . . Always here torrential
cascade words.

D'un dodelinement de vague, je saute
ancestral aux branches de ma

végétation.
Je m'égare aux complications
fructueuses.
Je nage aux vaisseaux
Je plonge aux écluses.
. . . . .
... Toujours ici torrentueuses
cascadent les paroles

But the two lines immediately preceding these have fixed the context within which this heroic undertaking is to be interpreted:

Buried repressions! desires, desires,
processional desires!

Refoulements enfouis! désirs, désirs,
processionnels désirs!

Clearly by his coding of desire repressed *(refoulements)*, Césaire has drawn us into the orbit of Freud. The violence of the succeeding movement proceeds—to borrow a term that Marcuse derived from his reading of the surrealists—in the manner of a repressive desublimation. The hero must savagely undo the work of centuries, cut through the unnatural knotting of his limbs and his veins. The dénouement of the poem occurs in the second movement, in a passage that must have struck André Breton as being the poetic realization of his own dialectical conception of the surreal:

Sounds link their hands and embrace
above me.
I wait. I wait no more.
Delirium.

Nothingness by day
Nothingness by night
a sweet attraction
in the very flesh of things
splashes.

[Nocturnal day
diurnal night]
exuded by
Plentitude.[10]

Les bruits se donnent la main et s'embrassent
par dessus moi.
J'attends. Je n'attends plus.
Délire.

Néant de jour
Néant de nuit
une attirance douce
à la chair même des choses
éclabousse.

[Jour nocturne
nuit diurne]
qu'exsude
la Plénitude.

The result of this attainment of the supreme (psychic) point at which opposites cancel out and opposition ceases is felt in the earth itself as a transmuted state of being:

And the Earth stretched. There was a cracking
In its knotted shoulders. There was in its veins
a crackling of fire.
Its sleep peeled off like a guava tree in August . . .

Et la Terre s'étira. Il y eut un craquement
A ses épaules nouées. Il y eut dans ses veines
un pétillement de feu.
Son sommeil pelait comme un goyavier d'août . . .

As the poem attains this final moment of realization, of identification, there is no longer a clear distinction between subject and object. The shoulders of the earth are no longer distinguishable from those of the speaker who, in shedding the constraints of rationality, has reached a state of cosmic fusion. This consciousness has felt itself penetrating, permeating, the natural universe:

As each thing was dying,
I found myself, I found myself enlarged—like the world—
and my consciousness wider than the sea:
Final sun.
I burst. I am the fire, I am the sea. The
world is undone. But I am the world!

A mesure que se mourait toute chose,
Je me suis, je me suis élargi—comme le monde—
et ma conscience plus large que la mer!
Derner soleil.
J'éclate. Je suis le feu, je suis la mer. Le
monde se défait. Mais je suis le monde!

This imaginary regression to primeval Chaos leads directly to an Orphic recreation, in the penultimate stanza, of the world through the word:

And I speak,
and my word is peace
and I speak and my word is world
and I speak!
and
Joy
Bursts in the sun renewed!
and I speak:
Through knowing grasses time slips.
The branches were gathering a surreal peace
And the earth breathed beneath the gauzy mists.
And the Earth stretched ...

Et je dis,
et ma parole est paix
et je dis et ma parole est terre
et je dis!
et
la Joie
éclate dans le soleil nouveau!
et je dis:

Par de savantes herbes le temps glisse.
Les branches picoraient une paix surréelle
Et la terre respira sous la gaze des brumes.
Et la Terre s'étira...

Here we witness the full force of Sartre's discovery of negritude as the voice of a black Orpheus. And it is on this very point that Sartre found himself for once in agreement with André Breton: "Because it is the living and dialectical unity of so many opposites, because it is a Complex resistant to analysis, only the multiple unity of a song [*chant*] can make manifest that flashing beauty of the Poem that Breton calls 'exploding-fixed.' "[11] This poem and others of Césaire's miraculous weapons were intended to inspire a new principle of cultural unity or, as Sartre put it, the being-in-the-world of the black. In this context what is the significance of the regressive-mythic ideal that "The Thoroughbreds" expresses? Once again the first issue of *Tropiques* provides the context for the poem. Directly following "The Thoroughbreds" (p. 27) there appears Suzanne Césaire's essay on "Leo Frobenius and the Problem of Civilizations." The reader today cannot escape the impression that these ten pages of hortatory prose, complete with an outline of the symbolism of plants, heavenly bodies, and numbers, was printed in this precise place to serve as a guide to Aimé Césaire's "The Thoroughbreds." Reread in this light, the poem—which is particularly noteworthy for its solar and vegetative imagery, its cosmic acceptance of a vital force, and its powerful refusal of technological civilization in favor of a primitive mysticism—stands as a beacon to those who must feel keenly their humiliation as servants of the Hamitic principle of civilization.

A central element of Frobenius' thought that Suzanne Césaire merely alluded to is the symbolic identification of the hero with the sun: "It is this grasp[12] [of time and of death] that is expressed for instance in all the rituals linked to the theme of the predetermination of the death of the god in a great number of civilizations. Similarly the light of the sun illuminating the world engenders the grasp of space, of spatial limitation, of delimited order." Using this concept as a hermeneutic device, one can establish that the moments in the hero's quest in "The Thoroughbreds" are expressed in terms of solar images, from the prelude—"the hundred whinnying thoroughbreds of the sun, / amongst the stagnation" ("les cent purs-sang [sic] hennissant du soleil, / parmi la stagnation")—through the purifying fire of the first movement, to the single line that bridges the second and final movements—"The last of the last suns falls" ("Le dernier des derniers soleils tombe"). The Sun is of course reborn with the Hero: "Joy / bursts in the sun renewed!" ("la Joie / éclate dans le soleil nouveau!").

"The Thoroughbreds" is the first of Césaire's poems to articulate in a demonstrable fashion both a metaphoric structure deriving from Frobenius and a model of consciousness that one recognizes as a surrealist version of Freud. Until the recent reprinting of *Tropiques* the earliest available text of "The Thoroughbreds" was that of the original (1946) edition of *Miraculous Weapons*. Therefore it is not generally known that some manifestly Freudian associations in the 1941 text were either dropped entirely (as was the case of the two lines on "Buried repressions! desires, desires, / processional desires!") or so radically transformed as to effectively obscure their coordinates. The second form of modification was used on the passage that since 1946 has read:

> flash of absolute snows
> cavalry of chemical steppe
> withdrawn from the sea at ibis tide
> the annihilated semaphor
> sounds in the tonsils of the coconut palm
> and twenty thousand whales blowing
> through the liquid fan
> a nubile manatee chews the coals of pearly orients

> éclair des neiges absolues
> cavalerie de steppe chimique
> retiré de mer à la marée d'ibis
> le sémaphore anéanti
> sonne aux amygdales du cocotier
> et vingt mille baleines soufflant
> à travers l'éventail liquide
> un lamantin nubile mâche la braise des orients

What common measure is there between these banal but surrealist metaphors of purity (construed as the work of the fires invoked in the line immediately preceding) and this text, which appears only in *Tropiques*:

The volcanos fire at point-blank range
Cities leveled, in a great crash of idols,
in the evil wind of prostitutions
and of sodomies.
Cities leveled and the wind blowing
amid the mucky explosion of their flesh
the excremental roar!

Les volcans tirent à bout portant
Les villes par terre, dans un grand bris d'idoles,
dans le vent mauvais des prostitutions
et des sodomies.
Les villes par terre et le vent soufflant
parmi l'éclatement fangeux de leur chair
le rugissement excrémentiel!

One need not be a clinical analyst to recognize in this section of the poem a utilization of anal erotism as weapon (*arme*) in the destruction of a civilization that the poet, like Jehovah leveling Sodom and Gomorrah, condemns as irretrievable. I draw the preliminary conclusion that in 1941 Césaire, following Freud's indications of the sexual implications of all desire, chose to exploit this realm of experience in a manner that he later preferred to push into the background.

Of the three types of affective organization that Freud related to the progressive displacement of the pleasure principle by the reality principle, the second—anal affectivity—is passed over with scarcely a comment in surrealist treatments of the subject, whereas it is subjected to a conspiracy of silence by society at large. In the most extensive essay on the subject by a surrealist one would search in vain for any positive appreciation of the liberating function of this form of archaic or primitive Eros, despite the repeated claim that "art, the proof of man's definitive submission to the pleasure principle, has as its goal play [*jeu*], to make us rediscover childhood, to reveal to us the content of the unconscious, and to overcome repression."[13] Notwithstanding their well-known predilection for de Sade, whose *Justine* is memorable for its representation of anal-erotic activity and their admiration for Norman O. Brown's *Life against Death*, the surrealists most closely associated with Breton seldom permitted their own imaginings of this type to be expressed in print. Brown's celebration of polymorphous perversity appears to have been interpreted by the surrealist poets in a remarkably innocent guise, thus permitting an easy integration to the mythic domain of the androgyne, *l'amour fou*, and in general, of women as mediatrix between the reality principle and the surreal (defined as erotic paradise). Robert Benayoun confirms the analytic naïveté of surrealism's interpretation of the unconscious: "Imbued with the lessons of de Sade and Fourier, of courtly love and of romanticism, [surrealism] would transcend the fundamental pessimism of Freud, restore to man his state of innocence, that is, of total playful pleasure of his body, enlighten and exalt erotic activity by the exercise of imagination, transform desire into action by creating a new *élan vital*, by provoking marvels of clairvoyancy that love conditions and excites."[14]

From the 1928 issue of *La Révolution surréaliste* devoted to "research on sexuality" to their more recent publications, the surrealists exercised in their poetic practice a surprising degree of self-censorship in this domain.[15] There are exceptions, to be sure: Henri Michaux, while not a member of Breton's group, would by any stylistic test qualify as a surrealist. His poem "My King" ("Mon Roi"), frequently reprinted in anthologies, develops its principal effects within the framework of anal erotism as weapon. But such examples, particularly in the official surrealist literature, are very rare. It is the surrealist painter or sculptor who is more likely to give a truly free rein to primitive sexuality through the deformation of the object of desire or its subordination to an "unnatural" function (witness the work of V. Brauner or M. W. Svanberg). And finally it is not a surrealist but Pierre Klossowski who calls our attention to the revolutionary psychic force of de Sade. Like Marcuse in his *Eros and Civilization* Klossowski has demonstrated that the perversions testify to an insubordination of the life forces. It follows that in the work of de Sade the act of sodomy is the typical and the purest example of integral monstrosity because it is "the act that strikes out against the law of propagation of the species within the individual."[16]

I would suggest that in the 1941 version of Césaire's "The Thoroughbreds" the Martinican poet does not embrace the position that Klossowski attributes to de Sade but rather exploits to a different end the full explosive force of this repressed form of Eros. The Sodomites metaphorically present in the poem are those whose rotten, corrupt civilization is to be brought down. Their perversion, moreover, is not to be emulated. Yet nowhere in his work does Césaire fall prey to the sensual illusion so dear to surrealism: the identification of uninhibited genital sexuality with the ideal socialist state. Not for him the return to romantic socialism typified by Breton's *Ode à Charles Fourier*. Perhaps for this reason his poetry, even when it is erotic and oriented toward myth, manifests considerable ambiguity toward the mysticoerotic ideal of the Eternal Feminine in its many guises. "Surrealist woman is a forgery concocted by males," concluded Xavière Gauthier after an exhaustive examination of the data.[17] Césaire's poem in 1941 functioned to express a mythic quest in which the speaker could hope to communicate symbolically the African's original reality; his exceptional use of anal erotism in the early version of the poem doubtless arose from an anger or frustration that demanded an extreme expression. It may be that after the war the modification of the passage was imposed by the censor within or simply by a different assessment of poetry's proper role in confronting unacceptable social conditions. More importantly for our understanding of Césaire's poetics, the hero's triumph in "The Thoroughbreds" affirms the inviolability of the self and its resources; indeed it transcends the opposition to its interests raised by quotidian reality and reaches the primitive state of being that is posited as anterior to opposition. In so doing it achieves the sublime state that Freud described in the same section of the essay on humor cited by Césaire in 1943. In short, Césaire seems to have leapt joyfully over the technical complexities of Freudian analytical thought to seize a poetic truth that he held in common with the surrealists before the celebrated meeting with Breton in April 1941.

The Naturalization of Surrealism

Between publication of its first and second issues *Tropiques* effectively transformed itself from a strictly local publication intent on stimulating a cultural renaissance among Martinicans into a quasiofficial organ of surrealism. We witness a fundamental shift from surrealism as a poetic mode, seen in Césaire's "The Thoroughbreds," to an unreserved adherence to surrealism as a movement.[18] Surrealist ideology was, so to speak, grafted onto the world view I have already described. The horticultural image corresponds accurately enough to the intention of *Tropiques* to acclimate surrealism to a new cultural climate. But there was a further primary and determining consideration: from its inception *Tropiques* followed surrealism in its efforts to identify and realize the potential of natural man. Frobenius certainly became a link between negritude and surrealism, and the reading of Freud proposed by *Tropiques* was likewise determined by this quest for the natural functioning of the psyche.

René Ménil, in the October 1941 issue of *Tropiques,* articulated the dual interest of psychoanalysis and ethnography in terms that leave no doubt whatever as to their common purpose in the eyes of the *Tropiques* group: "The truly current interest of psychoanalysis and ethnography is that they show luminously that neither individuals nor peoples act according to the motives that they give consciously for their acts . . . The latest anthropological discoveries finally open up to man the subject of man, that is they permit us to transcend the ludicrous zone of false reasons and to attain the level where our essential and vitally engrossing energies come into play" (pp. 60–61).

This heroic vision of the social sciences offered unlimited promise for ethics and politics, which, according to Ménil, would be so efficacious as to render the pathetic efforts of propaganda and political rhetoric utterly obsolete. There is something frighteningly naïve about these predictions when one considers that they are contemporaneous with Hitler's crowd-swaying speeches and the apogee of Leni Riefenstahl's film making in Nazi Germany, both of which appealed to the "vitally engrossing energies" in a culture. The radical innocence of this position is no less problematical with respect to aesthetics, insofar as the unleashing of the unconscious is posited as fundamentally beneficent: "But the drives that are the mainspring of our activity do not appear in consciousness in their furious nakedness. Physical and social taboos force them to be veiled . . . This is why they are known to us only in their transposition as symbols, metaphors, and their play sets the stage for dreams, reveries, tales, myths, and so on. It is in poetry therefore . . . that we can read what matters to us, I mean that for which we live and die" (p. 61).

Tropiques had rapidly fallen in step with the surrealist doctrine of a poetic revolution to be realized by breaking down the di-

visions between dreaming and doing. René Ménil made an unequivocal statement of the position that surrealism was to be the
final working out of the Hegelian Idea: "Since Hegel such a
divorce reveals itself as simply chimerical. The unity in man of
dream and of action . . . shows not only that it is possible to
conciliate our life with our dream but that it is necessary, in
accordance with a secret justice, to extract from the domain of
dream the lessons that will permit us to see clearly into this life
and consequently to effectuate the liberating transformation of
it" (p. 62).

In 1973 Ménil wrote a short essay, "For a Critical Reading of
Tropiques," in which he corrected the inadequacies of his position thirty years earlier: "Thus, at the level of aesthetics that remains essential to *Tropiques,* an insufficiently developed idealism
too often stuck in metaphysics stands face to face with a materialism that claims to be dialectical but that hesitates to accept
the ultimate consequences of the ideological world of the imagination."[19] Ménil's critique of *Tropiques* is that of a lifelong Marxist
whose politics have been in opposition to Césaire's since the latter's break with the Communist party in 1956. But in October
1941 the third issue of *Tropiques* was composed in such a way
that the reader of Ménil's "Introduction to the Marvelous" was
adequately prepared to grasp the import of Aimé Césaire's poem
"The Great Beyond" ("Au delà"). By composition I do not mean
to imply that Ménil's article was conceived as an illustration of
Césaire's poem but that both texts resulted from a remarkable
unity of purpose common to the principal contributors during
this period. I reproduce only the opening lines and the conclusion
of "Au delà" (p. 26):

> From below, from the furious congestion of appalling
>   dreams
> the new dawns
> rose
> rolling their free lion cub heads.

> D'en bas, de l'entassement furieux des songes épouvan-
>   tables
> les aubes nouvelles
> montaient
> roulant leurs têtes de lionceaux libres.

The initially frightening discoveries of the unconscious arise bearing the promise of a savage new freedom. The middle section of the poem contains a scene of struggle, of bloodshed, and of violent conquest, which closes on this scene of reconciliation suggestive of Freud's band of brothers after the assassination of the patriarch of the primal horde:

> And reconciled bands offer one another gifts in
> the hand of a woman assassinating the day.

The naturalization of surrealism was to develop along other lines as well. In the second issue an anonymous editorial note introducing the movement to the readers of *Tropiques* affirmed that "the encounter of André Breton with the Antilles takes on a singular significance when one realizes that it was in Negro art, Oceanic folklore, and pre-Columbian America that the post-war artistic revolution found one of its principal catapults." In the same issue (July 1941) *Tropiques* published the first text suggesting its intention to familiarize Martinicans with their natural surroundings. The brief article excerpted from the *Bulletin Agricole* on the vegetation of the French Antilles makes sense only within this broad perspective of a return to the natural defined as the primitive and good. *Tropiques* was to reinforce this naturalist aspect of its message periodically from 1941 through 1944. This naturalistic bent also helped accustom the reader to the frequent use of names of tropical plants in Césaire's poetry. In general European commentators have been baffled or put off by this feature of his work, sometimes dismissing it as tropical exoticism. This perspective ultimately reveals the cultural imperialism of those who persist in adopting it. Césaire's diction is often very concrete. Like that of any other poet it possesses its own theme words, which derive from his Martinican origins, but beyond this stylistic question there are important cultural implications in Césaire's insistence on a concrete idiom. Since he is obliged to write in French for purposes of communicating with a wide audience, it is only in this way that he can remind the reader that he is not an ersatz Frenchman. In short the issue is not exoticism but its contrary: authenticity. M. a M. Ngal's study of Césaire argues convincingly that the profusion of images of tropical vegetation in his poetry testifies to an effort to put down roots *(enracinement)*.

It is revealing to reread in this light Breton and André Masson's *Martinique charmeuse de serpents,* which collects texts (poems, articles, prefaces, and Masson's drawings) prepared during and after their 1941 visit. A good case can be made for the exoticism being entirely on their side or, to put it more accurately, consisting in their perception of Martinique through a European sensibility. Thus in Masson's erotic drawings a feminized and sexualized Martinique identifies Woman with Nature: "and always in the sun the gait of the *porteuses* / It is the foot of Gradiva— / Yes the soil is truly touched—the earth is pressed" ("et toujours au soleil la démarche des porteuses / C'est le pied de Gradiva— / Oui le sol est vraiment touché—la terre est appuyée").[20] The explicit reference to Freud's analysis of Wilhelm Jensen's *Gradiva* is typical of their tendency to interpret their sensory impressions in terms of a familiar European system of symbols. The title of their joint publication is taken from the painting by Henri Rousseau ("Le Douanier"), *La Charmeuse de Serpents,* to which they liken Martinique (p. 21). Breton's "Bearer without Burden" ("Porteuse sans fardeau") compares young Martinican girls to Baudelaire's poem "With Her Flowing and Pearly Garments" ("Avec ses vêtements ondoyants et nacrés," no. 27 in *Les Fleurs du Mal,* 2nd edition). The gratuitousness of the comparison is flagrant, considering that the second tercet of Baudelaire's sonnet constitutes an ironic denial of Breton's own vision. His poem "Providence Turns" ("La Providence tourne") represents the strange fruits of the island in terms of "those kings of the tropical forest whom Giorgio de Chirico delighted in immobilizing in their full force next to the head of Jupiter" (p. 43).

From the standpoint of Martinican reality this is exoticism. How much more concrete are the terms of Césaire's poem "Annunciation" ("Annonciation"), dedicated to Breton in 1946: "A movement of palms outlines the future body / of the *porteuses* with yellow breasts germinating harvest / of all hearts revealed" ("Un mouvement de palmes dessine le corps futur / des porteuses aux seins jaunes moisson germante / de tous les coeurs révélés").[21] Whereas the European artists introduce bookish reminiscences between self and world, Césaire as a Martinican writing on the identical subject presents nature as the everyday experience linking self and world. This is not to suggest that Césaire's poetics should be considered a purely natural upsurge of affect or emotion. Such a neoromantic reading of the negritude poets effaces the extraordinary complexity of Césaire's relation to modernism. At the same time it is equally important to recognize, as the foregoing examples permit us to do, that Césaire lacks the patent exoticism of the European surrealist. When Césaire practices a poetics of intertextuality, as he has frequently done, his intertexts are functional elements within his poems, not the references to the outside world that we find in Breton's and Masson's work.

Miklós Szabolcsi has advanced the thesis that as the surrealist movement was transplanted from the urban environment of Paris to other cultures it underwent a process of folkloricization. Surrealism in Martinique presents precisely those characteristics described by Szabolcsi: "The rejection of the present, the exposure of the lies of the established culture, the search for new values all contributed to the awareness of specific Negro features, *Négritude,* and helped to put into words and throw into relief, in opposition to the official and conservative trends in literature, the individual and the original."[22]

In an effort to bring *Tropiques* closer to the Martinican people Aimé Césaire and René Ménil joined forces in the issue for January 1942 to write a brief introduction to Martinican folklore. What they found in the existing fund of Creole tales is the triple legacy of slavery: hunger, fear, and defeat. Animal tales such as those retold by Lafcadio Hearn express for Césaire and Ménil the degradation of a people who, in the absence of any sense of collectivity, must fall back on the ruse of the trickster to save their own skin. As in previous issues, a document is appended to serve as an explanatory device for the two Creole tales collected and translated by Georges Gratiant. Four pages culled from Frobenius' *Kulturgeschichte Afrikas* point up the most obvious similarities between the wily rabbit of the Creole tales and the hare in the folktales of West Africa. The connection with surrealism not being immediately evident, it is supplied through the concept of the marvelous. Selected passages from *The Mirror of the Marvelous* by Pierre Mabille, who was among the first to introduce surrealist principles into psychiatry in France, provide the necessary link in the form of a magical realism.[23] These pages are the logical extension of Ménil's "Introduction to the Marvelous" and share his prophetic optimism.

There is an overworked and inauthentic quality to the pieces that Césaire and Ménil contributed to the folklore issue. One senses that Ménil's epistle entitled "Legendary Drama at Dusk" ("Drame légendaire au crépuscule") is supposed to suggest the collective function of folk tale. Yet his text harks back to an atmosphere reminiscent of the symbolism of Maeterlinck, and his evocation of Don Quixote atop a Martinican hill fails miserably. A European model intrudes even into his attempt at an autonomous Martinican art. A degree of everyday reality, however magically treated by surrealist metaphor, similarly weakens the effect of Aimé Césaire's Rimbaldian narrative poem "Living" ("Histoire de vivre") in the same issue. It is one of the poems printed in *Tropiques* that Césaire chose not to collect in his *Miraculous Weapons*. These flaws may well be symptomatic of a deeper problem. The intellectuals grouped around *Tropiques* diagnosed the sickness of Martinican culture using the same analytic reason that they fustigated in their theoretical and ideological statements of position. Is it not precisely because they were European trained that they were unable to bridge by themselves the chasm between analysis and the uniquely original Martinican art they fervently wished to create? The dilemma for Aimé Césaire and others of his generation has been their inability to create a literary form that does not rely on a European model. Césaire's goal, from the time of *Tropiques* through the sixties was to reach an accommodation that would not compromise his art.

In the tenth issue of *Tropiques* (February 1944) Césaire presented with obvious enthusiasm a Negro-Cuban tale as related by Lydia Cabrera: "Poem to desire, to fear, to death, to power, to catastrophe, to life: tragedy steaming with sadism, with the Oedipus complex; bitter drama of a social experience dominated by arbitrariness and slavery; pact of friendship with the sun, the moon, the stars, the animal, the forest; and especially a mad hymn to Freedom, vibrant epitome, *tafia* spiced with humor, its importance will be lost on no one" (p. 11). What is not lost on us is the special importance of the tale "Bregantino Bregantin" for Aimé Césaire. He saw in it the realization of his own ideal for Martinican literature, down to the muted presence of the old spirits who had given meaning to the lives of Martinican slaves and who survive still in Haitian voodoo, in its Negro-Cuban counterpart *santería*, and in Brazilian *macumba*.

There is more than a little nostalgia in the attitude of Césaire at this date. Born in a land where the only surviving traces of voodoo were tucked away in the most isolated hills, he had certainly never lived in contact with an active voodoo tradition. This element of nostalgia, of imaginary identification with African culture, cannot be dissociated from Césaire's interpretation of surrealism. As I have shown, surrealism was to serve the Martinican as an instrument for making contact with his own African heritage construed as biological and presumably waiting to be tapped in the reservoir of the collective unconscious. In the April 1942 issue this unsigned statement had introduced a short text by Frobenius in terms that draw together these several preoccupations: "There flows in our veins a blood that requires of us a unique attitude toward life. At the risk of failure . . . we, and the poet more than any other, must respond to the special dynamics of our complex biological reality. Tracing back one of our lines of force we encounter that immense phenomenon, Africa. The Africa of unique poetic gifts, of unique artistic, especially sculptural, production. Africa and its disdain for clever industrial brigandage" (p. 62).

The objective value of these claims is not at issue here, particularly since they involve such a high degree of subjectivity on the part of the editors of *Tropiques*. From time to time discussions of contemporary literature allude to an "African surrealism" that is to be understood as the natural product of a civilization whose motives and modes are assumed to be essentially different from the European. Without examining in detail whether the term conveys any specific meaning not better rendered by a more indigenous concept, we may retain it for its explanatory value in accounting for the collective conduct of the contributors to *Tropiques*. Investigation of the naturalization of surrealism in Martinique brings one to the point of glimpsing its underlying contradiction: the phenomenon imported from Europe was intended to liberate the psyche of Martinicans so that they might then live and know the spiritual existence of a culture not their own. This project was—in the strongest, surrealist sense—an imaginary one. As such it willingly sacrificed the categories of history for the norms of myth.

Not all young Martinicans concluded that the goal of this cultural revolution should be sought at so high a cost. A few years after the end of the war Frantz Fanon, psychiatrist and Marxist, expressed his doubt in these terms: "The Antillean of 1945 is a black . . . Now, turned toward Africa, the Antillean is going to hail her. He discovers in himself a transplanted child of slaves, he feels the vibration of Africa in the deepest regions of his being and aspires toward but one thing: to plung into the great 'black pit.' It seems then that the Antillean, after the great white error, is now in the process of living the great black mirage."[24] As Césaire was eventually to discover, myth could be but cold comfort when the issue for Martinique became economic and political survival.

Serving Surrealism

While they strove to naturalize surrealism in Martinique the *Tropiques* group adopted an aggressive posture of unconditional adherence to surrealist ideology. The extent to which they considered themselves to be a bastion of surrealist orthodoxy became apparent in October 1941 when they printed a sharp criticism of the Venezuelan neosurrealist publication *Viernes*. René L. F. Durand had published in Fort-de-France a *Lettre Vénézuélienne* in which *Tropiques* recognized an invitation to establish cultural relations with their neighbors in the Americas, a project that has always appealed to Aimé Césaire. Durand had cited Juan Vicente Gonzáles as an example of the direction in which Venezuelan culture ought to move: "Spin silk of your own making; collect your own honey; sing your song, for you have a tree, a hive and a nest." And he added that this indigenousness is the source of "the creolism, or if you like, the nationalism of the best literary production from *Peonía* by Manuel Romero García to the young author of 'La Guaracha,' Juan Radón, not to mention the celebrated author of *Doña Bárbara*, Romulo Gallegos nor Urbaneja Achelpohl" (p. 52). *Tropiques* extended the sense of internationalism by adding to these the names of three writers considered to represent the cultural renaissance of their respective nations: Pablo Neruda (Chile), César Vallejo (Peru), and Miguel Otero Silva (Venezuela). The last named was represented by a lengthy quotation in French of an anti-Yankee poem that bears little resemblance to a surrealist text.

The article that aroused the ire of *Tropiques* was published in *Viernes* (August-September 1940) by José Ratto-Ciarlo, who gave a lucid exposition of the paradoxical relationship between style and ideology in contemporary letters. He deplored the lack of sympathy toward surrealism on the part of many socialist writers who gratuitously cling to an outmoded classical dogmatism in their poetics and simultaneously criticized the reactionary attitude. His own position rejected what passes for socialist realism while insisting that surrealism be socially efficacious. The struggle that had pitted the Paris surrealists against one another throughout the previous decade cast its shadow on the nascent movements in the Americas as well. As reprinted in that issue of *Tropiques* (p. 57) Ratto-Ciarlo concluded that Breton's attitude was finally indefensible: "The intellectualized theory of André Breton has failed because the social and philosophical foundations of its aesthetic doctrine are fragile. Of course the poets of the *Viernes* group . . . have been influenced by surrealist lyricism, but *[Viernes]* wishes to avoid in time the serious errors of the French master."

The Venezuelan neosurrealists concluded by affirming that they incorporated the surrealist concern for synthesis in style within a socialist world view. A very difficult road to travel, to be sure, and one that *Tropiques* was not prepared to take in 1941. The unsigned editorial, which followed the reprint from *Viernes,* objects in the name of social commitment, but the core of its position is surrealist and subjective:

> Petty bourgeois fear of being duped. Dread of following through to the end.
> Come on! the moment—which already promises the dawn of a new age . . . —is not right for reticence.
> One does not choose surrealism.
> One does not flirt with life.
> It takes you. It breaks you—It carries you.
> Into the shadow. Into the light (p. 59).

Today one may well consider that the noble sentiments of *Tropiques* were unwisely invested. The fact of the matter is that after the war Césaire—somewhat more gradually than Fanon, and without breaking with Breton—moved toward a poetic and political position quite similar to that occupied by *Viernes* in 1940.

During the darkest period of the war *Tropiques* not only continued to defend surrealism but conceived of its role in terms of a growing surrealist international in which it placed great faith. The combined eighth and ninth issue (October 1943) is especially illuminating in this regard. Suzanne Césaire wrote with her customary conviction that "everywhere, in New York, in Brazil, in Mexico, in Argentina, in Cuba, in Canada, in Algiers, voices echo that would not be what they are . . . without surrealism" (p. 14). To be sure, many of the voices in question were those of French expatriates, but others reached Martinique from indigenous surrealist movements. From Santiago de Chile Jorge Cáceres contributed a poem "Una alondra polar me ha saludado al pasar" ("A Polar Lark Greeted Me in Passing"), which was printed in Spanish with French translation by René Durand. Cáceres was then editor of *Leitmotiv*, the little magazine founded by Braulio Arenas. In the same issue Charles Duits, a Harvard student who contributed to *VVV* in New York, offered two poems of which the best one can say is that they convey a strong impression of automatic writing. This surrealist technique continued to be held in high regard at *Tropiques* and, as though to prepare the reader for the poems of Duits and Cáceres, Franck Laurencine had written a paraphrase of *Poisson soluble* with the promising title "Fauna and Flora of the Unconscious." The ever-elusive concept of objective chance also received cursory treatment at the hands of S. Jean-Alexis, who concluded his somewhat circular reasoning by founding objective chance on the Kantian notion of internal finality.

Two further texts published in this same issue of *Tropiques* (October 1943) situate the Martinican surrealists with respect to poetry and ideology at the moment of their strictest orthodoxy. Aimé Césaire defined poetry as a necessary instance of self-defense against an unacceptable reality: "To defend oneself against the social by the creation of a zone of incandescence, on this side of which, inside which flourishes in terrifying security the extraordinary flower of the 'I' " (p. 7). Freud had defined the sublime as the triumph of narcissism. As I have indicated in the chapter on Césaire's modernism, this fundamental element of his poetics derives from Freud's essay on humor. Césaire goes on to relate this creative state to the mythic import of two great criminals: "Accursed poetry . . . Accursed, in the wake of Prometheus the thief, of Oedipus the assassin" (p. 8). The Promethean metaphor is further extended at the conclusion of the article: poetry is not Prometheus himself but rather his eagle, "endlessly devouring the liver of the world."

René Ménil, more concerned than Aimé Césaire with the logic of dialectics, discussed the rapidity of operations of the mind using a vocabulary intended to marry psychoanalysis with dialectical materialism. His favorite terms—*leap* and *bound*—suggest the nodal points of Hegelian and Marxist logic. The fifth of his fourteen propositions draws the parallel quite expressly: "In the mind as in nature changes in quantity give way, at certain points in the process of becoming, to changes in quality" (p. 27). The birth of surrealism (preceded by the multiplication of accursed poets after Nerval, Poe, Baudelaire, and Rimbaud) is presented as the most recent stage of the dialectical process. The last of his fourteen propositions optimistically predicts that surrealism will lead to the eventual appearance of a new Robespierre: "The ultimate destiny of poetry being to multiply itself dialectically into the naked force of the throng" (p. 32). The supposed link between Marxism and psychoanalysis is posited on a biological necessity: "Thought is bio-logical,—or it is not" (p. 29).[25]

That André Breton counted *Tropiques* among the publications of the surrealist movement during the war is attested by several documents. In March 1942 Breton was quoted in an interview with the London magazine *Arson* as including both Aimé Césaire and René Ménil among current surrealists. His wartime prolegomena to an eventual third manifesto contain this word of praise: "There is my friend Aimé Césaire, magnetic and black, who, having broken with all the old refrains—Eluardian and other—is writing the poems we must have today in Martinique."[26] And the 1943 American edition of B. Péret's *Péret Has the Floor (La Parole est à Péret)*, the introduction to his anthology of Mexican folklore, appeared in New York with a foreword signed by numerous surrealists. Among the foreign signatories are Braulio Arenas and Jorge Cáceres (Chile), Wifredo Lam (Cuba), and Aimé Césaire, Suzanne Césaire, and René Ménil (Martinique). There can be no doubt that Breton placed *Leitmotiv* and *Tropiques* on the same footing within the international movement. Given these facts one must qualify Césaire's statement to the effect that he "never wanted to belong to the surrealist movement."[27] Willy-nilly Césaire conducted himself and his magazine in the best traditions of surrealism from 1941 through early 1945 while he was writing the poetry of *Miraculous Weapons.*

The end of the Second World War brought with it a decided shift in the ideological position of *Tropiques.* The final issue (September 1945) refocused the magazine from the poetic, individual values of surrealism to the contemporary economic and political realities of Martinique. Existing social conditions were opposed unequivocally by Suzanne Césaire in her anticolonialist article attacking "The Great Camouflage." The final salute to Martinique was made in the name of still another "great man," one who had not previously figured in *Tropiques* but who was far more familiar to Martinicans than Breton, Freud, Nietzsche, or Frobenius: Victor Schoelcher, the French parliamentarian who more than any other individual had accomplished the liberation of the slaves in the French Empire in 1848. The peculiar institution as it applied to Martinique had been studied by Armand Nicolas in the issue for October 1943 ("La Traite des nègres," pp. 49–61). But the scholarly objectivity of that article was to be replaced in 1945 by a more urgent tone. Aimé Césaire's "Homage to Victor Schoelcher," the text of an address delivered on 21 July 1945 at the annual festivities devoted to the liberator, marks both the general change in climate and Césaire's move into the political arena. In the elections of 27–28 May he had won his first, unexpected political victory. After decrying the illness of democracy from 1918 to 1939, an illness characterized by shame at its own greatest republican moments, 1789 and 1793 to be sure, but also the Commune of 1871, Césaire took his stand well to the left: "And so we who are proud of our past of suffering and struggle, we who know that to love Victor Schoelcher is to give all one's strength to the creed of the Rights of Man; if there are in the midst of our labors thoughts that come to encourage us, surely the most stimulating is that perhaps the Martinicans of the future will say in speaking of our team of workers and proletarians: those were the men who rediscovered the mystique of Schoelcher. Those were the men who, by dint of gratitude, rediscovered the true spirit of Victor Schoelcher."[28]

These were the accents of the best political rhetoric. They foretell Césaire's eloquence at the centenary of the abolition of slavery in 1948 and his impassioned denunciation of colonialism in 1950. They are the words of the public man who emerged from the crucible of wartime Martinique, whose inspiration personally and poetically had come through surrealism, but whose future lay elsewhere in a highly individual pairing of imagination with the exigencies of socialism in a postcolonial world. At war's end *Tropiques* had run its course. As Césaire said in the interview he gave for the reissue of the magazine: "If suddenly, at the Liberation, we ceased publication, it was precisely because the *cultural struggle* was giving way to the political struggle" (p. viii).

Part II
HEROIC
NEGRITUDE

4

Miraculous Weapons

> Man today, stripped of myth, stands famished among all his
> pasts and must dig frantically for roots, be it among the most
> remote antiquities.
>
> Nietzsche, *The Birth of Tragedy*

EARLY IN 1946 Césaire's wartime poetry was published by Gallimard under the title *Les Armes miraculeuses (Miraculous Weapons)*. This collection rapidly established him as a
major surrealist poet but did little to extend his reputation to a
wider audience. It was the first of his writings to be made available
in postwar France, since *Notebook of a Return to the Native
Land*—with Breton's influential preface—was not to be distributed as a book until the following year. *Tropiques* was known to
a handful of French readers, if that many, through secondhand
accounts such as the one published by Etiemble in *L'Arche* just
prior to the liberation of Paris.[1]

My examination of Césaire's intention to create a Martinican
poetics that would meld the surrealist ethos with an African
world view as he then understood it tends to confirm the findings of Roger Bastide concerning Césaire's relationship to European culture. Bastide drew the provocative conclusion that Aimé
Césaire is a culturally "white" poet. Although the formulation
of the conclusion is paradoxical, the argument is solid: "Césaire's
Africa, then, is not a dictation from his unconscious but an intentional construction of his creative imagination, composed from
his readings—in short, an image of an ethnographic type."[2]

"Poetry and Cognition" articulated an orthodox surrealist history of modern French literature. Against the neoclassical aesthetics that had dominated France for roughly two centuries
Césaire set the modern tradition beginning with Baudelaire.
Within this tradition he singled out the effort of poets to restore
communication between man and the world in all its nonrational

aspects. In that paper Césaire alluded to the thesis of Frobenius concerning the Ethiopian principle of civilization, substituting the role of the poet for the collective life of a society: "Like the tree, like the animal, [the poet] surrendered himself to primal life; he said yes, he consented to that immense life which surpassed him. He rooted himself in the earth; he stretched out his arms; he played with the sun; he became a tree; he blossomed; he sang."[3] Two further passages tie Césaire's poetics still more closely to Frobenius. He suggests in an image the vast number of cave drawings that Frobenius collected and compared before establishing his broad generalizations: "The word of the poet, the primitive word: rupestral design in the stuff of sound" (p. 120). And finally, "In every true poem the poet *plays the game of the world*, the true poet wants to give the word up to its free associations, in the certainty that he is ultimately giving it up to the will of the universe" (p. 120; italics mine). Compare the conclusion of Frobenius' chapter 10 in *Histoire de la civilisation africaine:* "Civilization is born when the essence of things reveals itself to man, when, ready to surrender himself, he allows himself to be grasped by that essence. That permits man to *play with reality*."[4] When questioned about this idea in "Poetry and Cognition," Césaire replied to an interviewer that he had indeed found it in Frobenius: "Perhaps it isn't very scientific. [In Frobenius] there are great wingbeats; he has astonishing intuitions . . . As for me, I *love* that; it's more poetic than the dry monographs of French positivistic ethnologists."[5] Césaire further commented that Frobenius' concept of mankind being grasped by the world (rather than actively grasping it in the manner typical of Western civilization) suggested to him the essence of possession in voodoo. Here again a European thinker offered Césaire access to a mode of experience that has sometimes been taken to be uniquely Caribbean or neo-African.

For Césaire the poem was to be a miraculous weapon in a sense analogous to that which Frobenius described in chapter 36 of his *History*, "The Reflection of the Eternal": "From this point of view, the garden of civilization and of art still appears full of *miracles*, but not of magical spells. For the existence of spells supposes the possibility of interrupting or of changing the course of nature by phenomena contrary to it; whereas miracles represent a greater power of the data of nature. It is manifest that the marvelous appears in the spiritual creations and in the poetry and stories of humanity as a mystical phenomenon born of surrender" (p. 211). This is the meaning of the surrender Césaire claimed for the true poet in "Poetry and Cognition." The attitude of the poet is mystical and irrational; it is also profoundly religious. His activity can properly be called mythopoesis. The objects he fashions are, intentionally and perhaps inevitably, hybrids, "imaginative constructs to fill in the gaps in our knowledge," as Harry Levin has put it.[6] But at the time he composed his miraculous weapons Césaire would have insisted that mythopoesis was not a stand-in for science, pending further progress. Rather mythopoesis as it functions in *Miraculous Weapons* makes its claim as the response to an eternal need of the human spirit.

The context in which many of these poems were originally published in *Tropiques* is in itself an indication of the mythic import Césaire attached to them; yet no one has thought to apply Césaire's early conception of myth to *Miraculous Weapons* as a whole, a collection having a particular kind of relation among its parts. An important element of coherence within the collection is the repetition from poem to poem of similar structuring elements. These are not so much stylistic elements in a linguistic or technical sense as elements of an overall mythic construct— mythemes in short. In my earlier discussion of *Tropiques* I called attention to the sequential development of "The Thoroughbreds," a poem that is nearly programmatic in its unfolding of a mythic scheme plainly focused on a heroic figure. I stressed the dialectical tensions within that poem that resolve in a harmonious synthesis, a type of organization that is typical of one aspect of Césaire's practice in this 1946 collection. But he has of course varied the combination of elements within poems in such a way as to avoid, for the most part, monotonous repetition while developing the possibilities inherent in the mythic construct he has chosen to elaborate. The result is a sequence of poems in which now one, now another aspect of the myth is brought to the fore in a given poem.

I have already indicated in what sense we may construe the "miraculous" element of the title. The poetic foreword, "Avis de tirs," informs the reader that the verbal space to be traversed is a firing range. The "weapons" are thus situated at the outset. The framing device is completed by a "postface" characterized by a

near total absence of verb tense other than the present indicative
and the present participle; the time is, as the subtitle states, that
of myth.

"The Thoroughbreds" is the first poem in the collection, following the foreword. It sets the tone and orients the reader
toward the myth of the Hero who is reborn to a new cosmic consciousness. "The Thoroughbreds" is followed by the injunction
not to take pity on the poet, "N'ayez point pitié de moi." The
collection unfolds before the reader a series of compelling but
allusive symbols: "Serpent Sun" ("Soleil serpent"), "Water
Woman" ("Femme d'eau"), "Great Midday" ("Le Grand Midi");
a sequence of transitional states: "Perdition," "Survival" ("Survie"), "The Great Beyond" ("Au delà"); scenarios of revolt:
"Miraculous Weapons" ("Les Armes miraculeuses"), "Conquest
of Dawn" ("Conquête de l'aube"); intimations of ecstasies or
epiphanies: "Phrase," "A Poem for the Dawn" ("Poème pour
l'aube"), and "Visitation." The rhythm increases to a frenzy in
"Tam-tam I," "Tam-tam II," and "Batouque." This pitch is
maintained by two poems with a markedly iterative construction—"Secret Dungeons of the Sea and the Deluge" ("Les Oubli-
ettes de la mer et du déluge") and "The Woman and the Knife"
("La Femme et le couteau")—which prepare the reader for the
poem that combines all these elements in a ritual tragedy, "And
the Dogs Were Silent" ("Et les chiens se taisaient").

As he revised the collection for what was meant to be the
definitive edition of 1970 Césaire chose to heighten the formal
indications of an internal mythic structure. The most notable
modification concerns the poem originally entitled "Batéké."
The first half of the poem, which evoked the Batéké people of
the Congo in terms of a surrealist eroticism reminiscent of
Breton's "Free Love" ("L'Union libre"), was eliminated from the
new edition. The remainder of the poem metaphorically fuses a
regressive erotism[7]:

> I utter to the ligneous trough of the infantile wave of your
> breasts...

> je profère au creux ligneux de la vague infantile de tes
> seins...

with sexuality and freedom:

born of your sex on which hangs the fragile fruit of
freedom.

né de ton sexe où pend le fruit fragile de la liberté.[8]

This section of the original "Batéké" Césaire retitled "Mythology" ("Mythologie"). The poem entitled "The Irremediable"
("L'Irrémédiable") was replaced by a subject more in keeping
with the curve of the mythic evolution: "Prophecy" ("Prophétie").
"Water Woman" underwent a title change to "Nostalgic"
("Nostalgique"), suggesting the same intention of tightening the
collection.

To a remarkable degree the organization of *Miraculous
Weapons* suggests the stages in the life of the Hero from heroic
rebirth to his sacrificial death. Some observations arise directly
from the grouping of poems in the collection. Thus the reader
notes a distinct progression in the three poems arranged con-
secutively: "Perdition," "Survival," "The Great Beyond." The
Hero must be prepared to lose himself (an expression with a
range of meaning that runs from the notion of surrender to that
of ritual sacrifice) in order to survive spiritually, in order to attain a consciousness beyond *(au delà)* that of quotidian reality.
I have cited the last of these three poems as a poetic statement
of the potential of the marvelous. We can further refine our understanding of Césaire's hybridized view of mythopoesis by taking another look at the final image of the poem "Au delà" (p. 102):

and reconciled bands offer one another gifts in
the hand of a woman assassinating the day.

et des bandes réconciliées se donnèrent richesse dans
la main d'une femme assassinant le jour.

The presence of the woman among the band of men suggests
a frame of reference alien to Freud but central to one of the ritual
ceremonies related by Frobenius. As Frobenius understood it, the
ritual was intended as a propitiation of the spirit of an antelope
to be killed by a band of pygmies in the Congo forest. The sun
at daybreak restores life to the dead antelope, whose image had
been prepared upon the ground before the hunt. The initial prep-
arations are described in his *History* as follows:

The sun rose on the horizon. One of the men placed himself with his drawn bow near the cleared space on the ground. After a few minutes the rays of the sun illumined the drawing traced on the ground. At the same moment this scene took place with the speed of lightning: the woman raised her hands as though to grasp the sun while loudly shouting sounds I did not understand; the man let fly an arrow; the woman shouted other words; then the men sprang into the bush with their weapons; the woman remained there a few minutes more, then turned back toward camp (p. 110).

A connection can be made between Césaire's poem and this ritual activity with regard to the symbolism of light, the specific importance of dawn, a rapid and violent symbolic activity the result of which is joy (success in the hunt or the reconciliation of a social group), and the central figure of the female officiant in relation to the sun. The final observation on the ritual according to Frobenius likewise fits the overall implications of the poem: "According to this notion the star—the sun in this case—is related to life and to blood, as observations of other societies have confirmed" (p. 111).

There is a sufficient isomorphism between Césaire's poem and the account of the ritual to support the hypothesis that Frobenius' text may have served as a scenario for the creation of the poem. But to discuss Césaire's "The Great Beyond" on its own merits one must place equal stress on those elements that it neglects or uses differently. "The Great Beyond" is totally unrelated to the central motif and indeed to the purpose of the pygmy ritual: the propitiation of the spirit of the animal to be killed for food. Furthermore, in the ritual the woman's function cannot be construed as an assassination of the sun, or day. Just as significantly, the practical, realistic attitude of the pygmies is replaced in the poem by a network of images that conditioned the earlier, Freudian response: frightening dreams rising from the depths, carrying the promise of the freedom of lion cubs; desire related to blood, flowers, and a fierce eagle. The intertextual resonance of the poem proves helpful in situating the locus of Césaire's Africanism, partly imaginary, partly an amalgam of Frobenius and European irrationalism as interpreted by the surrealists. The final line of

"The Great Beyond," its final metaphor, forecloses the play of associations that, far from being free, has guided the reader to an imaginary grasp of a radiant future.

"Miraculous Weapons" follows "The Great Beyond" in the collection. If we read the poems as interrelated, the opening strophe of "Miraculous Weapons," with its dense sequence of associative metaphors, reveals a particularly rich texture. We move backward to the preceding poems and anticipate not only the development of this poem but the further evolution of the collection (p. 103):

> The great machete blow of red pleasure full in
> the forehead there was blood and that tree called
> flamboyant and which never deserves that name more
> than in the expectation of a cyclone and of plundered
> cities
> new blood red reason all the words of all
> the languages meaning to die of thirst and alone when
> dying had the taste of bread and earth and the sea a
> taste of ancestor and that bird calls to me not to
> surrender and the patience of howls at every turn
> of my tongue.

> Le grand coup de machette du plaisir rouge en plein
> front il y avait du sang et cet arbre qui s'appelle
> flamboyant et qui ne mérite jamais mieux ce nom-là
> que les veilles de cyclone et de villes mises à sac
> le nouveau sang la raison rouge tous les mots de toutes
> les langues qui signifient mourir de soif et seul quand
> mourir avait le goût du pain et la terre et la mer un
> goût d'ancêtre et cet oiseau qui me crie de ne pas me
> rendre et la patience des hurlements à chaque détour
> de ma langue.

This strophe draws together into one massive extended metaphor the thematic elements that run through the collection like so many threads. Pleasure and reason are reconciled through their association with blood and the color red. The new blood of red reason has an objective correlative: the stunning tropical tree called flamboyant. The natural violence of tropical storms is associated metaphorically with the unnatural violence of men looting and plundering cities; both images are prepared by the initial one—a great machete blow full in the forehead makes possible this renewal of life's true force. Death itself is included, its meaning transmuted, so as to bring together the ancestral past and the struggle for a better future. We learn at the poem's end (p. 105) that the Hero's revolt must continue "as long as we have not attained the stone without dialect the leaf without dungeon the femurless frail water the serous peritonium of spring-water nights" ("Tant que nous n'aurons pas atteint la pierre sans dialecte la feuille sans donjon l'eau frêle sans fémur le péritoine séreux des soirs de source").

This quest for the original transparency of language ("la pierre sans dialecte"), for the natural understanding of the world by man ("la feuille sans donjon l'eau frêle sans fémur"), for the interpenetration of all created things ("le péritoine séreux des soirs de source") typifies several of the longer poems and occasional shorter ones such as "The Great Beyond." A few poems concentrate on the necessary violence of the revolt itself without the happy synthesis of poems such as "The Thoroughbreds" or "The Great Beyond." These poems ("The Virgin Forest," "Another Season," and "Day and Night" are printed in series) share other features as well: the unrelieved typographical density of their layout intensifies the effect of the *métaphore filée* and suggests the surrealist practice of automatic writing; the text of "Jour et Nuit" echoes the title of "La Forêt vierge," reinforcing the notion of interrelated mythemes within the collection.

The religious connotations of the myth are kept in the foreground through the use of titles suggesting moments in the history of a quasidivine figure. These titles are to be found throughout the collection, but they do not seem to correspond to a specific mythic sequence. "Visitation," which immediately precedes "Mythology," could be taken in a Christian frame of reference as an allusion to Mary's visitation of her cousin Elizabeth, the future mother of John the Baptist. The text of the poem, on the other hand, moves from a tender and sensual evocation of the Hero's former life to a refusal of the Christian world (p. 98): "As for me I have nothing to fear I am from before Adam I am not answerable to the same lion / or the same tree I am from another hot and another cold" ("pour moi je n'ai rien à craindre je suis d'avant Adam je ne relève ni du même lion / ni du même arbre je suis d'un autre chaud et d'un autre froid"). The notion that the specific relationship to Christian mythology may be parodic or satiric is borne out by the 1946 edition of the poem "The Virgin Forest," in which Mary appears as the religious symbol of colonization: "solitary hour and the first for the Virgen de la Caridad and her pretty young face of colonial extortion" ("heure seule et la première pour la Virgen de la Caridad et son frais minois d'exaction coloniale").[9]

The poem "Prophecy" was new to the collection in 1970, replacing "The Irremediable." It dates from 1946, however, having first appeared in the magazine printing of the poem "To Africa" ("A l'Afrique") prior to the publication of *Beheaded Sun (Soleil cou coupé)* in 1948. The new title is taken from the final lines on p. 107: "where bathe prophetic / my mug / my revolt / my name" (où baignent prophétiques / ma gueule / ma révolte / mon nom"). In this case the revolt is directed against the Muslim slave traders of Africa (p. 106): "for having cursed my masters bitten the soldiers of the sultan / for having wailed in the desert" ("d'avoir injurié mes maîtres mordu les soldats du sultan / d'avoir gémi dans le désert"). But the historical aspect of the situation is not pursued. The final strophe resolves the conflict in the poem by turning to an epiphany, a revelation of future harmony. Other titles that function in a like manner are "Investiture" (p. 115), which again refuses Christianity—"O my eyes without baptism and without rescript" ("O mes yeux sans baptême et sans rescrit")—and "Annunciation," dedicated to André Breton.

All the techniques of mythopoesis practiced by Césaire came together in "And the Dogs Were Silent" ("Et les chiens se taisaient"), a splendid dramatic poem that from its inception he conceived as a tragedy of a rather special type. The Hero takes on a kind of symbolic identity that permits him, as the Rebel, to remain midway between the lyric and the drama. In the sacrificial action of his death he recapitulates the direction and meaning of the entire collection, integrating its several parts on a higher level of intelligibility.

A Tragic Poem

More than any other single poem in *Miraculous Weapons,* "And the Dogs Were Silent" deserves André Breton's appreciation of Césaire as a great poet in a major key. The contradictions that appeared irreconcilable in *Tropiques* and in its search for a specifically Martinican culture are here transmuted. They become the necessary antagonisms of tragic myth, expressing themselves as antiphonal voices.

Here too Césaire drew extensively on that fund of European literature that, for good and for ill, has become part of him without ever being entirely his own. "And the Dogs Were Silent" projects into the black experience of the modern world the tragic hero whose struggle, according to Freud, represents the keystone of all tragedy: Oedipus. And yet this is not a Freudian poem. The tragic knot and the riddle that founds a pessimistic culture on the implacable demands of sexuality are not homologous for Césaire. Mother and Lover are separate instances of the tragic situation in his poem. The Mother appeals to her son in the name of the human race and the religion of brotherhood. In this respect she represents the abstract love of humanity proposed by the humanist tradition. The female Lover holds forth the glowing promise of an eroticism that would deny the intolerable reality of the world in an orgastic ecstacy and the hope of a biological immortality (from the 1946 edition of *Les Armes miraculeuses*, p. 99):

> Embrace me: life is there, the banana-tree from its tatters draws its lustrous violet sex; a speck of dust strikes a spark, it is the fur of the sun, a lapping of red leaves, it is the mane of the forest . . . my life is surrounded by threats of life, by promises of life.

> Embrasse-moi: la vie est là, le bananier hors des haillons lustre son sexe violet; une poussière étincelle, c'est la fourrure du soleil, un clapotis de feuilles rouges, c'est la crinière de la forêt . . . ma vie est entourée de menaces de vie, de promesses de vie.

The Lover of "And the Dogs Were Silent" embodies all the erotic potentialities and unresolved contradictions that gravitate about surrealist woman as mediatrix. An important sign of Césaire's independence with regard to surrealist orthodoxy even in 1946 is the Rebel's refusal to seek the absolute through ephemeral orgastic plentitude. Césaire's Rebel does not aspire to the beatitude of the androgyne. He responds antiphonally:

O death in whom hunger ravages not, o sweet tooth, two black children on your threshold they are without parentage, fat death two emaciated children holding one another by the hand on your threshold, they are crepuscular and fallen.

O mort où la faim n'avarie, ô dent douce, deux enfants noirs sur ton seuil ils sont sans parentage, mort grasse deux enfants maigres se tenant par la main sur ton seuil, ils sont crépusculaires et faillis.[10]

Lover and Rebel continue to speak in contradictory—and equally surrealistic—metaphors of beauty (p. 100):

THE LOVER
Embrace me: the hour is beautiful; what is beauty if not the full weight of threats fascinated and seduced into impotence by the disarmed batting of an eyelid? . . .

THE REBEL
what is beauty if not the lacerated poster of a smile on the thunderstruck door of a face? What is dying if not the stony visage of discovery, the journey out of the week and out of the color and toward the sun?

L'AMANTE
Embrasse-moi, l'heure est belle; qu'est-ce que la beauté sinon ce poids complet de menaces que fascine et séduit à l'impuissance le battement désarmé d'une paupière? . . .

LE REBELLE
qu'est-ce la beauté sinon l'affiche lacérée d'un sourire sur la porte foudroyée d'un visage? Qu'est-ce mourir sinon le voyage hors de la semaine et de la couleur à l'envers du soleil?

This dialogue of Eros and Thanatos is taken up again and again in the several voices and diverse guises of the age-old antagonists in man. As the poem progresses the tension is heightened to an unbearable state, and the reader senses that the Rebel is moving ever closer to his own death in full consciousness of his destiny.

A device that serves Césaire particularly well is his use of the Chorus and two Narrators, male and female. The grave intonation of their speech with its rhythmic strophes reiterates a few theme words that take on an incantatory quality (pp. 118, 120):

> THE CHORUS *(chanting)*
> With your sandals of rain and of courage, rise loom immi-
> nent lord so near to tears rise in the desert like water
> and the rising of surging waters of corpses and of
> harvests; rise very imminent lord, the flesh flies in chips
> of dark Africa, rise very imminent lord, there will
> again be eyes like sunflowers of great amorous soyas
> banded by birds as beautiful as the ringing of an
> Adam's apple in the flash of brief wrath . . .
>
> THE NARRATOR *(very calmly)*
> step after step the king has set foot in the pit camouflaged
> with slippery smiles . . .[11]
>
> THE REBEL
> I had led this country to knowledge of itself,
> familiarized this land with its secret demons
> lighted in craters of heloderms and of cymbals
> the symphonies of an unknown hell, splendid,
> inhabited by haughty parasitic nostalgias
>
> LE CHOEUR *(psalmodiant)*
> Avec tes sandales de pluie et de courage, monte surgir im-
> minent seigneur tout près des larmes monte dans le
> désert comme l'eau et la montée des eaux houleuses
> de cadavres et de moissons; monte très imminent
> seigneur, la chair vole en copeaux d'Afrique sombre,
> monte très imminent seigneur, il y aura encore des
> yeux comme des tournesols ou de grands sojas amour-
> eux bandés d'oiseaux aussi beaux qu'une sonnerie de
> pomme d'adam dans l'éclair des colères brèves . . .
>
> LE RECITANT *(très calme)*
> pas après pas le roi a mis le pied dans la fosse camouflée de
> sourires glissants . . .

LE-REBELLE
j'avais amené ce pays à la connaissance de lui-même,
familiarisé cette terre avec ses démons secrets
allumé aux cratères d'hélodermes et de cymbales
les symphonies d'un enfer inconnu, splendide
parasité de nostalgies hautaines

This last speech occurs at the midpoint of a development in crescendo punctuated by the chant of the Chorus ("O standing king") which the Rebel repeatedly interrupts with the monologue of his fate. The directions for this section indicate a very distant historical past in which the Chorus mimes a scene of black revolution, accompanied by monotonous and savage chants. In the absence of any individualized antagonist the Chorus collectively fulfills that role by calling the Rebel to heel, by marshaling the forces of religion to convict him of his fault. Herein resides the principal dramatic tension of the poem. In one awesome scene (p. 123) the Fetishes appear but do not speak, and the Rebel must justify himself before them: "Why should I fear the judgment of my gods? / who said I betrayed?" ("pourquoi aurais-je peur du jugement de mes dieux? / qui a dit que j'ai trahi?"). In yet another the Chorus revitalizes its parodic theme of the Rebel as king or lord by conjuring up the specter of the past glories of Benin and Gao. These are offered in turn by various Tempters. All that the Rebel can claim as his own is the knowledge of who he is after centuries of enslavement and humiliation. His one indubitable proof of his own worth is his refusal to approve the order of things; his only freedom is the freedom not to capitulate. The grotesque episodic characters and the Chorus work to bring about the Rebel's death in ignominy, but they fail.

One is reminded of the traditional role of the chorus in ancient Greek tragedy, where it acts as the representative of conservative social forces and of religion, especially in Aeschylus. Césaire modifies the chorus of Aeschylean tragedy to fit his own contemporary needs: there is no longer any possibility of the real values of the community being served by the Chorus of "And the Dogs Were Silent." To begin with there is no community, only a master-slave relationship; and the tragedy is that of the slave who will not submit to bless the order and the morality of the master. In other words the blacks of Césaire's Chorus are zombies; their souls belong to the exploiters whom they serve. Thus the religion represented in the play is the religion of colonialism (this is how the Christian church is usually portrayed by Césaire).

It is in the conception of the agonistic hero that one finds a more stable notion of the meaning of tragic myth for Césaire. I have alluded to the Rebel as an Oedipal figure, and I have shown that the motif of kingship occurs, albeit as parody, in the speeches of the Chorus. As Thebes was decimated by the plague, so the setting of Césaire's poem is that of a collective disaster: a vast prison on the thirtieth day of famine, torture, and delirium. The Rebel states—in a passage quoted above—that he had led his country to a knowledge of itself before the present disaster befell them. Finally, the Rebel suffers a torture identical to that of Oedipus: he is blinded. The essential difference is to be found in the hero's intrinsic innocence. The collective disaster is not imputable to the Rebel, who fought against it. Nor does his blinding come by his own hand; he is attacked and punished by other prisoners whose lot is objectively the same as his own. It might appear that Césaire has taken the Sophoclean tragedy of *Oedipus the King* and turned it inside out.[12] But Césaire himself has stated that his attempt at "Greek" tragedy in "And the Dogs Were Silent" is related to Nietzsches' theory in *The Birth of Tragedy*.[13] This detail is valuable in that it confirms the conclusions suggested by an analysis of the text. In *The Birth of Tragedy* Nietzsche included a commentary on Sophocles' Oedipus that presents the tragic hero in a perspective akin to that of Césaire's Rebel: "Sophocles conceived doomed Oedipus, the greatest sufferer of the Greek stage, as a pattern of nobility, destined to error and misery despite his wisdom, yet exercising a beneficent influence upon his environment in virtue of his boundless grief."[14] For Nietzsche the interpretation of catharsis in the tragedy, as set forth by commentators on Aristotle and received into the Western tradition, is wrongheaded and absurd. Far from purging the spectators of the emotions aroused by the play, he goes on to say, the death of the hero represents a sacrificial act, the function of which is to renew the collectivity: "The profound poet tells us that a man who is truly noble is incapable of sin; though every law, every natural order, indeed the entire canon of ethics, perish by his actions, those very actions will create a circle of higher consequences able to found a new world on the ruins of the old" (p. 60).

Through the abrupt conclusion of "And the Dogs Were Silent," which conforms to the "exploding-fixed" type of closure described by André Breton in *L'Amour fou* we may see in the transformation of the male and female Narrators the working out of the poetic and metaphysical premises of Nietzsche's argument. Until the death of the Rebel the two Narrators ally themselves with the Chorus in its attempts to induce him to recant. His heroic death, however, brings about a profound modification of their attitude and their language. In the concluding pages they abandon the religious incantations of the Chorus and speak lyrically, as the Rebel had done. At one point the evocation of the sea is suggestive of the Dionysian nature of the hero's sacrifice (*Les Armes miraculeuses,* 1946, p. 190):

MALE NARRATOR
Orgy, orgy, divine water, heavenly body of luxurious flesh, vertigo
isles fresh rings in the ears of diving sirens
isles coins fallen from the purse of the stars

LE RECITANT
Orgie, orgie, eau divine, astre de chairs luxueuses, vertige
îles anneaux frais aux oreilles des sirènes plongées
îles pièces tombées de la bourse aux étoiles

But the Chorus does not relent (p. 191):

swarm of larvae, worthless talismans
isles
silent lands
truncated isles

grouillement de larves, talismans sans valeur
îles
terres silencieuses
îles tronquées

The final antiphonal lines of the two Narrators realize a lyrical closure, symbolic of a new consciousness (p. 191): "I come to you" / "I am one of you, isles" ("Je viens à vous" / "Je suis une de vous, Iles").

The *Mysteries of Ogun*

To what extent does Césaire's tragic poem approximate the vision of West African ritual that he sought to emulate elsewhere in his *Miraculous Weapons?* The question is inevitable, but the risk is that any attempt to answer it may rest on gratuitous associations. Since Césaire's knowledge of African traditions was at the time bookish by his own admission, one can only reasonably adduce for comparison sources with which Césaire either was, or can be assumed to have been, familiar. Until recently the colonialist attitude held that there was no tragedy in Africa; tragedy has been thought to be the unique creation of European civilization. Therefore in this view Césaire's "And the Dogs Were Silent," insofar as it is a tragedy, belongs by definition to European literature.

African scholars who have begun to study their own oral traditions outside the colonialist prejudice have obliged us to alter our preconceptions. One such valuable contribution to comparative literature is a book by Wole Soyinka, *Myth, Literature and the African World.* Soyinka has analyzed the *Mysteries of Ogun* in the dual context of traditional Yoruba belief and of Nietzsche's theory of tragedy. His study offers us the rare opportunity to confront the relationship of the *Mysteries of Ogun* to Nietzsche with the relationship of "And the Dogs Were Silent" to Nietzsche. I have shown that Césaire considered his Rebel a Nietzschean suffering hero. Soyinka's commentary on the *Mysteries of Ogun* suggests that it would be desirable to pursue further the nature of the hero's suffering.

After entertaining briefly the possibility of a Yoruba parallel to Nietzsche's Dionysos-Apollo brotherhood in the orishas, or gods, Ogun-Obatala, Soyinka dismisses it as too facile and not in keeping with the true nature of the Yoruba orishas: "But Obatala the sculptural god is not the artist of Apollonian illusion but of inner essence . . . Ogun, for his part, is best understood in Hellenic values as a totality of the Dionysian, Apollonian and Promethean virtues."[15] But the *Mysteries of Ogun* are, according to Soyinka, in other respects remarkably like the ancient Greek tragedies, which Nietzsche described as arising from the Mysteries of Eleusis. Most notably the hero is seen as representing the suffering god: "The first actor—for he led all others—was Ogun, first suffering deity, first creative energy, the first challenger, and

conqueror of transition. And his, the first art, was tragic art"
(p. 145). The *Mysteries* also present an analogue to the stages of
being of Dionysos: participating first in the original Oneness as
undifferentiated Being, then as Zagreus-Dionysos torn asunder
by the Titans, and finally, after the ritual suffering and sacrifice
of his individuality, reincorporated into a new harmony. Soyinka
obviously finds the *Mysteries of Ogun* important because they
demonstrate that "Yoruba metaphysics of accommodation and
resolution could come only after the passage of the gods through
the transitional gulf, after the demonic test of the self-will of
Ogun the explorer-god in the creative caldron of cosmic powers"
(p. 145). European commentators on African thought have generally denied the existence of such a struggle in traditional African
belief systems, preferring to see only the end result, "a harmonious will which accommodates every alien material or abstract
phenomenon within its infinitely stressed spirituality" (p. 146).
Aimé Césaire later attacked this European distortion of African
thought in his *Discourse on Colonialism*, seeing in it a justification
for the subjugation of Africans. The proper distinction between
an African view of tragedy in the *Mysteries* and a European view
may reside in the stress laid on the final, harmonious accommodation. Soyinka relates the structure of the *Mysteries* in distinctly
Nietzschean terms but with the appropriate African flavor:

> To fashion a bridge across [the experience of transition]
> was not only Ogun's task but his very nature, and he had
> first to experience, to surrender his individuation once again
> (the first time, as a part of the original Orisa-nla Oneness)
> to the fragmenting process; to be reabsorbed within univer-
> sal Oneness, the Unconscious, the deep black whirlpool of
> mythopoeic forces, to immerse himself thoroughly within
> it, understand its nature and yet by the combative value of
> the will to rescue and re-assemble himself and emerge
> wiser, powerful from the draught of cosmic secrets, orga-
> nising the mystic and the technical forces of earth and cos-
> mos to forge a bridge for his companions to follow   (pp.
> 153–154).

Concerning the purpose of the tragedy Soyinka has this to say:
"And what has the struggle of the tragic hero been, after all, but

an effort to maintain that innate concept of dignity which impels to action only to that degree in which the hero possesses a true nobility of spirit?" (p. 154). In all these respects a very striking parallelism can be drawn between the *Mysteries of Ogun* and the tragic poem "And the Dogs Were Silent."

Is this to say that in spite of all the obstacles Césaire has somehow created an authentically African tragedy? In answering that question one must bear in mind first that Soyinka has offered us the most attractive parallel imaginable by presenting the poetics of the *Mysteries of Ogun* in Nietzschean terms. Clearly Soyinka wished to show to European civilization that the traditional Yoruba culture includes features that had formerly been claimed as uniquely European. His essay is also intended to show contemporary Africans that their traditions contain elements that point toward a technological future (among Ogun's attributes is the knowledge of working iron). In this respect Soyinka also intends to offer the *Mysteries of Ogun* as an image of antinegritude. "The principle of creativity when limited to pastoral idyllism, as negritude has attempted to limit it, shuts us off from the deeper, fundamental resolutions of experience and cognition" (p. 150). No doubt here as elsewhere in this book (which never names or quotes Césaire) Soyinka is thinking primarily of Senghor and his epigones; but many readers will find Césaire guilty by association. However many times Césaire patiently explains that he never conceived of the black world as petrified for all time in a mythic past, it remains the sad fate of his *Notebook of a Return to the Native Land* that a few magnificent lines inspired by Frobenius are all that matter to some readers.[16] When the mythic import of *Miraculous Weapons* is properly understood, it too will probably be offered as evidence against Césaire.

Although it is highly unlikely that Césaire knew anything of the details of the *Mysteries of Ogun* in the forties, he did have access to an account of an African rite presented in terms of its analogies to European tragedy. Once again it is Leo Frobenius, whose *Histoire de la civilisation africaine* Césaire had read with such passion, who provides the most probable scenario for an Africanization of "And the Dogs Were Silent." In his discussion in *Histoire* of the rite of passage at puberty that he had observed in the Cameroons, Frobenius gives the following interpretation: "The motif of decline, agony, and death here joins that of resurrection and life: it is the 'renewal' that seems to us the culminating point . . . The young man must traverse a subterranean corridor where frightening masks of leopards and specters lie in wait for him. By going through the corridor the young man receives the consecration of renewal. This recalls burial in a funerary niche (and consequently death and subsequent resurrection), and all the symbols common to the group of peoples who celebrate the ceremonies of puberty" (p. 158). Frobenius concludes with some speculation on the life cycle of plants as the prototype of such a ritual, a type of speculation that had great appeal for the *Tropiques* group when Césaire was writing "And the Dogs Were Silent."

The issue, finally, is the purpose of a tragic poem such as "And the Dogs Were Silent." One can grasp it properly by insisting on the distinction between traditional myth and pseudomyth of the modernist variety. Myths in traditional societies, be they African or European, cosmogonic, ritual, or etiological, belong to the culture in which they were created and have their full significance only with respect to the complex mode of symbolic expression within that culture. Thus the outline of the *Mysteries of Ogun* given above is truncated and incomplete; it is a literary plot rather than the description of a ritual, as Soyinka himself implies in *Myth, Literature and the African World* when he states that "In contemporary [public] festivals of Ogun the usual intermingling of idioms has occurred—the ritual dismembering of a surrogate dog, enactment of the massacre at Ire, the dispute between Sango and Ogun, Ogun's battle triumphs, etc. The note is summatively festive" (p. 157, n. 7). The tragedy discussed so movingly by Wole Soyinka is then a reconstruction of what the *Mysteries of Ogun* may have been. Nor can we know how much the reconstruction may owe to Nietzsche's *Birth of Tragedy*.[17] But if Wole Soyinka is right in every particular, the *Mysteries of Ogun* must ultimately be considered as a collective phenomenon, reaffirming aspects of the life of the Yoruba people.

Not so the tragic poem "And the Dogs Were Silent." This is an aesthetic object made by an individual for other individuals. Its mode of communication is the solitary act of reading; Césaire did not envisage an audience of any sort beyond individual readers of poems. This particular aesthetic object is marked both by its time (as a modernist pseudomyth it may be compared to a work such as Camus's *Caligula*) and by the personal history of its author.[18] For these reasons and others the aspect of the suffering hero that Césare has stressed is his unqualified revolt (Camus again comes to mind)—he is the Rebel—and just enough pseudo-historical anecdote is given to situate him as the leader of a slave uprising on a Caribbean plantation in the unspecified past of an unnamed island. This high degree of generality is justifiable in the name of negritude, of course. But is it necessary to be the descendant of slaves to appreciate it? Nor is the humanism to which Césaire appeals a universal one. The tone and atmosphere of the play situate it as a hybrid of surrealism and existentialism, of which Aimé Césaire is beyond any doubt the great exponent.

"And the Dogs Were Silent" is finally no more or less African than "The Thoroughbreds" or other poems of Césaire's *Miraculous Weapons*. As a tragic poem of great lyric accomplishment it will take its place among the best modernist visions of the agonistic type, once criticism has disengaged it from the narrowly ideological quarreling over negritude. A twofold analysis of the poem reveals in conclusion that Césaire's *Miraculous Weapons* proceed from the myth of the birth of the Hero in "The Thoroughbreds" to the myth of the death and rebirth of the Hero in "And the Dogs Were Silent." It is easy to see how Césaire could have been drawn to the Nietzschean view of tragedy in the forties. Before Frobenius, Nietzsche in *The Birth of Tragedy* saw the ritual as a form of surrender, a voluntary sacrifice, an affirmation of the life force transcending an individual death. It is the collectivity that is represented as renewed, reborn as a result of the sacrifice. At the close of "And the Dogs Were Silent" the conversion of the Narrators orients the reader toward the eventual renewal of the society. *Miraculous Weapons* is composed in the manner of a cycle that, like a mythical cycle, opens onto a new beginning—at a higher level—just as it appears to end.

Epiphanies and Explosions

Césaire's surrealism in *Miraculous Weapons* has proved a stumbling block to those readers who have not approached it as a contribution to modern poetry. This is particularly unfortunate because some of the poems deserve to rank high among surrealist texts. If there is one effect that Césaire seeks consistently to produce in this collection it is that of a poetic epiphany, a momentarily dazzling revelation that, like a phosphorus flare, transforms everything it touches with its special illumination. Nowhere is this more apparent or striking than in those abruptly foreclosed poems in which Césaire achieves the convulsive beauty that Breton had said "will be erotic-veiled, exploding-fixed, magic-circumstantial or it will not be."[19]

The poem "Firing Range" ("Avis de tirs") features a syntactically iterative composition that gradually defamiliarizes the reader by presenting several sequences of metaphors of a given structure; then the poem seems to burst from its own pent-up energy in this movement (from *Poèmes*, p. 84):

> the white toothed black flag of the Vomito-Negro
> will be hoisted for the unlimited duration
> of the brush fire of brotherhood.

> le pavillon noir à dents blanches du Vomito-Negro
> sera hissé pendant la durée illimitée
> du feu de brousse de la fraternité.

On the one hand Césaire suggests explosive aggressiveness: Vomito-Negro is volcanic, brush fire is threatening, and in this context, the white-toothed black flag is scarcely comforting. But against this release of affective energy the poet sets a stabilizing, arresting element: unlimited duration, brotherhood. To a remarkable extent the conclusion of this first poem sets the tone and thus prepares the reader to apprehend poetically the miraculous weapons offered by the collection.

An interview Césaire gave to the late Michel Benamou goes part way toward explaining why the device of volcanic explosion is used so frequently in his work, adding a very personal note to a familiar surrealist practice. Césaire described what it means to call oneself "un Péléen": All Martinicans know what Mt. Pelée is. It's a mountain that has been considered extinct . . . for a very long time and that shows itself rarely, but when it shows itself it does so with violence. It is an explosion; it's the explosive type."[20] Césaire's violence has given pause to those who are interested primarily in finding a straightforward message in his poetry. *Miraculous Weapons* explodes frequently in a volcanic fire, but it is a fire that purifies. Brotherhood is its ultimate goal; hatred must be spent and consumed in the flames. Throughout his work, beginning with the *Miraculous Weapons,* there runs the conviction that only after the moment of convulsion (social, mythic, or psychic—these planes interpenetrate the density of the metaphor in most cases) is the new order of peace and true brotherhood possible. Poetry of this type has an overtly therapeutic purpose. On the individual level it says through its peculiar indirection that it is both right and necessary to give vent to the hostilities accumulated in a lifetime. With regard to the thematics of negritude that inform the collection, giving it a special substance, Césaire has made abundantly clear what he intended: "Victim of the colonial trauma and in search of a new equilibrium, the black man has not yet finished liberating himself. All the dreams, all the desires, all the accumulated rancor, all the formless and repressed hopes of a century of colonialist domination, all that needed to come out and when it comes out and expresses itself and squirts bloodily, carrying along without distinction the conscious and the unconscious, lived experience and prophecy, that is called poetry."[21] Although in this statement Césaire was ostensibly prefacing a new collection of poetry from the black world, nowhere has he given a more perfect commentary on his own poetic practice in *Miraculous Weapons.*

A dominant metaphor of transformation and renewal for Césaire is the swamp, teeming with life and bringing forth new forms out of the decomposition of the old. The poem "Take No Pity" (*Poèmes,* p. 94) is a mere sixteen lines long (it is among the shortest in the collection), and the abrupt conclusion is realized by means of a comparison expanded by an exploding-fixed metaphor: "—swamp— / like a viper born of the blond force of / dazzlement" ("—marais— / telle une vipère née de la force blonde de / l'éblouissement"). The next poem, "Serpent Sun" ("Soleil serpent"), maintains the same metaphoric frame, although the focus changes to the principal force of transformation, the vampirelike suction of the sun over its waters. The concluding line (p. 95) stands alone to indicate that the "sea teeming with islands" ("la mer pouilleuse d'îles") is in reality an avatar of the life-giving swamp: "the sugar of the word Brazil in the depth of the swamp" ("le sucre du mot Brésil au fond du marécage"). Neither prepared nor explained, the sweetness of this totally unexpected combination serves to transform positively the unpleas-

ant but vital swamp. An extensive study could be made of the
creative morass in Césaire's work, an image that appears, with
some modifications, from this collection to the 1960 collection
Shackles (Ferrements).

Occasionally Césaire prepares an exploding-fixed closure by
organizing the poem in a sequence of predominately nominal
statements, as in "Investiture" (*Poèmes*, p. 115):

> my eyes of India ink of Saint-Pierre assassinated
> my eyes of summary execution and of back to the wall
> my eyes that rise up against the proclamation of grace
> my eyes of Saint-Pierre braving the assassins beneath the
> dead cinder

> mes yeux d'encre de Chine de Saint-Pierre assassiné
> mes yeux d'exécution sommaire et de dos au mur
> mes yeux qui s'insurgent contre l'édit de grâce
> mes yeux de ville bravant les assassins sous la cendre morte

In this case the poet reserves for the conclusion the independent
clause containing the theme word of the title:

> I shall not let go the ibis of mad investiture from my hands
> in flames.

> je ne lâcherai pas l'ibis de l'investiture folle de mes mains en
> flammes.

Although the statement itself promises a resolution, a not letting
go, all the accumulated metaphoric tensions of the poem remain
intact with the flames consuming the hands for all time. A poem
of this type gains immeasurably by being assigned a place in a
loose progression suggestive of the stages in the life of a culture
hero. The mad investiture of this poem can await its final resolution in "And the Dogs Were Silent." At the same time this
state of extreme tension provides what many consider the hall-
mark of Césaire's poetry, his signature. In *Miraculous Weapons*
this type of poem maintains the reader's attention at a high level
of nervous response. Knowing that such a state cannot be maintained indefinitely, Césaire has taken care to intersperse poems

of the dialectical type—a long one, "The Thoroughbreds," at the beginning and shorter ones, such as "The Great Beyond," in the middle. The reader senses, even without consciously recognizing, that the exploding-fixed poems replicate the violence of the middle or antithetical movement common to the dialectical poems. Thus there is a unifying principle at work in the collection on the level of poetic structure as well as on the level of myth and mytheme.

A third type of poem relies on a percussive rhythm for its dominant effect. Three of these are quite short, suggestive of a rapid staccato movement of the tom-tom: "Tam-tam de nuit" (five lines), "Tam-tam I" (eight lines), and "Tam-tam II" (ten lines). They are related to the poems that build to an exploding-fixed closure, but their overall effect is still more intense; the whole brief movement explodes, as it were, without any introduction or preparation.

The poem of this type that has attracted the most attention is also the most complex: "Batouque." In the original edition of *Miraculous Weapons* Césaire gave the only footnote of the collection to this title: "Brazilian tom-tom rhythm." This indication has led some scholars to assume that the entire poem must be mimetic of a specific Afro-Brazilian drumbeat, whereas *Batouque* is a "generic term, designating black dances, whether profane or religious."[22] *Batuque* in Luso-Brazilian is an onomatopoeia for the drumbeat itself, and this was undoubtedly all that Césaire intended by the footnote, which he withdrew from subsequent editions.

Bernadette Cailler has offered a subtle, complex, and convincing interpretation of the title and the frequent repetition of the word *batouque* throughout the text: "The term *batouque,* as it is taken up in Césaire's poem, would thus be at one and the same time (1) an onomatopoeia (the sound of the drum), (2) the name of a dance (rhythmic sequence, movement of bodies in time and space), (3) a reference to a set of religious practices (rite of passage between the individual and the cosmos, between the profane and the sacred)."[23] Cailler is also correct in considering the overall effect to be incantatory, tending to produce a trancelike state. This is perfectly in keeping with Césaire's theory in "Poetry and Cognition." I am less convinced by her conclusion that a specific victory results from the speaker's metaphoric violence: "Reduced to its simplest formulation, Césaire's poetry is also [the poetry] of a drama in which the monster is fought, dies and in which the child, hale and hearty, comes into the world. In 'Batouque,' the victory is that of the black Sun which is going to strangle, cut up, rape, the night of the islands . . . and impregnate it" (p. 78). Cailler's reliance on a structuralist method has, in my view, produced a stimulating but unjustified conclusion. This is finally less important than her excellent observations on the poem's construction. Each sequence preceded by the strong stress accent "batouque of . . ." calls up before us another of the multiple tableaux of unequal length and rather disparate character (p. 79). The conclusion of "Batouque" is indeed suggestive of a resolution, unlike the purer examples of the exploding-fixed type of closure. This may well be a function of the poem's much greater length combined with the mind's tendency to find a resolution. I would propose, therefore, that the trancelike state the poem seeks to create is not really in keeping with a specific victory, even in the form of the deep structure that Cailler claims to have arrived at by way of Malinowski as reinterpreted by Lévi-Strauss. Something more on the order of a Gestalt emerges from the poem, one of those the-whole-is-greater-than-the-sum-of-its-parts visions dear to surrealism. Moreover, Césaire certainly does not seem to have found a resolution that wold flow naturally from the structure of the poem. Unlike the examples of poetic closure examined earlier, this one seems somehow forced, even trite (from *Poèmes,* p. 134):

> Freedom my only pirate water of the new year my only
>   thirst
> love my only sampan
> we shall run our fingers of laughter and gourd
> between the glacial teeth of the Sleeping Beauty.

> Liberté mon seul pirate eau de l'an neuf ma seule soif
> amour mon seul sampang
> nous coulerons nos doigts de rire et de gourde
> entre les dents glacées de la Belle-au-bois-dormant.

The first two lines are very beautiful, but "la Belle-au-bois-dormant" is disappointing to say the least.

Césaire's rhythmic effects are a further example of his Africanization of French prosody. These are not French rhythms; on that
score everyone is agreed. But are they truly African? Or are they
Afro-American, like jazz? Or specifically Antillean, deriving from
Martinican dance rhythms? Working in a language whose metrical system has been considered by many moderns to be a strait
jacket, Césaire has effectively created a hybridized prosody that
is very personal, extremely expressive, and at its best eminently
satisfying. G. E. Clancier has grasped an important point concerning Césaire's problematical relation to the French language:
"This language belongs to the whites whose domination the black
poet intends to destroy; it is therefore the very essence of an obsessive and abhorred universe; it is at the same time the black
poet's most precious possession, since it is one with his song, be
it of praise or revolt, since it is the locus and the soul of his
poetry."[24]

A fourth major type of poem in the *Miraculous Weapons*
turns on the surrealist automatism effect. Automatic writing is
among the most widely publicized and least studied of the techniques preferred by surrealists, who gave it new vigor and a degree
of artistic respectability. The association of automatic writing
with spiritualism as a means of communication with the great
beyond was intentionally cultivated by André Breton and his
associates, especially in the early stages of surrealist experimentation. Automatic writing in a nontechnical sense has thus come
to mean inspired nonsense or subconscious oracular statement.
In either case the producer of automatic texts has been able to
claim the irresponsibility of the Delphic oracle while simultaneously making a claim to its prestige. Most of what has been
written on surrealist automatism is consequently of no literary
critical value whatever.

Michael Riffaterre has formulated a theory of automatic texts
that considers their literariness. Automatism is a literary effect like
any other; it can be described and studied. Analyzing what he calls
the "automatism effect" in Breton's *Poisson soluble*, he concludes
that the surrealists created a new and distinct genre using old
topoi:

> Normally, that is, in a non-automatic text, discourse gen-
> erated under the restrictions of semantic and morphologi-

cal association and of rules of grammar, must also conform to the rules and requirements of the narrative. No verbal association is allowed to contradict the narrative or to deflect its progress, except as a parenthesis clearly subordinated like the rest to the overall telling of the story. In these texts, on the contrary, there are incompatibilities between the narrative and the discourse. The words and phrases generated by the lexical actualization of the narrative structure generate in turn associative chains that are aberrant in the overall context.[25]

We have here in condensed form a model for reading automatic texts including, of course, Césaire's. Eventually it should be possible to differentiate between the automatism effect in Breton, say, and in Césaire.

The work of revising *Les Armes miraculeuses* for inclusion in his *Oeuvres complètes* prompted a decision by Césaire that tells us something significant about his own view of automatism. In both the earlier editions of the collection (the original in 1946 and the so-called definitive edition of 1970) "The Virgin Forest" appeared as one of the longer texts (three pages) in which the automatism effect was announced by the poem's layout. In the 1976 collected works there suddenly appeared three poems ("La Forêt vierge," "Autre Saison," and "Jour et Nuit") where there had been but one. None of the three poems contains any new or rearranged material. What might at first appear to be a process of simple division actually corresponds to the internal logic of the genre. In fact each text is constructed according to a different generative principle: the abbreviated version of "The Virgin Forest" is based entirely on syntactic and semantic negation of a cultural norm; "Day and Night," an abbreviated version of the final third of the original text, contains elements of social protest coupled with a utopian vision of negritude; "Another Season," originally the middle section, couples a satire of military operations with a pronounced use of eroticism, which both opens and closes the poem. Whereas "The Virgin Forest" and "Day and Night" could conceivably have been considered two parts of a whole—and thereby lose a part of their unique flavor—"Another Season" corresponds to another *topos* entirely. Each poem as a poem has benefited from the separation. Furthermore, in "Day and Night"

Césaire has simply cut out roughly half the original. This is less a question of improving the aesthetic quality of the poem, I think, than one of reducing the number of associative sequences. Two distinct sequences have been removed or reduced to insignificance by this process: one dealing in blasphemy, which Césaire has also minimized in the revision of *Beheaded Sun,* and another that acts as a series of veiled allusions to Martinican realities of the forties. In the second instance the poem has been made to better approximate the "absolute language," Césaire's avowed goal; in the former he has signified his intention to refuse entry into the poem to an institutional religion that should not be equated with religious feeling.

Césaire intended his automatic texts to function as miraculous weapons of a type distinct from the exploding-fixed poems or the trance poems, which use an obsessive rhythm. All three types are themselves, within the context of the collection as an intentional construct, subordinate to the first or dialectical type. The dialectical poems provide an implicit thematic unity of a pseudomythological sort, linking the parts of the collection from "The Thoroughbreds" to "And the Dogs Were Silent." The decision to remove the lyrical version of "And the Dogs Were Silent" from the collected *Poèmes* in 1976 was in this regard an unfortunate one. From the standpoint of the lyrical quality of the collection, the text of *Miraculous Weapons* published by Gallimard in 1970 might be considered the best to date were it not for the old form of "La Forêt vierge," which Césaire rectified only in 1976. In all other respects the 1970 edition is superior in bringing the metaphorical and pseudomythological unity of the collection into a sharply defined relief that calls the reader's attention to the suffering hero of negritude.

5

The Epic of Negritude

The poetic spirit alone corrodes and builds, cuts out and quickens.

Seul l'esprit poétique corrode et bâtit, retranche et vivifie.
Césaire in *Martinique,* no. 1 (1944)

CÉSAIRE'S *Notebook of a Return to the Native Land* *(Cahier d'un retour au pays natal)* has become one of the classics of the literature of decolonization. It is in every sense a political poem as well as the account of the poet's effort to establish contact with himself by breaking down the barriers of alienation. From the first Césaire conceived of negritude as the struggle to transcend racism and the effects of colonization, including the colonization of the mind. The *Notebook* was a political act in that it plumbed the depths of the black Martinican's experience and revealed its horrors. The struggle, composed or recomposed so as to render a sense of process, gives the poem its ternary structure: an initial revolt against an intolerable present; a recollection of childhood and early youth that calls up images both fascinating and revolting, culminating in the recognition of an awful personal reality; and finally a shorter movement that swells with the surge of vital force renewed. Because it is a political poem, some commentators have read it as a document, passing over the significance of its poetic fabric. I hope to point out the balance of formal intention and ideological aim inherent in the *Notebook.*

The smallest unit of the poem is the strophe, whose limits are set by emotional completeness rather than by strictly governed metrical arrangement. In modern poetry Césaire's use of the strophe comes closest to that of Lautréamont in Maldoror's cantos. We may safely apply to Césaire's use of this flexible form the description he gave of Lautréamont's in 1943: "He declames with

the booming voice of the storm the surrealist strophe of mael-
stroms of blood."[1] In the same article Césaire declared that Lautréamont and Rimbaud represent complementary principles in
modern poetry. In the *Notebook* he has combined the theory of
Rimbaud with aspects of Lautréamont's practice in order to create a new hybrid. Like Lautréamont he gives a sense of immedi-
acy to his text through the apostrophe, the device with which
Césaire opens the first strophe of postwar editions of the *Notebook:*

> Beat it, I said to him, you cop, you lousy pig, beat it I
> detest the flunkies of order and the cock-chafers of hope.
> Beat it evil ju-ju, you bedbug of a petty monk.

> Va-t'en, lui disais-je, gueule de flic, gueule de vache, va-
> t'en je déteste les larbins de l'ordre et les hannetons de
> l'espérance. Va-t'en mauvais gris-gris, punaise de moinil-
> lon.[2]

Lautréamont, however, employed apostrophe to a different end.
Representatives of the natural world were addressed directly by
his speaker, Maldoror, who ironically preferred their monstrous
qualities to those of contemporary civilized man:

> O octopus with silken gaze! you whose soul is insepa-
> rable from mine; you most beautiful of terrestrial inhabi-
> tants and who reign over a harem of four hundred suckers;
> you in whom sweet communicative virtue and the divine
> graces nobly abide, as in their natural residence, by mutual
> agreement, by an indestructible bond, why are you not with
> me, your mercurial belly against my aluminum chest, seated
> together on some rock along the shore to contemplate this
> spectacle that I adore!

> O poulpe au regard de soie! toi dont l'âme est insépa-
> rable de la mienne; toi le plus beau des habitants du globe
> terrestre, et qui commandes à un sérail de quatre cents ven-
> touses; toi en qui siègent noblement, comme dans leur rési-
> dence naturelle, par un commun accord, d'un lien inde-

structible, la douce vertu communicative et les grâces divines, pourquoi n'es-tu pas avec moi, ton ventre de mercure contre ma poitrine d'aluminium assis tous les deux sur quelque rocher du rivage pour contempler ce spectacle que j'adore![3]

Not infrequently Lautréamont pulled out the stops in a style that parodies the worst excesses of romantic grandiloquence. Such is the effect of his hymn to the louse:

> I salute you, rising sun, celestial liberator, you invisible enemy of mankind. Continue to tell filth to couple with man in an impure embrace, and to swear to him with oaths not written in dust that she shall remain his faithful lover for all eternity . . . If the earth were covered with lice, like grains of sand on the seashore, the human race would be annihilated, suffering horrible pains. What a spectacle! I, with the wings of an angel, immobile in the ether, would contemplate it.

> Je te salue, soleil levant, libérateur céleste, toi l'ennemi invisible de l'homme. Continue de dire à la saleté de s'unir avec lui dans des embrassements impurs, et de lui jurer, par des serments, non écrits dans la poudre, qu'elle restera son amante fidèle jusqu'à l'éternité . . . Si la terre était couverte de poux, comme de grains de sable le rivage de la mer, la race humaine serait anéantie, en proie à des douleurs terribles. Quel spectacle! Moi, avec des ailes d'ange, immobile dans les airs, pour le contempler![4]

Césaire praised Lautréamont for having discovered "the chilling hysterical power of Parody" (p. 11). It may well be that the fundamental principle of Maldoror's strophe can be accounted for in terms of this surrealist version of parody. Césaire's modification of that strophic form involves a complex relationship to nineteenth-century literature and to more recent authors, a relationship in which parody per se plays a relatively minor role. If parody is a critical device that heightens the characteristics of the thing imitated, as one definition has it, then Lautréamont parodies a certain romantic style. Césaire does not parody Lautréamont; he takes him as a critical model to be turned toward the specific end required by his subject. Césaire embraces subversive excess, in the manner of Lautréamont, for the purpose of challenging entrenched positions, both literary and political. It is this subversion of a consecrated style for its potentially corrosive effect that initially provides grounds for comparison. From the outset Césaire's poem works to arouse a similar effect of nauseated disgust with the existing order.[5] *Order* must be understood simultaneously in its political and in its aesthetic ramifications if the reader is to first feel and subsequently analyze the import of corrosive poetics in the *Notebook*. To orient the reader, Césaire has, since 1956, begun the *Notebook* with the statement of hatred for "the flunkies of order and the cock-chafers of hope" quoted above. In the "petty monk" we sense the speaker's revulsion with his own role as dutiful student, laboriously absorbing the value system of oppression while awaiting his metamorphosis as a flunky of order.

A second look at the device of apostrophe reveals that it too is exploited self-consciously as Césaire gives its etymology in the text:

> Then I *turned toward* paradises lost for him and his kin, calmer than the face of a woman telling lies, and there, rocked by the flux of a never exhausted thought I nourished the wind, I unlaced the monsters and heard rise from the other side of disaster a river of turtle-doves and savanna clover which I carry forever in my depths . . .

> Puis je *me tournais vers* des paradis pour lui et les siens perdus, plus calme que la face d'une femme qui ment, et là, bercé par les effluves d'une pensée jamais lasse je nourrissais le vent, je délaçais les monstres et j'entendais monter de l'autre côté du désastre, un fleuve de tourterelles et de trèfles de la savane que je porte toujours dans mes profondeurs . . . (*Cahier*, p. 29, my emphasis)

The speaker turns away from the here and now in a movement that arouses the expectation of a return to paradise lost, the familiar poetic return to the delights of childhood in a natural world characterized by innocence and the splendid indolence of the tropics. But in the French Antilles even the presumably universal preserve of childhood has its political implications of class and race, a situation to which the poem "To Celebrate a Childhood" by Saint-John Perse bears haughty testimony:

> Palms . . . !
>   In those days they bathed you in water-of-green-leaves; and the water was of green sun too; and your mother's maids, tall glistening girls, moved their warm legs near you who trembled . . . (I speak of a high condition, in those days, among the dresses, in the dominion of revolving lights.)

> Palmes . . . !
>   Alors on te baignait dans l'eau-de-feuilles-vertes; et l'eau encore était du soleil vert; et les servantes de ta mère, grandes filles luisantes, remuaient leurs jambes chaudes près de toi qui tremblais . . . (Je parle d'une haute condition, alors, entre les robes, au règne de tournantes clartés.)[6]

Quite possibly in the conclusion of the following passage Césaire intended to parody this same poem. The parenthetical exclamation at the end, a device typical of Perse's style, is rendered parodic by the grating contradiction between the concept of the queen and her attributes (*Cahier*, p. 129):

> my queen of spittle and leprosy
> my queen of whips and scrofula
> my queen of squasma and chloasma
> (oh those queens I once loved in the remote gardens of spring against the luminations of all the candles of the chestnut trees!)

> ma reine des crachats et des lèpres
> ma reine des fouets et des scrofules
> ma reine des squasmes et des chloasmes
> (oh ces reines que j'aimais jadis aux jardins printaniers et lointains avec derrière l'illumination de toutes les bougies de marronniers!)

But in the main Césaire's speaker turns away from what is symbolized in the Caribbean poetry of Saint-John Perse, an order that includes him only insofar as the black servants fill in the background of the picture in much the same way as do the insects or the ripe fruit falling from the trees:

> . . . Then those flies, that sort of fly, and the last terrace of the garden . . . Someone is calling. I'll go . . . I speak in esteem.
> —Other than childhood, what was there in those days that there no longer is?
> Plains, Slopes! There
> was greater order! And everything was glimmering realms and frontiers of lights. And shade and light in those days were more nearly the same thing . . . I speak of an esteem . . . Along the borders the fruits
> might fall
> without [joy] rotting on our lips.
> And men with graver mouths stirred deeper shadows, women more dreams with slower arms.

> . . . Puis ces mouches, cette sorte de mouches, et le dernier étage du jardin . . . On appelle. J'irai . . . Je parle dans l'estime.
> —Sinon l'enfance, qu'y avait-il alors qu'il n'y a plus?
> Plaines! Pentes! Il y
> avait plus d'ordre! Et tout n'était que règnes et confins de lueurs. Et l'ombre et la lumière alors étaient plus près d'être une même chose . . . Je parle d'une estime . . . Aux lisières le fruit
> pouvai choir
> sans que la joie pourrît au rebord de nos lèvres.
> Et les hommes remuaient plus d'ombre avec une bouche plus grave, les femmes plus de songe avec des bras plus lents.[7]

In the *Notebook* we find the poetic negative of Saint-John Perse's songs of praise. Césaire's speaker articulates a vitriolic statement of the degradation of those same blacks whose labor made possible the motionless, hieratic beauty of the planter class. Here too there is immobility, but it is the stagnation of a stratified order that adamantly refuses change (p. 33):

At the end of the wee hours, this flat town—sprawled, toppled from its common sense, inert, winded under its geometric weight of an eternally renewed cross, indocile to its fate, mute, vexed no matter what, incapable of growing with the juice of this earth, self-conscious, clipped, reduced, in breach of fauna and flora.

Au bout du petit matin, cette ville plate—étalée, trébuchée de son bon sens, inerte, essoufflée sous son fardeau géométrique de croix éternellement recommençante, indocile à son sort, muette, contrariée de toutes façons, incapable de croître selon le suc de cette terre, embarrassée, rognée, réduite, en rupture de faune et de flore.

A single strophe suffices to fix, quite incomparably, the contradictory qualities of this urbanized mass, which is still rural in its reactions but cut off from what poor roots it can be said to have had (pp. 33, 35):

In this inert town, this strange throng which does not pack, does not mix; clever at discovering the point of disencasement, of flight, of dodging. This throng which does not know how to throng, this throng, clearly so perfectly alone under this sun, like a woman one thought completely occupied with her lyric cadence, who abruptly challenges a hypothetical rain and enjoins it not to fall; or like a rapid sign of the cross without perceptible motive; or like the sudden grave animality of a peasant, urinating standing, her legs parted, stiff.

Dans cette ville inerte, cette étrange foule qui ne s'entasse pas, ne se mêle pas: habile à découvrir le point de désencastration, de fuite, d'esquive. Cette foule qui ne sait pas faire foule, cette foule, on s'en rend compte, si parfaitement seule sous ce soleil, à la façon dont une femme, toute on eût cru à sa cadence lyrique, interpelle brusquement une pluie hypothétique et lui intime de ne pas tomber; ou à un signe rapide de croix sans mobile visible; ou à l'animalité subitement grave d'une paysanne, urinant debout, les jambes écartées, roides.

Either of the foregoing images of the island woman could be isolated for its beauty: the first because it might seem initially to continue the long tradition of poetic images of the tropics, including some of Baudelaire's best; the second for the graphic wildness, the stark, untamed quality that sometimes occurs in Saint-John Perse. But to isolate is to distort. The final image of the strophe supplies the caustic element that corrodes the facile lie that has transformed the islands into a never-never land for the imagination of the French. The concrete image functions in Césaire's poem to radically negate the presentation of the black as Other that characterizes the literature of colonialism. Therein reside both its uniqueness and its collective value as statement. The "peasant, urinating standing, her legs parted, stiff" denies the projection of white erotic fantasy onto the "lyric cadence" of the thighs of the city woman, who by the 1930s had become a cliché in the collective dream of domination.

The next strophe draws the reader toward the double sense of domination via its concrete meaning "to stand above." The statue of Joséphine, Empress of the French (and symbol of the Martinican planter class), dreams high above the niggers ("la négraille"). The statue in question, which dominates the esplanade at the heart of Fort-de-France, the "city" of the *Notebook*, had been erected under the imperial patronage of Joséphine's grandson, Napoleon III. The statue of the conquistador mentioned in the same strophe was spanking new when Césaire wrote his poem, having been erected to commemorate the third centenary of Martinique's acquisition by the French in 1635. It bears the inscription: *To Pierre Belain d'Esnambuc, Founder of French Power in the Antilles*. In the poem the black crowd has no share in this scorn, this freedom, this audacity. The *Notebook* extends its corrosive power even to the official hero of blacks in the French Empire, Victor Schoelcher, who had been the principal advocate of the abolitionist movement in the French legislature. He is surely the liberator "fixed in his whitewashed stone liberation" ("figé dans sa libération de pierre blanchie") whose statue in fact stands paternally over the Place du Palais de Justice. Even he is separated by his whiteness from the "free" descendants of slaves.

Freedom does not exist as an abstraction in the *Notebook*. We are invited to contemplate a vision of crushing poverty that grows more personal as it approaches home (p. 43):

The carcass of wood, which I call "our house," comically perched on minute cement paws, its coiffure of corrugated iron in the sun like a skin laid out to dry, the main room, the rough floor where the nail heads gleam, the beams of pine and shadow across the ceiling, the spectral straw chairs, the grey lamp light, the glossy flash of cockroaches in a maddening buzz . . .

La carcasse de bois comiquement juchée sur de minuscules pattes de ciment que j'appelle "notre maison," sa coiffure de tôle ondulant au soleil comme une peau qui sèche, la salle à manger, le plancher grossier où luisent des têtes de clous, les solives de sapin et d'ombre qui courent au plafond, les chaises de paille fantomales, la lumière grise de la lampe, celle vernissée et rapide des cancrelats qui bourdonne à faire mal . . .

The poem takes a brief turn in the direction of pathos with this reflection on the futile attempt to maintain a semblance of respectability in such conditions (p. 53):

A cruel little house whose demands panic the ends of our months and my temperamental father gnawed by one persistent ache, I never knew which one . . . ; and my mother whose legs pedal, pedal, pedal, night and day, for our tireless hunger, I was even awakened at night by these tireless legs which pedal the night and the bitter bite in the soft flesh of the night of a Singer that my mother pedals, pedals for our hunger and day and night.

Une petite maison cruelle dont l'intransigeance affole nos fins de mois et mon père fantasque gringnoté d'une seule misère, je n'ai jamais su laquelle . . . ; et ma mère dont les jambes pour notre faim inlassable pédalent, pédalent de jour, de nuit, je suis même réveillé la nuit par ces jambes inlassables qui pédalent la nuit et la morsure âpre dans la chair molle de la nuit d'une Singer que ma mère pédale, pédale pour notre faim et de jour et de nuit.

If Césaire is here drawing on his own family's poverty, as his readers have generally assumed, it is for a purpose that is finally collective rather than individual. We can usefully compare this aspect of the *Notebook* with the exploitation of pathos by a European author and Césaire's contemporary, who creates an intensely personal vision out of a reality that inspired the populist novelists and poets as well. In *Death on the Installment Plan (Mort à crédit)* Céline had represented Bardamu's father as a grossly exploited employee of a large and impersonal insurance company. Bardamu's mother courageously made ends meet by selling her needlework in suburban marketplaces. It need not concern us that Céline distorted some facts of his autobiography for stylistic purposes, except to point out that our interest ought properly to focus on the way in which style reinforces ideology. By the same token it is inconsequential whether Césaire had six brothers and sisters rather than five, whether his father was subject to one gnawing misery or several, or whether his mother ever owned a Singer. The value of Césaire's art in the *Notebook* depends not on its degree of mimetic accuracy but on its rendering of a collective dilemma as embodied in the lives of individuals. For Céline the relation of the antihero to his world is one of paranoia. The collective plight of French shopkeepers around the turn of the century served as backdrop to the individual romance of Bardamu, the Parisian schlemiel who is sucked ever deeper into the maelstrom of night. At the end of episodes in *Journey to the End of the Night (Voyage au bout de la nuit)* the reader is lulled into complicity by the rhythmic repetition of the all-encompassing but finally empty symbol of the Night.

In his *Notebook* Césaire uses night lyrically to heighten our rhythmic perception of a maternal figure whose labors are endless because they can never overtake the pace of hunger and want. This rhythmic circularity then provides the reader with a frame within which to comprehend the formless misery of the father (p. 41) "whom an unexpected sorcery could lull to melancholy tenderness or drive to towering flames of anger" ("qu'une imprévisible sorcellerie assoupit en mélancolique tendresse ou exalte en hautes flammes de colère"). The lyrical movement develops a prior thematic statement, set off typographically to introduce it: "the teratical bulb of night, sprouted from our vileness and our renunciations" ("le bulbe tératique de la nuit, germé de nos bassesses et de nos renoncements"). In the *Notebook* the symbol of night is tied to a past characterized by an ignominy that must be recognized, acknowledged, and transcended. So too the device that gives a measure of formal coherence to the successive vignettes of Martinican life—the constant repetition of the anaphora "At the end of the wee hours . . ." ("Au bout du petit matin . . .")— offers a bright promise beyond the night and beyond this poem. No more than a half-dozen pages are devoted to this personal, lyrical evocation, and these are positioned between the nervous gaiety of a Christmas feast and a further description of the black section of a town in colonial Martinique (p. 55):

> And this rue Paille, this disgrace
>
> an appendage repulsive as the private parts of the village which extends right and left, along the colonial highway, the grey surge of its shingled roofs. Here there are only straw roofs, spray browned and wind plucked.

> Et une honte, cette rue Paille,
>
> un appendice dégoûtant comme les parties honteuses du bourg, qui étend à droite et à gauche, tout au long de la route coloniale, la houle grise de ses toits d'aissantes. Ici il n'y a que des toits de paille que l'embrun a brunis et que le vent épile.

Just as the evocation of his house prepares the reader to appreciate the collective misery of the city, so the family drama reproduces in small the history of the race. An important signifying element of the French text that again suggests Céline's style is the systematic repetition of nouns, in both nominative and objective position, to heighten their effect (pp. 53, 55):

> And the bed of boards from which my race arose, my whole entire race from this bed of boards, with its kerosene case paws, as if it had elephantiasis, that bed, and its kid skin, and its dry banana leaves, and its rags, yearning for a mattress, my grandmother's bed . . .

> Et le lit de planches d'où s'est levée ma race, toute entière ma race de ce lit de planches, avec ses pattes de caisses de

> Kérosine, comme s'il avait l'éléphantiasis le lit, et sa peau
> de cabri, et ses feuilles de bananes séchées, et ses haillons,
> une nostalgie de matelas le lit de ma grand-mère . . .

This combination of repetition with syntactic inversion, mod-
eled on working-class speech, created a startling effect when
Céline used it in *Journey* in 1932. Céline had created a lyrical
narrative. Césaire's use of the device, while seemingly more appropriate to a poem with a narrative component, in fact ran
against the grain of poetic practice in France. The tradition of
noble language dies slowly, and here Césaire was defying it by
insisting that conditions of extreme poverty be expressed in the
style of the poor, who are also, in this case, speakers of a Creole
idiom.

Language, Reason, Order

The second movement of the poem mutes this corrosive representation of reality so as to articulate a more open revolt. The
goal is to challenge directly an order that legitimizes an oppressive
reality. Consequently the speaker's relationship to language and
style undergoes a metamorphosis. The text that indicates the
passage from the first to the second movement was added by
Césaire in 1947, doubtless for this purpose. Structurally it is the
point of articulation; thematically it is a modulation. One senses
that the legendary Rimbaud is present at the speaker's leave-
taking (p. 57):

> To go away.
> As there are hyena-men and panther-men, I would be a
> jew-man
> a Kaffir-man
> a Hindu-man-from-Calcutta
> a Harlem-man-who-doesn't-vote . . .

> Partir.
> Comme il y a des hommes-hyènes et des hommes-pan-
> thères, je serais un homme-juif
> un homme-cafre
> un homme-hindou-de-Calcutta
> un homme-de-Harlem-qui-ne-vote-pas . . .

The principle of corrosive poetics does not disappear entirely, however, even though it becomes less prominent, somewhat in the manner of a musical theme that is displaced by a new one. The panther-man in the passage just quoted recalls the chapter entitled "Syracuse or the Panther-Man" ("Syracuse ou l'Homme-Panthère") in a collection of racist fictions by Paul Morand, *Black Magic (Magie noire,* 1928). By considering the intertextual resonance of the term *panther-man* one can readily understand how a book like Paul Morand's could serve as a critical or creative irritant in the genesis of the *Notebook.* A recurring motif cynically exploited in *Black Magic* by this successful cosmopolitan entertainer is the formula, scratch a nigger or even a light-skinned mulatto and you'll discover an unrepentant savage. In "Syracuse or the Panther-Man" Dr. Lincoln Vamp, the self-made chief executive of a black financial empire in Syracuse, New York, totally loses his wits—his thin veneer of civilization. He imagines himself transformed into a roaring panther after a visit to an exhibit of tribal life in the Belgian Congo.

Paul Morand's tales were edifying in the sense that they reinforced the colonialist axiom that the savagery and inferiority of nonwhite cultures justify the atrocities committed against them. In this respect Morand's tales were the necessary by-product of colonialism. Césaire's strategy in the *Notebook* is to deny the pretensions of colonialism by attacking its ideological assumptions with derision. In the second movement especially Césaire's speaker adopts the point of view of the panther-man to lash out at the racism epitomized by Morand and the ideology he represented. The catalogue device—the sequence of semantically interchangeable terms—extends the context beyond this possible single referent. Thus freed, *panther-man* takes its place beside *jew-man* in an affirmation of the values of cultures that have been massively repressed. Césaire's speaker has surpassed the Satanic monstrosity of Lautréamont's Maldoror in the direction of the actual situation of the black in a white society that would deny his humanity. He would recognize in himself (p. 57) "the torture-man you can grab anytime, beat up, kill—no joke, kill—without having to account to anyone, without having to make excuses to anyone" ("l'homme-torture on pouvait à n'importe quel moment le saisir le rouer de coups, le tuer—parfaitement le tuer—sans avoir de compte à rendre à personne sans avoir d'excuses à présenter à personne").

But even as Césaire prepares this movement of revolt he allows by way of transition an occasional resurgence of the romantic re-affirmation of Otherness, as in this arch metaphor (p. 59) of re-morse "perfect as the stupefied face of an English lady discovering a Hottentot skull in her soup-tureen" ("beau comme la face de stupeur d'une dame anglaise qui trouverait dans sa soupière un crâne de Hottentot"). In his relation of a season in Hell had not Rimbaud evoked the negation of the consecrated image of Beauty as the first step to be taken? "One evening I seated Beauty on my knees.—And I found her bitter. —And I insulted her" ("Un soir, j'ai assis la Beauté sur mes genoux.—Et je l'ai trouvée amère. —Et je l'ai injuriée").[8] Césaire likewise envisages an alchemy of the Word (p. 59):

> I would rediscover the secret of great communications and great combustions. I would say storm. I would say river, I would say tornado. I would say leaf. I would say tree. I would be drenched by all rains, moistened by all dews. I would roll like frenetic blood on the slow current of the eye of words turned into mad horses into fresh children into clots into curfew into vestiges of temples into precious stones remote enough to discourage miners. Whoever would not understand me would not understand any bet-ter the roaring of a tiger.

> Je retrouverais le secret des grandes communications et des grandes combustions. Je dirais orage. Je dirais fleuve. Je dirais tornade. Je dirais feuille. Je dirais arbre. Je serais mouillé de toutes les pluies, humecté de toutes les rosées. Je roulerais comme du sang frénétique sur le courant lent de l'oeil des mots en chevaux fous en enfants frais en caillots en couvre-feu en vestiges de temple en pierres précieuses assez loin pour décourager les mineurs. Qui ne me com-prendrait pas ne comprendrait pas davantage le rugisse-ment du tigre.

But for Césaire the goal of the process of disalienation that is out-lined in the *Notebook* is not poetic expression for its own sake; it is not conceived as an individualist goal at all. Césaire's speaker, early in the second movement of the poem, imagines the return to his native land, which we now understand to be both a geo-graphically real place and a metaphor of his existence in the world. He sees himself as both poet and leader, the spokesman for a people not yet aware of their uniqueness (p. 61):

> I would go to this land of mine and I would say to it: "Embrace me without fear . . . If all I can do is speak, it is for you I shall speak."
> And again I would say:
> "My mouth shall be the mouth of those calamities that have no mouth, my voice, the freedom of those who break down in the solitary confinement of despair."

> Je viendrais à ce pays mien et je lui dirais: "Embrassez-moi sans crainte . . . Et si je ne sais que parler, c'est pour vous que je parlerai."
> Et je lui dirais encore:
> "Ma bouche sera la bouche des malheurs qui n'ont point de bouche, ma voix, la liberté de celles qui s'affaissent au cachot du désespoir."

From the first to the second movement of the *Notebook* Césaire has recapitulated critically several steps in the literary origins of surrealism.[9] In the second movement of all postwar editions of the poem this process leads to a clearly surrealist practice. It is important to note that those parts of the *Notebook* most commonly recognized as surrealist—they constitute more than one-third of the second movement—were all added after the war; they must be considered a direct result of Césaire's experimentation with surrealism in *Tropiques* from 1941 to 1945. Most of the passages discussed here are contemporaneous with the collection *Miraculous Weapons*, while some few were added as late as 1956, after the publication of *Beheaded Sun* and *Lost Body*. In view of the composite nature of the text, which has grown by accretion, it makes little sense to continue to consider the *Notebook* that is actually read as though it were a prewar poem. In many important respects it is not.

In the second movement words must be transmuted, wrenched from an imprisoning syntax, and be allowed to reform according to the logic of desire (p. 73).

Words?
Ah yes, words!
Reason, I crown you evening wind.
Your name voice of order?
To me whip's corolla.
. . . . .
Because we hate you
and your reason, we claim kinship
with dementia praecox with the flaming madness
of persistent cannibalism

Des mots?
Ah oui, des mots!
Raison, je te sacre vent du soir.
Bouche de l'ordre ton nom?
Il m'est corolle du fouet.
. . . . .
Parce que nous vous haïssons vous
et votre raison, nous nous réclamons de la
démence précoce de la folie flamboyante
du cannibalisme tenace

This suggestion of an alchemy of the Word is followed by another Rimbaldian imperative, the calculated disordering of all the senses (p. 73):

And you know the rest

That 2 and 2 are 5
that the forest meows
that the tree plucks the maroons from the fire
that the sky strokes its beard
etc etc . . .

Et vous savez le reste

Que 2 et 2 font 5
que la forêt miaule
que l'arbre tire les marrons du feu
que le ciel se lisse la barbe
et caetera et caetera . . .

The odd arithmetic is probably a direct borrowing from that other great prophet of irrationalism, Dostoevsky, whose underground man had devoted several of his notes to the necessity of purposeful madness (even in the event human motivations could be reduced to categories and tables). Dostoevsky had used as the paradigm for contemporary scientism the arithmetic law that "twice two make four." His argument concludes with the irrational proposition that in order to preserve the human person one must affirm against the very laws of nature that " 'twice two make five' is not without its attractions."[10] Césaire has retained the irrationalist imperative so neatly condensed in Dostoevsky's illogical logical proposition while integrating it into a poetic proposition. This one line devoted to the necessity of madness recapitulates the thematic element introduced by *dementia praecox*, but it introduces in turn three further propositions, each of which defies a law of nature: the forest meows, and so on. The expression "getting the chestnuts out of the fire" is in French culture a commonplace for altruistic behavior; one need not search as far afield as La Fontaine's fable of the monkey and the cat. Whether or not "that the sky strokes its beard" is similarly identifiable, it has an identical poetic function: from the point of view of the speaker this strophe illustrates the phenomenon of a systematic distortion of sensory experience.

Jahn confidently assured readers of his book *Muntu* that the impossible arithmetic is really a coded reference to the symbolic function of the twins (*marassa)* in voodoo: "Their vévé [a symbolic design representing their attributes] is mirrored, like the pattern of playing cards: this horizontal division signifies that man is half mortal and half deathless . . . ; the vertical division splits them into male and female, from which there results a third: marassa-three. Twins two and two give *five,* literally as *quint*essence of life."[11] As a gloss this is ingenious and fascinating, but it does not fit the poetic context, and there is no evidence that Césaire in the 1930s had any but the most rudimentary knowledge of the voodoo pantheon. Jahn's exegesis of the remaining lines is motivated primarily by a desire to present the poet as historian. Therefore "that the forest meows" refers historically to runaway slaves calling one another. That "the tree plucks the [chestnuts] from the fire" is coded as follows: *fire* represents the danger inherent in escaping from slavery; *marrons* in French can be escaped slaves or maroons rather than chestnuts; and *the tree* stands for the safety of the tree line to which the maroon would presumably flee. We are then to understand the line as a cipher meaning that the tree line was a refuge for runaway slaves. The final image—"that the sky strokes its beard"— is rather more fanciful: the white man's bearded god remains indifferent to the crimes committed in his name. Such a reading insists on the mimetic aspect of the *Notebook*. The most articulate statement of this position seems to proceed from the odd assimilation (not uncommon in the modern French tradition) of *poem* to the more restrictive term *lyric poem:* "The *Notebook* is not a poem . . . , but a text in which the imaginary marked with a negative sign alternates with realistic descriptions and the speech of an orator."[12] There are occasional realistic touches in the *Notebook* that serve to connect the poem in the reader's mind with social problems, notably with slavery and its disastrous aftermath. Zadi Zaourou has traced some of these historical details to Victor Schoelcher's writings on slavery.[13] The fact that parts of the poem can be read literally or historically indicates that Césaire's surrealism is not to be considered merely as an extension of the European movement.

Were we to take the term *dementia praecox* to be another borrowing (from Breton and Eluard's *L'Immaculée Conception*, 1930), we would find that the style of the Paris surrealists in their literary simulation of dementia praecox reveals notable differences. A representative excerpt from the original will suffice to demonstrate them: "On dansotte sur des pincettes pendant Aladin quiquiqui. Pierre est syllogone en pipe de mucèdre en or et en donc, matrès et matrop. L'étage au-dessous est occupé par Paris. L'x exaspaltère le feu de Seltz. Batavoir et roulêtre en devise de queue de rat décorent supertin l'Oniphonalgérianglaise."[14] The Paris surrealists were interested at this date in exploring what they took to be supranormal mental states for their potential as keys to the surreal. The passage quoted defies translation precisely because of its multiple semantic equivocations: "en or" translates as "in gold"; "or" is also the coordinating conjunction "but," which justifies by association "et en donc" ("and in therefore"). Any attempt to translate this phrase would have to maintain both possibilities simultaneously. Several other examples of related plays on syntax and semantics could be cited in this short passage alone. Breton and Eluard effectively maintain the reader's mind in a state of suspended judgment by stringing the reader along on a mental tightrope.

As a literary exercise this text is a specialized variety of the automatic style. Although Césaire developed his own approach to it in *Miraculous Weapons*, nothing of the sort occurs in the *Notebook*. A thematic development is always in sight. Dementia praecox leads directly to the metaphoric expression of Africanism reborn in "persistent cannibalism," a suggestion that the black's special reality has been there all along and awaits only the new relation to language and order to liberate it: in a word, the revenge of the panther-man (p. 75):

> Who and what are we?
> A most worthy question!
>
> From staring too long at trees I have
> become a tree and my long tree
> feet have dug in the ground large
> venom sacs high cities of bone
> from brooding too long on the Congo
> I have become a Congo resounding with forests and rivers
> where the whip cracks like a great banner
>
> Qui et quels nous sommes?
> Admirable question!
>
> A force de regarder les arbres je suis
> devenu un arbre et mes longs pieds
> d'arbre ont creusé dans le sol de larges
> sacs à venin de hautes villes d'ossements
> à force de penser au Congo
> je suis devenu un Congo bruissant de
> forêts et de fleuves
> où le fouet claque comme un grand étendard

Reason, already transformed into the whip's corolla, now "cracks like a great banner," presaging freedom. What links Césaire most significantly to the surrealists in this poem is his heavy investment in the imagination as an efficacious force. It is an act of mind that transforms the speaker into a Congo (p. 75) "where the angerbolt hurls its greenish axe forcing the boars of putrefaction to the lovely wild edge of the nostrils" ("où l'éclair de la colère lance sa hache verdâtre et force les sangliers de la putréfaction dans la belle orée violente des narines"). There is a dialectic present in the poem that allies the liberating force of imagination with the blacks' real potential—symbolized in the Congo— and against the colonial reality presented as both savage and decayed—"the boars of putrefaction."

Just as clearly, Césaire's notion of dialectics at this early stage in his writing reflects the idealist interpretation of Freud that characterized the first *Manifesto of Surrealism* (p. 87):

> Words? while we handle
> quarters of earth, while we wed
> delirious continents, while
> we force steaming gates,
> words, ah yes, words! but
> words of fresh blood, words that are
> tidal waves and erysipelas
> malarias and lava and brush
> fires, and blazes of flesh,
> and blazes of cities . . .

> Des mots? quand nous manions des
> quartiers de monde, quand nous épousons
> des continents en délire, quand
> nous forçons de fumantes portes,
> des mots, ah oui, des mots! mais
> des mots de sang frais, des mots qui sont
> des raz-de-marée et des érésipèles
> des paludismes et des laves et des feux
> de brousse, et des flambées de chair,
> et des flambées de villes . . .

The true self, which according to the surrealists resided in the unconscious, motivates a splendid metaphor of rebirth (pp. 87, 89):

> I am [forcing] the vitelline membrane that separates me
> from myself,

I am [forcing] the great waters which girdle me with blood

Je force la membrane vitelline qui me sépare de moi-
même,
Je force les grandes eaux qui me ceinturent de sang

A provisional synthesis is realized within the second movement of the poem through a positive valuation of eroticism. The
regeneration of the black world is expressed in a lyrical mode
that renders rebirth in terms of love, conception, and pregnancy
(pp. 113, 115):

under the reserve of my uvula there is a wallow of boars
under the grey stone of the day there are your eyes which
are a shimmering conglomerate of ladybugs
in the glance of disorder there is this swallow of mint
and broom which melts always to be reborn in the tidal
wave of your light
. . . . .

and you, star, please, from your luminous foundation,
draw lemurian being—of man's unfathomable sperm the
yet undared form

carried like an ore in woman's trembling belly!

il y a sous la réserve de ma luette une bauge de sangliers
il y a tes yeux qui sont sous la pierre grise du jour un-
conglomérat frémissant de coccinelles
il y a dans le regard du désordre cette hirondelle de menthe
et de genêt qui fond pour toujours renaître dans le raz-de-
marée de ta lumière
. . . . .

et toi veuille astre de ton lumineux fondement tirer
lémurien du sperme insondable de l'homme la forme non
osée

que le ventre tremblant de la femme porte tel un minerai!

For the European surrealist Eros functioned primarily as an
ontological gateway with woman as the mediatrix between

alienated self and the fullness of being. The most typical example may well be Eluard's poem "Elaine's Towers" ("Les Tours d'Eliane"), written to "illustrate" Man Ray's drawing of a full-figured young nude, shown seated in a frontal position, her open thighs superimposed on the twin towers of a Romanesque *château fort* whose narrow door is her vagina as well. Eluard's text is gnomic: "An insane hope / Window at the bottom of a mine" ("Un espoir insensé / Fenêtre au fond d'une mine").[15] Césaire at this point in the *Notebook* regards Eros as the means to biological transcendence: the continuation of the black ideal in one's progeny seen as purified by the ardor of love. The symbol shares with surrealist Eros the quality of the sublime, but it surpasses the individual to establish an idea of regenerated community. From present disorder Eros, likened to a swallow, will be reborn in the tidal wave of light emanating from the beloved. Renewed order is implicit in the as yet unborn new form that will emerge from her womb. The important passage from the individual to the collective plane is assured in a subsequent strophe that makes explicit the identity of the beloved: she is the city regarded in all the positive beauty of her future; she is the collective form of the people (pp. 121, 123):

> and here at the end of these wee hours is my virile prayer
> that I hear neither the laughter nor the screams, my eyes
> fixed on this town which I prophesy, beautiful,
> . . . . .
> . . . Make my head into a figure-head
> and as for me, my heart, do not make me into a father, nor
> a brother
> . . . . .
> . . . but the lover of this unique people.

> et voici au bout de ce petit matin ma prière virile que je
> n'entende ni les rires ni les cris, les yeux fixés sur cette ville
> que je prophétise, belle,
> . . . . .
> . . . Faites de ma tête une tête de proue
> et de moi-même, mon coeur, ne faites ni un père, ni un frère,
> . . . . .
> . . . mais l'amant de cet unique people.

The Dialectics of Blackness

The representation of blackness, of negritude, embraces the same dialectical rhythm as do those other elements of the poem discussed above. The following analysis is phenomenological: it presupposes the consciousness of a reader who responds to the shifting values associated with images of blackness.

In the first movement of the poem (pages 29–57 in the Présence Africaine bilingual edition of 1971) images of blackness are in fact rare. There are no more than three in all: "the nigger scum" ("la négraille," p. 35); a reference to "this sleepy little nigger" ("négrillon," p. 39); and by association with the people who inhabit this neglected section of the town, the "black, funereal sand" ("sable . . . noir, funèbre," p. 55). More importantly, all three terms assume a view of the black experience from the outside—a hostile view: *négraille* and *négrillon* are racist terms highly charged with negative connotations. In general Césaire in the *Notebook* uses the noun *nègre* in ways that show it to have been inadequately defined by and for blacks. When his speaker assumes the attitude of the black Martinican alienated from his own ethnicity, *nègre* in the text corresponds to *nigger* in English. Nowhere in his poem does Césaire use *noir* (Negro) as a noun. The reader is expected to understand that the situation of the black is one of racist oppression; the language of the poem is quite unequivocal on this point.[16] It is important that the reader perceive in the first movement of the poem what potential violence lies beneath the flat, soulless, zombielike appearance of the city and its black inhabitants. Only if one's perception is so conditioned by the text will the turbulence and contradiction of the second movement make sense.

The infinitive *to go away* ("partir") is set off from "that other dawn in Europe" ("cet autre petit matin d'Europe") by a suspended thought and a break in the text scarcely larger than that between strophes within a movement (p. 57). As we have seen, Césaire's much longer middle development involves a negation of the European colonial perspective. Thomas A. Hale has made a good case for there being more than one return in the *Notebook*. After several years as a student in Paris, Césaire spent the summer of 1936 in Martinique. It was a period of great disillusionment; nothing had changed. According to Hale, "the first *partir* (p. 57) refers to a departure from Martinique, rather than from Europe, while the second *partir* refers to the projected departure from Europe to return to the island."[17] The second movement, which begins at the first *partir*, develops dialectically with the abundant imagery of blackness passing from the representation of the black as nigger that characterizes the opening, through a period of marked tension, to a provisional synthesis in which blackness is promoted to a position of splendid past glory, which must in turn be negated to arrive at a true appreciation of present reality, of actual possibility.

"Haiti where negritude rose for the first time" is set off dramatically against the dominant images of the present (p. 67):

> and the funny little tail of Florida where the strangulation of a nigger is being completed, and Africa gigantically caterpillaring up to the Hispanic foot of Europe, its nakedness where Death scythes widely.

> et la comique petite queue de la Floride où d'un nègre s'achève la strangulation, et l'Afrique gigantesquement chenillant jusqu'au pied hispanique de l'Europe, sa nudité où la Mort fauche à larges andains.

Having established the contradictions inherent in the present, Césaire can allude to blackness indirectly; his speaker (p. 67) can refer confidently to "my fingerprint" ("mon empreinte digitale") and to "my calcaneum on the spine of skyscrapers and my filth in the glitter of gems!" ("mon calcanéum sur le dos des gratte-ciel et ma crasse dans le scintillement des gemmes!") The earlier reference to Haiti has prepared the reader for the relatively long variation on the theme of Toussaint Louverture. Images of blackness have been so thoroughly valued as positive that they reinforce, by opposition, the introduction of whiteness as synonymous with death (pp. 69, 71):

> What is mine
> a lonely man imprisoned in whiteness
> a lonely man defying the white screams of white death
> (TOUSSAINT, TOUSSAINT LOUVERTURE)
> a man who mesmerizes the white hawk of white death
> . . . . .
> death expires in a white pool of silence.

Ce qui est à moi
c'est un homme seul emprisonné de blanc
c'est un homme seul qui défie les cris blancs de la mort
    blanche
(TOUSSAINT, TOUSSAINT LOUVERTURE)
c'est un homme qui fascine l'épervier blanc de la mort
    blanche
. . . . .
la mort expire dans une blanche mare de silence.

Césaire's strategy is simple but effective. The dialectic of negritude, at this moment of negation of the dominant value system, articulates perfectly with the same moment in the dialectic of reason and order. The evocation of the imprisonment of Toussaint Louverture in the snowy Jura mountains immediately precedes the proclamation of a surrealist use of language: "Reason, I crown you evening wind. / Your name voice of order? / To me whip's corolla" (p. 73). The reader, if he is white or an alienated black, has been brought to the antipodes of his cultural starting point. Césaire has inverted the European matrix of values so that now reason is to oppression as whiteness is to death. Blackness, however, stands in relation to regeneration as surrealism does to liberation.

    With the exception of such obvious symbols of blackness as the Congo (p. 75) and the Zambesi (p. 77), the term *nègre* and associated images of blackness are dispensed with for the next twenty pages. When the reader again encounters *nègre* (p. 91) he is fully prepared to see it as a biting satire on racism and its simple-minded psychology:

(niggers-are-all-alike, I-tell-you vices-all-the-vices-
believe-you-me
nigger-smell, that's-what-makes-cane-grow
remember-the-old-saying:
beat-a-nigger, and you feed him)

(les nègres-sont-tous-les-mêmes, je-vous-le-dis
les vices-tous-les-vices, c'est-moi-qui-vous-le-dis
l'odeur-du-nègre, ça-fait-pousser-la-canne
rappelez-vous-le-vieux-dicton:
battre-un-nègre, c'est le nourrir)

In the same derisive vein Césaire introduces the old chestnuts on natural rhythm and lubricity, concluding, "My dignity wallows in puke" (p. 93). Just as the poem overall aims to inculcate a new awareness of the positivity of blackness, this part of the *Notebook* must force home an awareness of the abjection attendant on the fact of being black in a society dominated by white racist attitudes.

The overarching dialectic that subsumes those under discussion is Freudian in certain of its suppositions. One cannot pass directly from oppression to a glorious future in freedom. The intermediary stage—the dialectical antithesis or moment of negativity—involves the dredging up of the repressed contents of the psyche: in this case the refusal by blacks to recognize the extent of their own alienation. Césaire's originality in this respect derives from his realization that resignation to racism is collective and cultural, not an individual neurosis of the sort envisaged by the psychoanalyst. Césaire knew as well, probably from his own experience, that the initial reaction to such probing of unconscious motivations sets up a strong reaction. Consequently his poem takes a decidedly narrative turn at just this point. Condensations of black history in the Caribbean alternate with vignettes of Martinican life, bringing the reader gradually to an acceptance of the awful realities of his past. There is of course an unavoidable divergence here between the response of the black and the white reader, at least in the Americas. If the black reader must come to terms with his past in slavery, the white reader is called upon to recognize his collective past as slaver. By reader response I have in mind not the individual, Freudian variety but the reader's responsibility to question his own cultural axioms.

The black reader is thus obliged to refuse the temptation to project his cultural identity backward to an ideal Africa (pp. 97, 99):

> No, we've never been amazons of the king of Dahomey, nor princes of Ghana with eight hundred camels, nor wisemen in Timbuktu under Askia the Great, nor the architects of Djenne, nor Madhis, nor warriors . . . I may as well confess that we were at all times pretty mediocre dishwashers, shoeblacks without ambition, at best conscientious sorcerers and the only unquestionable record that we broke was that of endurance under the cat-o-nine-tails . . .

> Non, nous n'avons jamais été amazones du roi de Dahomey, ni princes de Ghana avec huit cents chameaux, ni docteurs à Tombouctou Askia le Grand étant roi, ni architectes de Djénné, ni Madhis, ni guerriers . . . je veux avouer que nous fûmes de tout temps d'assez piètres laveurs de vaisselle, des cireurs de chaussures sans envergure, mettons les choses au mieux, d'assez consciencieux sorciers et le seul indiscutable record que nous ayons battu est celui d'endurance à la chicotte . . .

Césaire's speaker insists on his status as an Afro-American, not an African. The resolution of the blacks' dilemma through mythic projection—the attempt to identify with someone else's African history—is thus presented as a false synthesis, the project of a false consciousness of one's present condition. His goal is the stimulation of an awareness of black history: "I have sworn to leave nothing out of our history" ("j'ai juré de ne rien celer de notre histoire"). But the process of raising the level of black consciousness is a complex one, according to Césaire, and it must pass through a painful period of recognizing that one has interiorized the racist view of oneself. Returning to the context of psychoanalysis that the poem itself has suggested, we see that the *Notebook* assumes the introjection by blacks of their image as it has been disseminated by a white society. This introjected self-image can be challenged and effectively destroyed only if one recognizes that it has determined the mode of one's behavior, both imaginary and real.

Nor is the white reader let off with a good conscience on the pretext that none of his antecedents were slavers. Césaire is perfectly right in assuming that the objective fact of slavery has continued to influence in very direct fashion every contemporary society in which slavery played a significant role. The bite of this strophe is by no means limited to Martinique or to the Caribbean; it concerns the United States just as directly as the European empires built on slavery (p. 99):

> And this land screams for centuries that we are bestial brutes; that [the] human [pulse stops] at the gates of the slave-compound; that we are walking compost hideously promising tender cane and silky cotton and they would brand us with red-hot irons and we would sleep in our

excrement and they would sell us on the town square and
an ell of English cloth and salted meat from Ireland cost
less than we did, and this land was calm, tranquil, repeating that the spirit of the Lord was in its acts.

Et ce pays cria pendant des siècles que nous sommes des
bêtes brutes; que les pulsations de l'humanité s'arrêtent
aux portes de la négrerie; que nous sommes un fumier
ambulant hideusement prometteur de cannes tendres et de
coton soyeux et l'on nous marquait au fer rouge et nous
dormions dans nos excréments et l'on nous vendait sur les
places et l'aune de drap anglais et la viande salée d'Irlande
coûtaient moins cher que nous, et ce pays était calme, tran-
quille, disant que l'esprit de Dieu était dans ses actes.

The figure of Toussaint Louverture in the poem has a mythic
quality that corresponds to an impossible return to the noble
past of black peoples. The lyrical mode that conveys the symbolic
value of Toussaint Louverture gives way to a narrative description of a representative contemporary black man in an everyday
situation. The speaker begins by announcing that he is confess-
ing the extent of his cowardice (pp. 101, 103):

One evening on the streetcar facing me, a [nigger].
A [nigger] big as a pongo trying to make himself small
on the streetcar bench. He was trying to leave behind, on
this grimy bench, his gigantic legs and his trembling fam-
ished boxer hands. And everything had left him, was leaving him. His nose which looked like a drifting peninsula
and even his negritude discolored as a result of untiring
tawing. And the tawer was Poverty.

Un soir dans un tramway en face de moi, un nègre.
C'était un nègre grand comme un pongo qui essayait de
se faire tout petit sur un banc de tramway. Il essayait
d'abandonner sur ce banc crasseux de tramway ses jambes
gigantesques et ses mains tremblantes de boxeur affamé. Et
tout l'avait laissé, le laissait. Son nez semblait une péninsule
en dérade et sa négritude même qui se décolorait sous
l'action d'une inlassable mégie. Et le mégissier était la
Misère.

The neologism *négritude* occurs here for the second time in the poem. It no longer hails the past glories of Haiti; in context *négritude* signifies the abjection of the nigger while denoting his blackness. The speaker's confession is a statement of his complicity (pp. 103, 105):

> He was a gangly [nigger] without rhythm or measure.
> A [nigger] whose eyes rolled a bloodshot weariness.
> A shameless [nigger] and his toes sneered in a rather stinking way at the bottom of the yawning lair of his shoes.
> Poverty, without any question, had knocked itself out to finish him off
>
> . . . . .
>
> He was COMICAL AND UGLY,
> COMICAL AND UGLY for sure.
> I displayed a big complicitous smile . . .
> My cowardice rediscovered!

> C'était un nègre dégingandé sans rythme ni mesure.
> Un nègre dont les yeux roulaient une lassitude sanguinolente.
> Un nègre sans pudeur et ses orteils ricanaient de façon assez puante au fond de la tanière entrebâillée de ses souliers.
> La misère, on ne pouvait pas dire, s'était donné un mal fou pour l'achever
>
> . . . . .
>
> Il était COMIQUE ET LAID,
> COMIQUE ET LAID pour sûr.
> J'arborai un grand sourire complice . . .
> Ma lâcheté retrouvée!

This self-deprecatory tone—which requires that *nègre* be translated as *nigger*, rather than either *black* or *Negro*—is maintained for several pages, making it difficult to misconstrue the function of the passage; it marks the nadir of the final dialectic in the second movement. Against the free verse in which this entire passage is written Césaire sets a single classical alexandrine that, read out of context, could easily pass for the moment of revelation in the heart of a Racinian protagonist: "Mais quel étrange

orgueil tout soudain m'illumine?" (p. 111). The balanced rhythm
and the gravity of this line—which unfortunately do not survive
the translation as "But what strange pride suddenly illuminates
me?"—trigger an expectation of imminent, dramatic change in
a reader of the French tragic poets. It announces the synthesis of
the second movement of the *Notebook*. Directly following the
prophetic announcement of a future "carried like an ore in
woman's trembling belly" (p. 115) the reader encounters the
third, decisive statement of negritude, now reconciled to itself
(p. 117):

> my negritude is not a stone, its deafness hurled against the
> clamor of the day
>
> . . . . .
>
> my negritude is neither tower nor cathedral
>
> it takes root in the red flesh of the soil
> it takes root in the blazing flesh of the sky
>
> . . . . .
>
> Eia for the royal Cedrat!
> Eia for those who never invented anything
> for those who never explored anything
> for those who never conquered anything
>
> but yield, captivated, to the essence of all things

> ma négritude n'est pas une pierre, sa surdité rueé contre la
> clameur du jour
>
> . . . . .
>
> ma négritude n'est ni une tour ni une cathédrale
>
> elle plonge dans la chair rouge du sol
> elle plonge dans la chair ardente du ciel
>
> . . . . .
>
> Eia pour le Kaïlcédrat royal!
> Eia pour ceux qui n'ont jamais rien inventé
> pour ceux qui n'ont jamais rien exploré
> pour ceux qui n'ont jamais rien dompté
>
> mais ils s'abandonnent, saisis, à l'essence de toute chose

The anti-Promethean attitude that Césaire's speaker adopts in

the eleven pages leading up to the final movement of the poem
is equally confusing to the white reader and to the black who is
aware of the notable discoveries, inventions, and conquests made
by blacks even during and despite slavery. *Tropiques* indirectly
clarified the question in its dissemination of the theses of Frobenius. The point at issue here is the supposed Ethiopian strain in African civilization, with which Césaire had manifestly identified
himself. The values associated with it by Frobenius are in the main
those evoked in the lines quoted above, values discussed at some
length in the two preceding chapters. This is a case of bad ethnography contributing to good poetry. Within the overarching dialectic of the poem these pages reiterate the speaker's acceptance of
(not resignation to) his history in slavery and its present-day aftermath in poverty, an acceptance that transmutes degradation into
patient strength and that finally transmutes negritude itself (p.
137):

> I accept [negritude], no longer cephalic index, or plasma,
> or soma, but measured by the compass of suffering . . .

> j'accepte [la négritude], non plus un indice céphalique, ou
> un plasma, ou un soma, mais mesurée au compas de la
> souffrance . . .

The much briefer third movement of the poem is turned entirely toward the future. Its fundamental thematic trait is the
struggle between the "bon nègre"—the "good nigger" or Uncle
Tom—and the "mauvais nègre," who represents the black man
of the future.[18] The opening of the final movement is startling:
the focus shifts abruptly from the specifically historical context
of negritude to a cosmic vision of the speaker-hero giving new
life to his world:

> Suddenly now strength and life assail me like a bull and
> the water of life overwhelms the papilla of the morne, now
> all the veins and veinlets are bustling with new blood and
> the enormous breathing lung of cyclones and the fire
> hoarded in volcanos and the gigantic seismic pulse which
> now beats the measure of a living body in my firm [con-
> flagration].[19]

> Et voici soudain que force et vie m'assaillent comme un
> taureau et l'onde de vie circonvient la papille du morne, et
> voilà toutes les veines et veinules qui s'affairent au sang
> neuf et l'énorme poumon des cyclones qui respire et le feu
> thésaurisé des volcans et le gigantesque pouls sismique qui
> bat maintenant la mesure d'un corps vivant en mon ferme
> embrasement.   (pp. 137, 139)

The transformation of the speaker from observer to committed
participant and then to inspired leader involves, in this final
avatar, a very considerable leap. Some readers have chosen to
see this as the peculiarly African attribute of the poet-priest,
whose word magically creates its object.[20] This is the interpretation offered by those who stress the Africanism of Césaire's work.
The undeniable thematic and lexical reminiscences that create a
network of African echoes do not, however, account for the underlying structure of the poem. The initial strophe of the third
movement invokes a life force that is readily comprehensible
within the broadly surrealist framework established earlier in
this chapter. It requires no knowledge of African *Nommo*—
spiritual forces—on the part of the reader or, for that matter, on
the part of the poet.[21] At the time he was writing the *Notebook*
Césaire was reading Frobenius with passionate interest; a part
of his representation of negritude is directly attributable to that
reading. Many other details in this and other poems have a similar
origin. Had they predominated there would have been no poetic
composition; the stuff of poetry would never have become a poem,
and the text would have remained only a notebook. It is in the
dialectical composition of the poem that we find the principle of
cohesion that holds together its disparate—indeed contradictory
—elements.

The speaker's leap to a new consciousness, to a new qualitative
relationship with the natural world and with his own cultural
community, bears the stamp of Hegel rather than Marx. The
radical break between the second and third movements coincides
with the nodal point at which the accumulated tensions of the
process of contradiction are themselves overcome in a new synthesis, according to the Hegelian dialectic. The synthesis is expressed by Césaire quite clearly in every aspect of the poem
considered to this point. One important metaphoric complex re-

produces the etymological sense of the Hegelian synthesis, which is sublated *(aufgehoben)*. Just so the city and its population are at the beginning of the poem (p. 33) "flat . . . sprawled . . . inert" ("plate . . . étalée . . . inerte"); negritude (p. 67) "rose for the first time" ("se mit debout pour la première fois"); and finally, in the second strophe of the third movement (p. 139), "We are standing now, my country and I" ("nous sommes debout maintenant, mon pays et moi"). While the Uncle Tom progressively disintegrates (p. 147), a passage developing the motif of the slave ship concludes with "The nigger scum is on its feet" ("elle est debout la négraille"). As the poem draws rapidly to a close the images of erectness, of uprightness proliferate. Césaire evaluates blackness in its new, triumphant state by replacing with a positive *she* ("elle") the most deprecatory of terms in French, *la négraille*. In the first movement of the poem "la négraille" connotes "the niggers," collectively, or "nigger scum." It is a value judgment imposed from outside, a racist denial of value. Césaire's poem seeks to transform consciousness of the black experience from within. Thus "la négraille," when it reappears in a prominent position in the conclusion of the third movement, must be transformed as well (p. 149):

> standing and no longer poor madwoman in her maritime
> freedom and destitution gyrating in perfect drift
> and there she is:
> most unexpectedly standing
> standing in the rigging
> standing at the tiller
> standing at the compass
> standing at the map
> standing under the stars
>   standing
>   and
>   free

> debout et non point pauvre folle dans sa
> liberté et son dénuement maritimes girant
> en la dérive parfaite
> et la voici:
> plus inattendument debout

debout dans les cordages
debout à la barre
debout à la boussole
debout à la carte
debout sous les étoiles
   debout
      et
        libre

The painful birth of the new black out of the transformation of the old nigger has its parallel in the birth of a new style. The poet-leader is, in a strictly textual sense, the product of the poem, not its cause. At the outset the Martinican poet, whose literary culture is essentially European, cannot but use the elements of style provided by the colonizer. The language and the literary forms at his disposal belong to the very tradition that he must attack in order to affirm the uniqueness of his own community. This initial reaction determines the corrosive poetics that dominates the first movement of the poem.

In the thirties the literature of France offered a promise of spiritual renewal in the self-proclaimed revolutionary posture of the surrealists, who as a collective entity had existed for a scant decade when Césaire first encountered their writings. In the second manifesto of surrealism (1930) André Breton claimed that surrealism had salvaged the Hegelian dialectic from the disaster of pure idealism. However much the second manifesto may today strike one as exemplary only in its intellectual legerdemain, in the mid-1930s it must have had a powerful appeal to a young mind keenly aware of being disinherited and repressed by the value system of French society. Surrealism as an ethical posture of systematic opposition then became the mediator between Freud, Hegel, and Marx as thinkers and Césaire's nascent strategy of disalienation. His *Notebook*—more accurately the postwar versions of it—resulted from the active exploration of the self and its social context, using techniques borrowed from the surrealists.

The heroic figure who emerges in the final movement of the poem calls upon the wind, his Lord, to assure his bond with the black world to and for which he claims to speak (p. 155):

and bind, bind me without remorse
bind me with your vast arms to the luminous clay
bind my black vibration to the very navel of the world
. . . . .
then, strangling me with your lasso of stars
rise,
Dove
rise
rise
rise

et lie, lie-moi sans remords
lie-moi de tes vastes bras à l'argile lumineuse
lie ma noire vibration au nombril même du monde
. . . . .
puis, m'étranglant de [ton] lasso d'étoiles
monte,
Colombe
monte
monte
monte

The pitch of the poem has been rising too in an insistent staccato
rhythm that, like a tom-tom, bursts forth in an explosion of
energy, a paroxysm of desire accomplished. One could not find
a more perfect example of poetic closure in which beauty achieves
André Breton's definition of *exploding-fixed* (p. 155):

I follow you who are imprinted on my ancestral white
cornea,
rise sky licker
and the great black hole where a moon ago I wanted to
drown
it is there I will now fish the malevolent tongue of the night
in its motionless veerition!

Je te suis, imprimée en mon ancestrale cornée blanche.
monte lécheur de ciel
et le grand trou noir où je voulais me noyer l'autre lune

c'est là que je veux pêcher maintenant la langue maléfique
de la nuit en son immobile verrition!

The "motionless veerition" realizes the proper end of a poem
with respect to which all revolution is future. Its swirl is seized
provisionally, artfully as object of contemplation and is so offered
to the reader. But as the thematic development of the dialectic
indicates, the poem makes a deep existential appeal to its reader,
in whom a spiritual revolution may now commence. The speaker's progress in the poem is of a therapeutic type. The poem
speaks to those who have yet to make the painful voyage from
alienation to authenticity.

The *Notebook* also intended to speak for and to a collectivity.
Césaire adopted a mixed form that relates it, however loosely, to
the epic. The lyrical bursts in the surrealist vein are subordinated
within the poem to a flexible narrative strophe characterized by
a reliance on the figure of anaphora. Like the epic of ancient
Greece, it claims to save from oblivion the past of a cultural community. Like the *Aeneid* it conveys a sense of origin and collective destiny. The *Notebook* begins and ends *in medias res*, as epic
should do according to Friedrich Schlegel, a formal characteristic
that coincides with Hale's biographical comment that there is
more than one return in the poem. If Césaire does not conform
to Hegel's notion that the epic is expressive of nationalism per
se, we observe nonetheless that the arousal of ethnic consciousness in the poem serves a similar end. For one African commentator the *Notebook* "is an epic with extraordinary power and
depth," although *epic* in his sense is scarcely a true generic term.[22]
And it certainly satisfies Ezra Pound's terse definition of epic as a
long poem including history.

Notebook of a Return to the Native Land is a very ambitious
poem. Although its subject matter is blackness in a white world,
its forms are a sophisticated hybridization of many elements of
modern European literary tradition. Césaire frequently corrodes,
or parodies, European modes and even specific works, yet his tone
never falls into the burlesque that has so frequently swallowed up
critical parody. The epic intention and a surrealist brand of seri-
ousness constantly draw him back to the high road. In the loose,
modern sense Césaire created in the *Notebook* the epic of
negritude.

6

Politics and Poetics

A civilization that proves itself incapable of solving the problems occasioned by its own functioning is a decadent civilization.
Césaire, *Discourse on Colonialism*

THE DECADE from 1946 to 1956 was especially disappointing for Aimé Césaire. During those years he represented
Martinique in the French legislature as a Communist deputy. His
political impact in Paris was limited, although at home in Fort-
de-France, where he held the office of mayor, he successfully in-
stituted urban renewal projects and contributed to such significant improvements in the quality of life as the installation of a
modern urban sanitation system. But while his local black constituents came to treat their representative with respect and trust,
Césaire saw little progress in the areas that meant most to him.
He had fought hard to change the political and administrative
status of the four overseas dependencies of Réunion, Guadeloupe,
Guiana, and Martinique from colonies to departments—administrative units identical to those in metropolitan France. But the
assimilation into France proper did not bring with it the desired
changes in local life. To be sure, the new bureaucracy resembled
that of France. Civil servants were imported in greater numbers,
but their presence soon created a privileged caste disdainful and
suspicious of the local inhabitants whose lives they were to
administer. Moreover, local people who had held administrative
positions were displaced in favor of the metropolitan imports.
Resentment increased as black Martinicans discovered that they
would remain second-class citizens of France. The new order,
which has changed only in details over a thirty-year period, resulted in a form of neocolonialism that is especially hard to combat as colonizer and colonized now appear to be united.

One of Césaire's important publications in the crucial year 1956
was his preface to Daniel Guérin's book *Les Antilles décolonisées*.

He admitted the possibility that the French Antilles might eventually participate in a Caribbean confederation of small island states united by their geography and their economy, although separated for centuries by cultural traditions imported from Europe. The scheme appears utopian, perhaps more so today than when it was initially articulated. That Césaire in 1956 could have envisaged such a confederation at all testifies to his enduring conviction that the values of negritude can transcend the particularities separating islanders with different colonial pasts. For however great the political failure of the departmentalization of Martinique, Césaire maintained that a national consciousness had been born. That Martinican consciousness had resulted, paradoxically, from a reaction to the progressive alienation of Martinicans politically, economically, and socially within the structure imposed by the new political status of the overseas departments. In the years since 1956 Césaire has gradually moved toward favoring a federalist status for Martinique. In the 1960s he called for autonomy in the affairs of the overseas departments and specifically for the recognition of the Martinican nation within France. That his constituents have been reluctant to rally to the idea is an unhappy fact of Aimé Césaire's political career.

That same year Césaire broke openly and spectacularly with the French Communist party in his scathing open *Letter to Maurice Thorez*. The *Letter* is seldom discussed in detail and has long been out of print in English. It deserves more than passing attention in considering Césaire's difficult political evolution during the first decade of the postwar period. Its political and ideological importance places it in a category apart from the numerous defections of French intellectuals throughout the fifties. Quite naturally Césaire took the party to task for its position on Martinique and the Caribbean dependencies generally:

> I think of [Martinique] only to note that communism has succeeded in passing the noose of assimilation around her neck; that communism has succeeded in isolating her within the Caribbean basin; that it has succeeded in thrusting her into a sort of insular ghetto; that it has succeeded in cutting her off from the other Antillean countries whose experience could be both instructive and fruitful to her (for they have the same problems as we and their democratic evolution is

impetuous); finally that communism has cut us off from Black Africa whose evolution henceforth takes shape in a direction contrary to ours.[1]

This angry cry for recognition illuminates the position outlined in Césaire's introduction to Guérin's book.

In a more general sense Césaire questioned whether the orthodox Marxist analysis of a capitalist economy even applies to Martinican conditions. Can the urban proletariat (which scarcely exists in Martinique) really be the vanguard of the revolution? Césaire concluded in the negative. He was among the first western Marxists to point to the example of Maoist China as a model for rural developing nations. Moreover—and this section of the *Letter* was to have particularly far-reaching repercussions—Césaire called for the creation of an African brand of socialism. This insistence on recognizing the particular nature and needs of societies in what has since come to be called the Third World assures Césaire of a modest place among those who have gradually transformed Marxist theory. It is ironic that he was addressing himself to the general secretary of the most hidebound Stalinist party in Western Europe. The opening section of the letter expressed shame, pain, and stupefaction at the recent revelations by Khrushchev and others, at the Twentieth Party Congress, of Stalin's crimes and at the French Communist party's reluctance to denounce them. Césaire was especially unwilling to admit the theoretical necessity of a dictatorship of the proletariat, which he saw as not so very different from capitalist exploitation. The tentacular bureaucracy of Soviet-style communism he condemned in the name of the principles of socialism.

In the final analysis it was Césaire's experience as a colonized black and his reflection on the values of negritude that gave both depth and a convincing ring to this critique, expressed in the *Letter,* of the Soviet monolith as it existed during the Cold War.

A fact of capital importance in my view is this: we people of color, in this precise moment of our historical evolution, have in our conscience taken possession of the entire area of our singularity . . .

Singularity of our "situation in the world," which can be mistaken for no other. Singularity of our problems,

which can be subsumed under no other problem. Singularity of our history, interrupted by terrible transformations
that belong to it alone. Singularity of our culture, which
we intend to quicken in ever more real ways.   (p. 8)

The publication of the *Lettre à Maurice Thorez* by Présence Africaine with a foreword by the editor, Alioune Diop, assured that
it would be read by every potential leader of the states of black
Africa then under French or Belgian colonial rule. Its immediate
impact was doubtless greater in West Africa than that of all of
Césaire's literary publications combined. And although Césaire
has never had a similar following in the African nations formerly
under British rule, it is noteworthy that Alioune Diop prepared a
separate English-language edition of the *Letter* in 1957.

When black African writers comment on the political import
of Césaire's work, his plays and the *Discourse on Colonialism* are
most frequently cited. The nations of Africa in which Césaire is
considered an important voice, even a prophet, are among the
more conservative; they maintain close ties with France and with
the West: Ivory Coast, Cameroon, Senegal. In 1969 Marcien Towa
called Aimé Césaire the "prophet of the revolution of black people." His article, published in Yaoundé, Cameroon, restates the
case for Césaire's version of negritude: "In a word, the importance
of the role played by Césaire in the movement to emancipate black
people is due to this: he announced the freedom of the Black
[Nègre], he prophesied with his great voice the 'Beautiful City', a
world in which the Black could be himself, master of his destiny."[2]
The first black African author of a book on Césaire, M. a M. Ngal,
was dean of arts and letters at the University of Lubumbashi in
Zaïre. His book was published in Senegal (whose president from
1960 to 1980 was L. S. Senghor) by a government-subsidized press.
B. Kotchy-N'Guessan, writing in an official organ of the University
of Abidjan, Ivory Coast, defined Césaire's political significance in
terms of a mystical negritude that Césaire would surely not wish
to call his own.[3] Claims such as this, made by people who consider
themselves followers of Césaire, ill serve his reputation and distort his thought. They are demagogic and essentially uncritical.
The demagogic aspect of Kotchy-N'Guessan's position is revealed
in his interpretation of the conclusion of *The Tragedy of King
Christophe*. According to him, Henri Christophe failed because

"the people do not yet understand that the construction of the citadel requires their complete abnegation" (p. 193). Small wonder that the orthodox Marxist detractors of negritude (Adotevi, for instance, whose position is outlined in chapter 1) argue that the movement is a reactionary mystification of the African masses.

Aimé Césaire's political writings have had the result of angering other Marxists—with whom he is frequently in agreement as to ultimate ends—and of attracting obscurantists who interpret his work in the most conservative manner. The misunderstanding is a permanent one, owing in part to the profound irrationalism that served as the basis of his early formulation of negritude, prior to his affiliation with a Marxist political party. It raises the important question, to what extent is Césaire a Marxist thinker?

A Practical Marxist

I have shown that up to 1945 Césaire's thinking was not Marxist but utopian, in the tradition that runs from the romantics to the surrealists. Without having considered a career in politics Césaire found himself catapulted overnight from teaching, for which he was splendidly qualified, to a seat in the Chamber of Deputies as a member of the French Communist party, Martinican section. Something of his preparedness for political action can be gauged by this lapidary formula that appeared in his "Panorama" of the Martinican scene published in *Tropiques* (no. 10, February 1944, p. 9): "The Martinican Revolution will be made in the name of bread, certainly; but also in the name of air and poetry (which amounts to the same thing)."

The years immediately following the war were marked by a prolonged struggle to have the new departmentalization law implemented, to ensure adequate primary school facilities, to improve the housing of the wretchedly poor, and to extend to the new Overseas Departments the social legislation that, in France proper, covered old-age pensions, health insurance, unemployment insurance. The realities of political action impressed on Césaire the inertia of the class in power and the unrelieved oppression of poverty, which materially and spiritually crushed his constituents. For Aimé Césaire a new phase in the history of negritude was born of this conflict between his aspirations and the realities of his political situation. The Marxist theory of the class struggle would remain fixed in Césaire's thought, although by 1956 he would accommodate it to the concrete problems of blacks as he saw them.

There is little evidence available as to when Césaire began to read the theoreticians of Marxism, but we know that while he was a student at the Ecole Normale Supérieure he read *Commune*, of which Louis Aragon was an editor. The undeniably dialectical nature of much of his writing throughout the war years was in touch with an idealist, even a spiritual principle; it owed little or nothing to dialectical materialism. Césaire's joining the French Communist party during the war should doubtless be seen primarily as an act of patriotism, given the repressive and racist nature of Admiral Roberts' administration of Martinique in the name of the Vichy government. The anti-Nazi and anticollaborationist fervor of the resistance made the discipline and organization of the Communists attractive to many who would not otherwise have gravitated to them. Césaire prepared a brief official statement for the party brochure, *Pourquoi je suis communiste*, in 1946. It stated his position succinctly: "I joined the Communist party because, in a world not yet cured of racism, where the fierce exploitation of colonial populations still persists, the Communist party embodies the will to work effectively for the coming of the only social and political order we can accept—because it will be founded on the right of all men to dignity without regard to origin, religion, or color."[4]

For a time at least the party was willing to overlook Césaire's more visible idiosyncrasies such as his close association with André Breton.[5] Césaire proved to be a particularly useful comrade in the aftermath of the war. His considerable talents as an orator were noted in the Paris press during the debates on the proposed new constitution by the First Constituent Assembly in April 1946. At the time the combined socialist and communist left held a voting majority. Alongside his old friend Senghor he led the debate linking the new constitution to the abolition of colonialism and capitalism.[6] In late September 1946 the press was again remarkably united in its praise for Césaire's oratorical style —quite apart from the newspapers' political preferences—in his speeches before the Second Constituent Assembly. Clearly the party was reaping benefits from the attention being paid to its new representative. Within the next few years Césaire was invited to represent the party at international meetings: In Wroclaw, Poland (August 1948) and in Bucharest, Rumania (March 1949), where he was introduced by both Aragon and Malraux. By October 1949 he was persona non grata in the United States; and the Department of State denied him a transit visa, presumably because of his party membership.

Césaire eventually broke with the Communists for the same reason he had joined them: having placed in the party his hopes for the economic and political liberation of blacks, and having found the party reluctant to move in these areas, Césaire could scarcely have taken a different course of action. His attitude toward the French communists' rigid Stalinism was similar to that of many white intellectuals who left the party in the fifties; but in his case the prolonged reflection on the values of negritude was the determining factor. Of the major texts that reveal the evolution of Césaire's ideological position, the earliest in date is the speech he made in 1948 to commemorate the centennial of the abolition of slavery.[7] The speech is ostensibly an homage to Victor Schoelcher, without whom, in Césaire's words, France might have had as bad a record for holding slaves as the United States or Brazil. But Césaire's party affiliation made itself felt when he blamed the entrenched interests of the French middle class (including its spokesmen Tocqueville, Guizot, and Montalembert) for attempting to defer and possibly to defeat the abolitionist movement. He cited an 1844 workers' petition to the Deputies asking in the name of human brotherhood that slavery be abolished. The construction of Césaire's speech clearly suggests the Marxist dialectic of the class struggle in which the date 1848 is especially hallowed. The "magnificent Parisian working class" thus becomes the true hero of abolition, and the party of the working class can be seen as the standard-bearer of the same goals in the present. The political right reacted with predictable outrage at Césaire's evocation of the workers' movement and the conditions of revolution in which the abolition of slavery had been achieved by France. This was but a pinprick, however, in comparison to the attack Césaire was to launch two years later.

The *Discourse on Colonialism* deserves a place alongside the great polemical pieces written in French. It was never a speech, although it may be considered the speech Césaire would have liked to make in the National Assembly. The title refers to the author's rhetorical stance. He opens his attack on capitalist democracy with a summary judgment of postwar Western society as decadent: "A civilization that chooses to close its eyes to its most crucial problems is a diseased civilization. A civilization that compromises its principles is a moribund civilization."[8] The first major point Césaire makes is to equate colonialism with racism, a feature of the *Discourse* that sets it apart from the standard Marxist analysis of imperialism as a necessary stage in capitalism brought on by the need for new markets. Césaire does touch all the bases required in the Marxist argument, but he does so rapidly, reserving his best moments for a condemnation of European racism.

Tactically Césaire intends to surprise his reader with a damning quotation from a completely unexpected source. His references to Nazi racism were, in 1950, completely unimpeachable. Every good Frenchman could be expected to join the chorus of outraged conscience. We read this statement, believing it to be by Adolph Hitler: "We aspire not to equality but to domination. The country of foreign race shall once again become a country of serfs, of agricultural day laborers, and of industrial workers. It is not a matter of doing away with the inequities among men, but of amplifying them and making a law of them" (p. 363). This cynical apologia of racial conquest came from the pen of the author of the "Prayer on the Acropolis" ("Prière sur l'Acropole"), a model of nineteenth-century humanism. Ernest Renan is only the most striking example of authors whose works are made to incriminate them in the *Discourse:* Joseph de Maistre ("the mystical mode"), Ernest Psichari (a grandson of Renan and novelistic apologist of empire), Emile Faguet (an arbiter of literary fashion early in the century), and at the lowest level of taste, Jules Romains: "I have on occasion faced a row of twenty or so pure blacks . . . I won't even blame our negroes and negresses for chewing gum. I will mention only that this movement has the effect of accentuating their jaws, and the thoughts that pass through your head take you closer to the equatorial rain forest than to the Olympic games . . . The black race has not yet produced, will never produce an Einstein, a Stravinsky, a Gershwin" (p. 375).

Having maneuvered his adversary into an awkward moral position, Césaire attacked the good conscience of the moralizers of colonialism who piously allege the white man's burden. At this point Césaire's anticlericalism all but gets the better of him. In fact his condemnation of Father Placide Tempels's book on Bantu philosophy[9] appears to go well beyond what he himself believed. It is true of course that this Belgian missionary priest had provided a convenient justification for white domination of blacks through his representation of Bantu ontology; but it does not necessarily follow—and Césaire has not always believed—that African religion is merely the opiate of the black masses. In a footnote (p. 383) Césaire does distinguish between what the Bantu think and the exploitation of their thought, but in the main Césaire's readers have taken from the *Discourse* a conviction that the author was basically irreligious.

It is on this last point that Césaire in the *Discourse* comes closest to a doctinaire Marxism. On another page we find him dismissing with a pun both Jaspers and Nietzsche.[10] But by 1956 Césaire was to cite Nietzsche as an authority on culture, barbarism, and style.[11] His sheer facility with the language and his improvisational brilliance carried Césaire into a pyrotechnic display that has nothing to do with Marxism per se nor even with politics.

Why such a heavy-handed approach? Césaire understood that in 1950 the forces supporting a colonial empire were not yet sufficiently vulnerable on their own ground. Another decade would pass before the Algerian war would wear France down to the point where the principle of empire could be abandoned. In 1950 it appeared that the French would be able to maintain their hold on Indochina and Madagascar as well. At the time the efficacious tactical maneuver was to tie colonialism so tightly to racism as to undermine the stronger position by attacking the weaker. The approach was fresh and its shock value considerable. Moreover, it is difficult today not to see the connection, in part because Césaire made it so well.

At exactly this time Gabriel Marcel was writing *Man against Mass Society*, in which he dwelt on what he called the "techniques of degradation" recently employed by the Nazis. The measured prose of the Catholic essayist could offend no right-thinking individual. Mutatis mutandis, Césaire's thesis that the exploitation of colonialism degrades the colonizer was practically identical, and it was shocking. The difference lies not in the truth of the proposition—which I take to be generally conceded today—but in the style.

Césaire attempted in *Discourse on Colonialism* to rectify some current notions about his idea of history in general and of African history in particular. This part of the text has a double thrust: to push aside the image of Aimé Césaire the surrealist and poetic mythologizer and to better establish in Marxist circles his credentials as a historian. Césaire's argument *pro domo sua* has often been taken at face value and applied retrospectively to the *Notebook*. Since the *Discourse on Colonialism* is among Césaire's most accessible writings, it has been tempting to accept unquestioningly his equivocation on the term *return* in this passage: "It seems that in certain circles they claim to have found in me an 'enemy of Europe' and a prophet of the return to a pre-European past. As for me, I try in vain to find where I could have uttered such words; where I can be seen to underestimate the importance of Europe in the history of human thought; where I have been heard to preach any *return* at all; where I can be seen to claim that there could be a *return*" (p. 370). Césaire would have one believe in 1950 that the *return* to the native land was only historical and sociological, in conformity with the requirements of Marxist political analysis. The irrationalist resonances of Spengler, Frobenius, and Bergson that are to be found in the *Notebook*—and throughout *Miraculous Weapons*—are dismissed as nonexistent. Many readers have approached the *Notebook* by way of the *Discourse*, giving what one may call the ambient socialist reading. Mazisi Kunene's gloss of the "Eia for those who never invented anything" passage is typical of this reading: "Clearly Césaire is not claiming that there is merit in the failure to invent, as some have understood him to say. He is talking tongue in cheek against the glorification of technology by the European, the bloody conquests and destruction of peoples by colonization."[12]

The facts are not quite so simple. Césaire's writing through 1945 had been concerned with an alternative to the rationalist histories that he equated with European repression and domination. However, he did not at that time envisage the alternative as Marxist. By 1950 he had undoubtedly found that the irrationalist current in his poetry had become a hindrance to him as a Marxist deputy. Without excusing his tactic, one must observe that the momentary solution was to deny the evidence. Certainly Césaire did not promote a back-to-Africa movement, nor did he recommend that the clock be turned back in Europe's colonial empires. But just as certainly he had written poetry that presented a pseudomythical alternative to the present, and that alternative can be seen as a return to ancient spiritual values.

At times Césaire's Marxism in the *Discourse* is curious, to say the least. This approach to Lautréamont as a social critic for instance: "I believe a day will come when, having collected all the documents, analyzed all the sources, clarified all the circumstances of the work, it will be possible to give a historical, materialist interpretation of the *Chants de Maldoror* that will bring to light a much misunderstood aspect of this frenzied epic, the implacable denunciation of a very precise form of society that could not escape the sharpest of gazes around 1865" (p. 390). The thesis is novel and may deserve attention, but the reference is decidedly odd, as is the quotation from quatrains two and three of Baudelaire's "The Ragmen's Wine" (Le Vin des chiffonniers"), taken to represent the working class.

A careful reader of Césaire may notice that these last reference points were also among the major ones of his essay on "Poetry and Cognition" in 1944; and his principal source on African societies before European conquest remained in 1950 none other than Frobenius. In short the *Discourse on Colonialism*, although it has the necessary Marxist superstructure, does not appear to arise from a Marxist grasp of history. The only one of Césaire's writings to be consistently well received in Marxist circles, the only one published in English by a Marxist press, can at most be said to have taken the idealist dialectic of "Poetry and Cognition," turned it upside down, and declared it to be Marxist.

The position Césaire adopted in the *Discourse on Colonialism* must have been a difficult one for him: feeling himself obliged to deny the inspiration of a significant part of his poetry, he also had to subordinate the particularities of the black experience outside Africa to the totalizing process of a dialectic that required that the urban proletariat be presented as "the only class that still has a universal mission" (p. 401). The *Discourse on Colonialism* is thus a watershed for Césaire. At the same time that it represents Césaire's effort to accommodate himself to Marxist orthodoxy, it also marks the tension between his political commitment on the one hand and the sources of his personal vision on the other. Twenty years later this problem was still central to Césaire's dual role as politician and writer. He said to Lilyan Kesteloot in

1971: "The writer is all alone with his mind, with his soul; the politician, not to mention the party hack, unfortunately has to take contingencies into account; he tries to lead but he also has to come to terms with contingencies, and if a *mot d'ordre* is not linked to the reality of things, that *mot d'ordre* is only literature. Consequently I find that there is no contradiction between what I write and what I do; they are merely two different levels of action."[13]

Politics and Poetics

Césaire's ultimate break with the Communist party came in large part because of pressures to conform to the official line on critical realism. In the mid-fifties Louis Aragon was in a position to establish norms for aesthetics and to apply pressure to those writers within the party who failed to comply. Since the war years Aragon had returned to a regular French prosody with some interesting modifications in rhyme (*Le Musée Grévin, Les Yeux d'Elsa, Le Crève-coeur*). Under his leadership the poets of the party had adopted a more straightforward, accessible verse in which a clear message expressed itself more or less handsomely. Césaire for his part continued to insist on the value of surrealist poetics in putting the poet in touch with himself, a goal that orthodox Marxists viewed with more than a little suspicion as excessively individualistic. One day we may know the details of the strained relations between Aragon and Césaire during this period; in 1955 Césaire himself brought the quarrel into the open.

Aragon had recently discussed in *Les Lettres françaises,* and Charles Dobzynski had echoed in *La Nouvelle Critique,* a theory of national poetry that proscribed free verse, pilloried formal individualism, and generally tied the traditional prosody of France to the interests of the revolutionary working class. However absurd this may seem in retrospect and in outline form, the question appeared sufficiently important for *Présence Africaine* to open its pages to an extension of the debate outside those magazines dominated or run by the party. To understand the full import of Césaire's participation and the tone he took, it is helpful to know something of his relations with René Depestre, a promising young Haitian poet whose collection *Végétations de clarté* Césaire had prefaced in 1951. As a Communist, Depestre was in exile in Brazil at the time these exchanges over poetics and ideology began.

René Depestre had written to Dobzynski to realign himself with Aragon's position; his attitude was one of submission to authority: "Thanks to Aragon I am in the process of resolving the conflict my 'formal individualism' was struggling with. I have in theory rallied to Aragon's decisive lessons, and before long there will be agreement between the new awareness I have acquired of realism in poetry and the emotional means my sensibility is called upon to use to illustrate my understanding of the problems raised and resolved by the 'Diary of national poetry.' "[14] The jargon is part and parcel of the problem: the old dichotomy of subject matter and form is maintained, with form subordinated to content.

Césaire appears to have chosen the occasion of Depestre's letter to signify his own displeasure with Aragon's ideological regimentation of poetry. He prepared a poetic epistle, "Reply to Depestre, Haitian Poet" ("Réponse à Depestre poète haïtien"), which he subtitled "Elements of an Ars Poetica" ("Eléments d'un art poétique"). It is rather a good poem despite its didactic purpose, but that very combination tends to weaken the argument that socialist art must return to a preestablished mold. Césaire appealed to Depestre not to abandon the values of negritude that are his Haitian heritage: "Can it be / that the rains of exile / have unstretched the drumskin of your voice" ("se peut-il / que les pluies de l'exil / aient détendu la peau de tambour de ta voix").[15] In a direct reference to intraparty affairs (p. 114) Césaire wrote: "To hell with it Depestre to hell with it let Aragon talk" ("fous-t-en Depestre fous-t-en laisse dire Aragon"). As for the forms of traditional prosody, Césaire dismissed them as "the solemn wretchedness of an impoverished tune" ("la gueuserie solennelle d'un air mendié") and urged Depestre to heed the powerful voodoo (spirit) of his blood. In a word, the direction indicated by Aragon signified for Césaire the very cultural assimilationism that he had combatted since the days of *Tropiques* ("Réponse à Depestre," p. 114):

> It's true they're turning out this season nicely fashioned
> sonnets

for us to do it would bring too much to mind
the sugary juice that back there the distilleries dribble down
    the hills
when the slow lean oxen make their circle to the humming
    of mosquitoes

C'est vrai ils arrondissent cette saison des sonnets
pour nous à le faire cela me rappellerait par trop
le jus sucré que bavent là-bas les distilleries des mornes
quand les lents boeufs maigres font leur rond au zonzon des
    moustiques

Césaire took an important stand in this text. He agreed that
poetics and ideology cannot finally be separated, but he put the
problem in such a way as to focus attention on two aspects of
dialectics that still divide Marxists: to wit, can ethnic or cultural
particulars be maintained within the totalizing process of the
dialectic, and can a socialist attitude express itself in an inno-
vative form? Depestre reflected further on Césaire's pointed questions and replied in a long, interesting, but somewhat self-contradictory statement. His most telling point is that:

> It is not the linguistic or racial community that determines
> the national character of a culture but, in the last analysis,
> the [economic] conditions of life, the conditions of histori-
> cal development proper to each country. Outside of that
> illumination of the national we risk falling into the trap of
> "negritude," which denies the evidence of the diversity of
> material conditions of evolution, which considers the cre-
> ative sensibility of blacks as a homogeneous cultural block
> without frontiers, interchangeable in its expressive mani-
> festations. And to speak of "black poetry" in general is a
> myth as confused as the metaphysical notion of negritude.[16]

This was basically the position of Aragon, within which Césaire
could be criticized as a reactionary. It assumes that Césaire is
interested primarily in pigmentation, an argument taken up more
recently by Adotevi. Césaire joined the combat with an incisive
commentary on Depestre's reply. Early on in his original letter
Depestre had noted that "it would be an error on our part, a

denial of nationality, to ignore the *African side*" of Haitian culture, but later he had concluded that it would be necessary to ascertain what part of it could be "harmoniously integrated into the French prosodic heritage" (p. 37). As Césaire saw it, the Marxist dialectic was being used to subordinate the particularities of the culture of colonized blacks to the dominant culture shared by the colonizer and the French Marxists alike. In Césaire's eyes, for a colonized black obliged by history to write in a European language the truly revolutionary attitude would be to disrupt the conservative forms of European discourse. More specifically an original, creative use of the language would presumably allow the distinctive features of the black poet's culture to find appropriate modes of expression. Césaire's argument with Depestre was that in subordinating one's experience as a black poet to European (or for that matter African) forms established a priori, one risked stifling the vitality of that experience. In so doing one would at the same time destroy poetry. Although he certainly overstated his case by adopting the position diametrically opposed to Aragon's and Depestre's, Césaire in his "Réponse" basically aligned himself with a familiar surrealist proposition: "The poetry of Rimbaud is not his stylistics; it is his revolt. The poetry of Whitman is not his *verset*, it is . . . his 'great heart' " (p. 41).

Césaire was on firmer ground when in defense of his own poetic practice he coined the neologism *marronner*. The verb is used transitively in Césaire's epistle to Depestre to allude to that corrosion of European modes that he had begun in the earliest version of his *Notebook*. A *marron* or "marroon" was a fugitive slave who had successfully escaped the plantation to live in freedom in the hills ("Réponse à Depestre," p. 114):

> Let's escape them Depestre let's escape them
> as in the past we escaped our whip-wielding masters

> Marronnons-les Depestre marronnons-les
> comme jadis nous marronnions nos maîtres à fouet

Just as in the past Caribbean slaves had escaped physical and legal bondage, so Césaire recommends to the descendants of slaves that they escape the shackles of European prosody. The analogy with surrealist practice is clear; Césaire's poetics, as I have indicated, drew from surrealism the means of expression required by the concrete realities of Martinican life. It is just as clear why Aragon could not approve; as far as he was concerned, he had seen it all before with André Breton in 1932. Césaire's continuing good relations with Breton did not simplify matters at all; rather they aggravated his situation.

This debate should not be left on the purely descriptive level. Its elements have recurred in Marxist theory not once but several times. Indeed at the very moment when *Présence Africaine* was organizing a debate on the conditions of a national poetry among black peoples, György Lukács was lecturing on critical realism in capitalist societies before audiences in the German Democratic Republic, Poland, Italy, and Austria. His *Realism in Our Time (Die Gegenwartsbedeutung des kritischen Realismus)* addressed itself primarily to the novel, but the parallels with Aragon's theory of critical realism in poetry are striking. Both are attacks on modernism, including the sense of anguish typical of existentialists and the recourse to the unconscious common to surrealists. The grotesque assessments of Joyce and Beckett that resulted from Lukács's position are well known. The intellectual conservatism of the Marxist position is revealing here, for it is not theoretically necessary. The *Tel Quel* group after 1968 took the position that a disruption of discourse was a necessary prerequisite to practical revolutionary activity. This position, as delineated by Kristeva and others, posited an alternative Marxism based— or so it was thought at the time—on the Chinese cultural revolution.[17]

This is not to suggest that there is some unsuspected affinity between the activity of *Tel Quel* and that of Aimé Césaire in the fifties. The significant common denominator is the effort to establish a poetics construed as revolutionary that would disrupt the stranglehold on the culture maintained by the class in power. The point of the analogy is that whether Césaire's position on the language of poetry be judged reactionary or progressive is essentially a function of where one stands.

Culture and Colonization

The First International Congress of Negro Writers and Artists was held in Paris in September 1956. It brought together a large number of black intellectuals from North America and the Caribbean as well as from black Africa and Europe. The views expressed at the meeting were as varied as the backgrounds of those attending. But though the delegates failed to agree on the nature of "The Crisis of Negro Culture," the Congress engendered a great deal of excitement. John A. Davis, introducing the collective volume *Africa from the Point of View of American Negro Scholars* (Présence Africaine, 1958), attributed the foundation of the American Society of African Culture directly to the Paris meeting. To properly appreciate the context in which Aimé Césaire gave his paper on "Culture and Colonization" ("Culture et Colonisation") one would have to read the entire special edition of *Présence Africaine* devoted to the Congress.[18] Accounts of the Congress, including James Baldwin's in *Nobody Knows My Name*, suggest that Aimé Césaire fairly dominated the proceedings. His contribution came as a shock to many North American delegates, whose position was broadly integrationist, particularly when early in his paper Césaire declared them to be "artificially placed—within a great modern nation—in a situation that is comprehensible only with reference to colonialism, abolished to be sure, but whose aftershocks yet reverberate in the present."[19] Césaire fully intended to establish the connection *racial discrimination = neocolonialism*. The wounded reaction of John A. Davis gives some indication of the state of mind of his North American audience: "America [read the United States] has always taken an anti-colonialist position; from George Washington down to Dwight Eisenhower, every president has taken this position."[20] Those who shared Davis's view certainly found Césaire's paper extremist and in the context of the Cold War dismissed it as communist propaganda. Marxist it is, but as we might expect from the preceding analyses of the *Discourse on Colonialism* and Césaire's position in the debate on a national poetry, it helps us understand the evolution of his thought in these crucial years.

Compared to the polemical brilliance of the *Discourse*, "Culture and Colonization" is generally moderate, even scholarly in tone. There are two main points on which Césaire's arguments turn. The first is the conviction that the culture of black peoples everywhere in 1956 was stifled, bastardized, corrupted by the nature of colonialism. It is unfortunate that Césaire's theses required that the North American experience correspond quite so strictly to that of blacks elsewhere in the world, since much that he had to say was otherwise unobjectionable. In a careful development of his thesis—really a more reflective version of his position in the *Discourse*—Césaire demonstrated through references to non-Marxist social scientists that the end of colonialism was the sine qua non of a worldwide black cultural awakening. The references Césaire selected can be taken to indicate an effort not to offend listeners who would be put off by Marxist oratory. He cited English-language works by Margaret Mead, Bronislaw Malinowski, Arnold Toynbee, Alfred Kroeber. More importantly for us now, he was right in his conclusions.

The second major aspect of Césaire's paper would have been less obvious to his hearers in 1956. It is a reflection on the nature of the distinction between a national culture and a civilization, obviously prompted in part by Césaire's need to justify negritude within the Communist party. After making an excellent point, Césaire seems to have partially undermined the distinction by neglecting to adhere to it rigorously later in his paper. In sum Césaire declared his agreement with the principle that a *culture* must be national, but he was quick to point out that a *civilization* —the more comprehensive term—can be supranational. Thus he could maintain in "Culture et Colonisation" that important elements of African civilization are preserved even after the destruction of a specific African culture (by colonialism or through the disruption caused by the random dispersal of slaves); and he was eager to add that "even in the United States" there are fringes, not to say centers, of "this Negro-African civilization" (p. 436). It was crucial for Césaire to establish a theoretical and historical basis for negritude at a time when L. S. Senghor was propagating a metaphysical version.[21] Césaire was by this date at the opposite pole from the position he and Senghor had shared some twenty years earlier. Césaire's political experience had taught the painful lesson that cultural renaissance cannot advance far in the absence of political change. Césairean negritude had instilled a new pride in African civilization and had, although not to so great an extent as he wished to believe, helped to foster a national consciousness in Martinique and elsewhere. What was still lacking was the political change prerequisite to the creation of truly national cultures.

With an eye toward convincing his Marxist colleagues of the

rightness of his view Césaire shored up both arguments in "Culture et Colonisation" with appropriate quotations from Hegel and, far more pertinently, from Marx and Lenin. In Lenin's *Philosophical Notebooks* Césaire found an underscored quotation from Hegel's *Philosophy of History* that he took to mean "a political and social regime that suppresses the self-determination of a people kills the creative potential of that people at the same time" (p. 440). So as to reinforce his concept of the particularity of a nation within a capitalist or socialist civilization, he cited Marx's *Capital* to excellent advantage. In the third volume of *Capital* he found a long paragraph in which Marx does indeed argue that particular factors, including racial ones, present a vast array of empirical variations and gradations from a given economic base. Furthermore, Marx called for the analysis of these empirical circumstances in a given society. Césaire's conclusion, surely Marxist in its intent, claimed for colonized blacks the right and the necessity of preserving the African legacy. Another lapidary phrase of the type Césaire has so often used affirmed that "the shortest road to the future is always the one that goes through the thorough study of the past" (p. 439).

Whether or not this phrase and the thought it represents so well can be reconciled with dialectical materialism, conditions in the French Communist party in 1956 were not conducive to a healthy discussion of it. Césaire had, even in this effort to play by the party rules, demonstrated that his thought was too particularist for Marxist orthodoxy. What discussions may have occurred within the party over Césaire's speech, which received considerable attention, we do not know. Precisely thirty-five days after addressing the congress Césaire sent his now famous *Letter to Maurice Thorez*. Two years later he founded the independent Parti Progressiste Martiniquais (PPM), which has returned him to his seat in every subsequent legislative election.

Part III
CRISIS AND CONTINUITY

7

Beheaded Sun

I am besieged. Europe patrols within my veins like
a pack of filaria at the stroke of midnight.

Europe sherd of cast iron
Europe low tunnel where oozes a bloody dew
Europe old dog Europe worm-drawn coach
Europe peeling tatoo Europe your name
is a raucous gurgling and a muffled blow
    Césaire, "At the Floodgates of the Void"

je suis investi. L'Europe patrouille dans mes veines comme
une meute de filaires sur le coup de minuit.

Europe éclat de fonte
Europe tunnel bas d'où suinte une rosée de sang
Europe vieux chien Europe calèche à vers
Europe tatouage pelé Europe ton nom est un gloussement
rauque et un choc assourdi
      "Aux écluses du vide"

READERS of *Beheaded Sun (Soleil cou coupé)* who
know the collection only in the revised edition published in
Cadastre in 1961 can hardly appreciate the surrealist flavor of
the original. *Beheaded Sun* was first released in 1948 by the publishing house K, which specialized in surrealist authors. In it
Césaire used more surrealist associative metaphors than ever before. The work has been thought to conform to the commonly
held assumptions concerning automatic writing: that the metaphors are gratuitous and the poem undoubtedly incoherent. These
assumptions usually derive from an uncritical acceptance of the
most frequently cited definition of surrealist automatic writing
as a direct dictation of the unconscious. The fact that Césaire in
revising this collection either omitted or abridged significantly
most of the poems of this type—the omissions number thirty of

the original seventy-two poems—has encouraged commentators who feel uncomfortable with surrealist poetry to assume that the author had simply come to his senses between 1948 and 1961. It is true that the extreme modification of this collection, which surely ranks among the most extensive of editing jobs by a postwar poet, is related to a shift in Césaire's poetics during the late fifties. The reasons for Césaire's severity with the 1948 text are, however, far more complex than he has suggested in such statements as the following, made to an interviewer the year *Cadastre* was published: "I did automatic writing under the influence of Breton, but the result seemed contrived . . . These poems reflected my personality no more and no less than those I wrote normally."[1] Césaire intended this statement to justify his minimizing of automatic writing in the recently released collection. He made two points generally accepted by his commentators: that automatic writing is somehow not normal and that the true purpose of automatic writing is to express the author's personality in its unconscious aspects. Compare André Breton's claim in the 1938 *Dictionnaire abrégé du surréalisme:* "For years I counted on the torrential flow of automatic writing for the definitive cleaning of the literary stable. In this respect, the will to open wide the floodgates will no doubt remain as the generating idea of surrealism."[2]

Such claims as these have given an aura of nonliterariness to surrealist texts, with the result that all too often they have been regarded as inspired nonsense. Contrariwise, but for the same reason, surrealist texts seem to authorize and even to invite the reductive activity of most psychoanalytic commentary, which is presumed to reveal the true personality of the writer. In the face of a half-century of obscurantism of this sort it is forgivable that Césaire's commentators to date, with very few exceptions, have decided to follow their author's lead in abandoning the original version of *Beheaded Sun* without further examination. Some of Césaire's automatic texts in *Beheaded Sun* cannot be dismissed on such nonliterary grounds. By showing that these poems have an order and a significance of their own, one makes the case that their exclusion from the revised edition must be ascribed to other motives. One may also legitimately suppose that careful consideration of the excluded poems will reveal aspects of the shift in Césaire's poetic practice, thus illustrating concretely what the preceding chapter dealt with at the level of poetic theory as it impinges on political thought and ideology.

The Automatism Effect

The poem "The Sun's Knife-Stab in the Back of the Surprised Cities" ("Le Coup de couteau du soleil dans le dos des villes surprises") is an ideal text to examine in this light. It is a good poem qua poem and therefore supports the contention that Césaire's reasons for suppressing it were not exclusively aesthetic. A descriptive reading of the page-long text reveals a composition in two parts of approximately equal length. The first part is in the form of the speaker's vision of three fabulous animals; the second part evokes the speech of a prophetic voice, concluding with the associative metaphor that gives the piece its title. In recent years some excellent contributions to the poetics of surrealist narrative have made it possible to discuss poems such as this in a more literary vein. Michael Riffaterre has noted that: "The automatism effect within a predictable narrative . . . results from two types of deviant lexical derivation: in the first type, lexical sequences make sense (seem referential) but in a way that deviates from the narrative. In the second, they do not deviate from it, but they do not make sense."[3]

The Césaire poem in question belongs to the second type. It is not manifestly referential and in that respect only does it not make sense. A second contribution to the poetics of surrealist narrative to which I shall refer throughout this section has been made by Laurent Jenny. The major points as they bear on the poem under discussion are as follows: "The 'automatic' narrative is just as reluctant to abandon [its] 'narrative cover' as to realize it consistently. The thread of a narrative is clearly visible, but intermittent or imperfect . . ." "The narrative forms are . . . perverted and returned to a pure poetic function, just like the components of a metaphor," which has the effect of negating the text's status as narrative. Jenny discovers in the automatic narrative, however, a paradigmatic logic that he defines as "the tendency of any paradigmatic unit introduced into the text to *decline* other elements of the paradigm to which it belongs," thereby conferring on the text a semantic coherence and a degree of verisimilitude. Finally, the intertextual network of different types of discourse within the same narrative "occasions a general circulation of meaning" or "a dialogue of discourse."[4]

Césaire's poem "The Sun's Knife-Stab in the Back of the Surprised Cities" corresponds, in varying degrees, to all the points outlined above.[5] Its three visions and a prophecy not only borrow the mode of discourse and diction from the Book of Revelation in the New Testament; they reproduce metonymically a rather large number of its details, generally in the identical narrative sequence, although with some deviation. The degree of paradigmatic semantic coherence in this poem is consequently much higher and more uniform than in the texts of *Poisson soluble* studied by Riffaterre and Jenny. Furthermore, when Césaire deviates momentarily from a given intertext of Revelation to another in the Gospel according to St. Matthew, the broader paradigm of biblical discourse of the prophetic type is nonetheless maintained. The reader who is sensitive to the biblical tenor of the text but not to the specific borrowing will not even notice the deviation. The poem presents, in the third vision, a further deviation from the details of Revelation, if not from its sequence. In this instance the intertext appears to be an Afro-Cuban tale with which Césaire was familiar. However, even here the narrative cover of Revelation is respected so that Césaire limits rather severely that free circulation of meaning that Jenny finds in Breton's *Poisson soluble*. The pertinent passages of Césaire's poem appear below in their normal progression, and the borrowed passages of the King James translation of Revelation 13–18 appear in their corresponding order.

1. And I saw a first animal / it had a *crocodile body*[a] *equine feet*[b] the *head of a / dog*[c] but when I looked more closely in place of *the buboes*[d] there were *scars*[e] left at different times / by storms on a body long subjected to obscure trials

   Et je vis un premier animal / il avait *un corps de crocodile*[a] *des pattes d'équidé*[b] une *tête de / chien*[c] mais lorsque je regardai de plus près à la place *des bubons*[d] / c'étaient des *cicatrices*[e] laissées en des temps différents par les / orages sur un corps longtemps soumis à d'obscures épreuves

   Intertext: Revelation 13:1–3
   And I stood upon the sand of the sea, and saw *a beast*[a] rise up

out of the sea,[a] . . . And the beast which I saw was like unto a leopard, and his feet were as the *feet of a bear,*[b] and his mouth as the *mouth of a lion*[c] . . . And I saw one of his heads as it were *wounded to death*[d]; and his deadly *wound had healed*[e] . . .

2. and I saw a second animal / it was lying beneath *a dragon tree*[a] from both sides of / its *musk-deer*[b] muzzle / *two rostra*[c] with inflamed pulp stood out like *mustachios*[c]

   et je vis un second animal / il était couché sous *un bois de dragonnier*[a] des deux côtés de / son museau de *chevrotain*[b] comme des *moustaches*[c] se détachaient / *deux rostres*[c] enflammés aux pulpes

   Intertext: Revelation 13:11
   And I beheld another beast coming up out of the earth; and he had *two horns*[c] like *a lamb,*[b] and he spake as *a dragon.*[a]

3. I saw a third animal which was *an earthworm*[a] but a / *strange will*[b] animated the beast with a long narrowness and it stretched / out on the ground losing and growing anew rings that one / would never have thought it strong enough to carry and which pushed / life back and forth among them very fast like a very obscene password

   Je vis un troisième animal qui était *un ver de terre*[a] mais *un / vouloir étrange*[b] animait la bête d'une longue étroitesse et il s'étirait / sur le sol perdant et repoussant sans cesse des anneaux qu'on / ne lui aurait jamais cru la force de porter et qui se poussaient / entre eux la vie très vite comme un mot de passe très obscène

   Intertext: "Bregantino Bregantin" (see commentary below)

4. *the motley exploded*[a] given up by *the veins of a nocturnal giantess*[b]

   le bariolage sauta[a] livré par *les veines d'une géante nocturne*[b]

   Intertext: Revelation 16:18
   And there were voices, and thunders, and lightnings; and *there was great earthquake,*[a] such as was not since men were upon *the earth,*[b] so mighty an earthquake, and so great.

5. o *the house built upon rock*

ô *la maison bâtie sur roc*

Intertext: St. Matthew 7:24–27
Therefore whosoever heareth these sayings of mine, and doeth them, I will liken him unto *a wise man, which built his house upon a rock* . . .

6. *the woman ice cube of the bed*[a] *catastrophe*[b] / *lost*[c] like a needle in a haystack

la femme glaçon du lit[a] *la catastrophe*[b] / *perdue*[c] comme une aiguille dans une botte de foin

Intertext: Revelation 16:19–20
and *the cities of the nations fell*[b]: and *great Babylon*[a] came in remembrance before God . . . And every island fled away, and the mountains *were not found.*[c]

7. *an onyx rain fell*[a] and broken seals upon a hillock *whose / name has never been spoken by any priest of any religion*[b] and *whose / effect*[c] can only be compared to the whiplashes of a star / on the rump of a planet

une pluie d'onyx tomba[a] et de sceaux brisés sur un monticule *dont / aucun prêtre d'aucune religion n'a jamais cité le nom*[b] et *dont / l'effet*[c] ne peut se comparer qu'aux coups de fouet d'une étoile / sur la croupe d'une planète

Intertext: Revelation 16:21
And *there fell* upon men *a great hail*[a] out of heaven, *every stone*[a] about the weight of a talent: and men *blasphemed God*[b] because of the plague of the hail; for *the plague thereof was exceeding great.*[c]

8. on the left abandoning the stars to arrange the "vever" of their / numbers *the clouds*[a] to anchor in no sea their reefs *the black heart*[b] / huddled in the heart of the storm. . .

sur la gauche délaissant les étoiles disposer le vever de leurs / nombres *les nuages*[a] ancrer dans nulle mer leurs récifs *le coeur noir*[b] / blotti dans le coeur de l'orage. . .

Intertext: Revelation 14:14
And I looked, and behold *a white cloud,*[a] and upon *the cloud*[a]
one sat like unto *the Son of man,*[b] having on his head a golden
crown, and in his hand a sharp sickle.

9. *we founded*[a] upon tomorrow with in our pockets the *very
violent / knife-stab of the sun*[b] in the back of *the surprised
cities*[c]

nous fondîmes[a] sur demain avec dans nos poches le *coup de
couteau / très violent / du soleil*[b] dans le dos *des villes surprises*[c]

Intertext: Revelation 18:5, 18, 8
And upon her forehead was a name written, MYSTERY,
BABYLON THE GREAT, THE MOTHER OF HARLOTS[c]
AND ABOMINATIONS OF THE EARTH. / And the woman
which thou sawest is *that great city,*[c] which reigneth over *the
kings of the earth.*[a] / . . . and *she shall be utterly burned with
fire*[b]: for *strong is the Lord God*[b] who judgeth her.

The marking of words and syntactic units in Césaire's poem
and in the corresponding texts of Revelation shows quite a remarkable parallelism in narrative sequence, a feature that testifies to the use of Revelation as the dominant narrative cover of
this automatic text. When one considers as well just how many
precise details can be traced from the opening lines of "The Sun's
Knife-Stab" to Revelation 13:1–3, (five shared *topoi* in three lines
strains any belief in chance), one is certainly justified in concluding that Césaire's poetics, however surrealist from a stylistic standpoint, derive from a concerted and consistent will, not from some
naïvely conceived dictation of the unconscious. The reader of
"The Sun's Knife-Stab" is rapidly caught up in the context and
mood of apocalyptic discourse.

All that is actually required of the reader—assuming some
familiarity with surrealist poetic practice—is the recognition of a
prophetic or apocalyptic design and its typical narrative sequence.
This will suffice for a satisfying reading of the poem. It is entirely
fortuitous that "The Sun's Knife-Stab" also corresponds so closely
in detail to Revelation 13–18. The formal requirements of the
automatism effect as these have been described by Riffaterre and
Jenny are met without recourse to the more learned operation of

identification of a specific intertext in one part of the book of
Revelation. A systematic analysis of the formal relations pertain-
ing within the poem succeeds in placing it with reference to an
established branch of modernist poetry—the automatism of the
surrealists. An interpretation of these findings will further reveal
the poem's relation to Césaire's conception of negritude in 1948.

The Prophet as Antichrist

In "The Sun's Knife-Stab in the Back of the Surprised Cities"
the first animal of the vision "had a crocodile body equine feet
the head of a dog." This appears to be a monstrous beast belonging to no single family of animals, the creature of nightmare
and of the cultural nightmare we call apocalypse. But Césaire
has given the reader cause to consider that there may be a real,
social formation of Antillean monstrosity, while remaining well
within the diction and stylistic devices of Revelation. The first
strophe quoted above contains a principle of transformation that
the prophetic speaker reveals: "But when I looked more closely
in place of the buboes there were scars left at different times by
storms on a body long subjected to obscure trials. . ." It is the
closer look of the speaker himself that reveals the truth of the
monster and not, as in Revelation, a transcendent allegorical sign.
Put another way, the monstrosity of the phenomenal beast, its
otherness, results from an uncomprehending gaze. Therefore its
truth is presented as immanent, within the scope of human
activity.

The poem is so constructed that the prophetic voice of the
second strophe can speak forcefully only after the preliminary
movement of empathetic comprehension has been realized. A
further qualification of the first beast ties the truth of the poem
more closely to the Caribbean islands and to Martinique, whose
principal city, Saint Pierre, was never fully rebuilt after the great
eruption of Mt. Pelée in 1902. From p. 31 (my italics), "It had I
have said the head of the *mangy dogs* that are seen prowling
around the volcanoes in the cities that men have not dared re-
build and that the souls of the departed haunt" (sa tête je l'ai dit
était des *chiens pelés* que l'on voit rôder autour des volcans dans
les villes que les hommes n'ont pas osé rebâtir et que hantent éternellement les âmes des trépassés"). Already at this point the

reader begins to understand that the monsters are being presented sympathetically, unlike the beasts of Revelation, which as agents of the Evil One, the dragon, are incarnations of evil. This negative hermeneutic principle extends to the entire poem, which then becomes an antiapocalypse—the apocalypse of negritude.

The second of the three beasts (see strophe number 2) is identi- fied only by allusion: "and I saw a second animal / it was lying beneath a dragon tree [*dragonnier* or dracaena] from both sides of / its musk-deer muzzle / two rostra with inflamed pulp stood out like mustachios." This metaphoric synthesis, or fusing, of the plant and animal kingdoms is typical of Césaire's representation of Martinican, or more generally, of human reality. There is an interpenetration of human experience by both, which one might relate to the correspondences of Baudelaire's celebrated sonnet, on the condition that they be seen as horizontal and immanent rather than vertical and transcendent. The intertextual herme- neutic supplied by Revelation once again obliges the reader to take note of Césaire's resolute treatment of the spirit as being in and of this world. The revelation of Saint John the Divine presents the dragon as the incarnation of "that old serpent, called the Devil, and Satan, which deceiveth the whole world" (12:9) and, in 13:11, as a horned beast. There is nothing otherworldly about Césaire's dragon, which is at once musk deer and dracaena. The dracaena, when cut, oozes a reddish liquid called dragon's blood in French. This is suggested by the inflamed pulp of the two rostra, the botanical equivalent of beaks or horns. The rostra themselves are replicated, by another metonymic displacement, as mustachios.

The third beast in Césaire's vision (strophe 3) has in common with the biblical apocalypse only the features provided by the narrative cover established earlier: "I saw a third animal which was an earthworm but a / strange will animated the beast with a long narrowness and it stretched /out on the ground losing and growing anew rings that one / would never have thought it strong enough to carry and which pushed / life back and forth among them very fast like a very obscene password." Clearly the connotation of the strophe is positive. Those attributes that the dominant value system takes to be disgusting, obscene, or simply ugly are accepted by the speaker and transmuted positively. But in another sense this inversion of values strikes the reader as

biblical too: it is written that the last shall be first and that the
meek—the worms—shall inherit the earth.

In the Afro-Cuban tale "Bregantino Bregantin," collected by
Lydia Cabrera and introduced with great enthusiasm by Césaire
in *Tropiques* (February 1944), a worm does in fact inherit a
kingdom and marry the beautiful princess before disappearing
underground. In his introduction Césaire had stressed the tragic,
Oedipal qualities of the tale. This reading locates the Afro-Cuban
model as an intrusion in Césaire's poem, or more properly, as a
second intertext superimposed on the model of Revelation and
extending it. One should not conclude from this observation that
Césaire's poem is either less good in the more traditional sense
of coherence or less automatic, in the sense described by Riffaterre
and Jenny. It is more appropriate to see in the multiple resonance
of Césaire's intertextual play another characteristic of his poetics
in the late forties. Césairean negritude, in order to realize itself
as a positive value system, must pass through a dialectic of opposites, as the chapters on *Miraculous Weapons* and *Notebook
of a Return to the Native Land* have already demonstrated. In the
first half of "The Sun's Knife-Stab" the monstrous animals are
necessary to the moment of recognition and understanding that
will permit the speaker to prophesy truly. As I have indicated
earlier, a closer scrutiny shows the first monster to be a creature
whose suffering is understandable and presumably mutable. The
second monster remains monstrous only until one recognizes in
it the embodiment of the marvelous natural synthesis common
to much surrealist writing. The third monster possesses an obscure and unexpected strength that renders it strangely vital.

At this point in the poem a full stop and a new strophe inter-
rupt the vision, which is followed by the prophetic utterance.
The biblical resonance is maintained by several images, including
the *"catastrophe* lost like a needle in a haystack" (passage 6),
which sustains the eschatological and apocalyptic framework,
and "o the house built upon rock" (passage 5), which unmistak-
ably represents the foundations of tomorrow's society ("we
founded upon tomorrow. . .") in terms of Christ's parable in St.
Matthew 7:24–27. Finally (passage 7) the poem as a whole makes
its claim for prophetic utterance: "an onyx rain fell and broken
seals upon a hillock whose / name has never been spoken by any
priest of any religion and whose / effect can only be compared to

the whiplashes of a star / on the rump of a planet." The strong
spiritual sense of the passage is, however, insistent in its denial
of a transcendent god. The divinity that liberated or gave up
(*livré*) the motley phenomenal world to its fate (passage 4) is in
fact named, although in the fashion peculiar to surrealism. The
chthonic goddess, or nocturnal giantess (passage 4), shifts the
focus well away from the God of the Christians to a modernist,
and immanent, version of the Great Mother, whom Césaire
venerates now as surrealist woman, now as Omphale, and here
as the archaic female divinity of the underworld. The whole
strophe (passage 8) progressively assumes a cosmic dimension
that nonetheless leaves room for the *merveilleux quotidien* dear
to surrealism. The perfectly matter-of-fact "on the left" removes
all possibility of the otherworldly or, as Nietzsche would say,
of the afterworldly, from one's interpretation. The lightness
of the touch approaches Supervielle's deft handling of cosmic
imagery in *Gravitations* or in *The Fable of the World (La Fable
du monde).*

"Vever," the mandala of voodoo, introduces a strictly Caribbean and Creole element that further specifies the nature of this
faith both geographically and, I am tempted to say, spiritually as
well, while maintaining the magical numbers of Revelation.
Césaire has gradually come to recognize in the voodoo cult the
embodiment of the values of negritude in their popular manifestation. It is a synchretic system in which diverse and half-
remembered divinities and beliefs of widely separate African
provenance have come to an easy but heterodox cohabitation with
Christianity. Thus St. Patrick banishing the snakes becomes the
voodo *loa* (spirit) Damballa-wèdo, himself represented by the
serpent; St. James the Great, shown on a charging steed, is considered in voodoo to be the warrior *loa* Ogun.[6] Voodoo has in
effect appropriated those aspects of Christianity that it could use
without regard to any theological or ritual purity. The example
is useful to the reader of Césaire's surrealist poetry because he
too has appropriated aspects of the dominant Christian culture
that are common to all Martinicans, as they are common to all
those raised in other Christian societies. But Césaire has transformed the images and the religious texts, setting them like
precious stones in a new design of his own, just as voodoo has
done with Christian iconography. The final associative metaphor

of "The Sun's Knife-Stab" sums up in its dynamic density this prophetic aspect of Césairean negritude: "we founded upon to-morrow with in our pockets the very violent / knife-stab of the sun in the back of the surprised cities." Cities are generally seen by Césaire as corrupt, venal, and worthy of destruction; the Sodom and Gomorrah strophe in "The Thoroughbreds" proceeds from the same attitude. On this one point the negative herme-neutic I have outlined above does not work; Césaire and Revela-tion are in complete agreement here. In the same vein "the woman ice cube of the bed" (passage 6) replicates both the narrative function and the negative connotation of the whore of Babylon in Revelation 16:19 and 17:5. But rather than a metaphysical evil, Césaire identifies a social evil, and his prophecy envisages a social rather than a metaphysical cataclysm. It is especially important to recognize how systematically, in all other respects, Césaire has emptied the transcendent, allegorical narrative of the poem of its original hermeneutic principle. We find the black heart of negritude (passage 8) taking the place of the Son of Man, and the natural symbolism of the sun (passage 9) displaces the super-natural agency of the Lord God. Rather in the manner of Nietz-sche's celebrated alter ego, Césaire's prophetic speaker in "The Sun's Knife-Stab" takes upon himself the mantle of the Anti-christ.

This reading of the poem bears on the recurrent problem in the interpretation of Césaire's powerful prophetic voice. In one view Césaire as the heir to an African cultural tradition had a mysterious and direct access to the Logos or Nommo of African prophetic utterance. At a much higher level of critical reflection Bernadette Cailler has taken into account both the sophisticated use of surrealist syntax and metaphoric structure in Césaire's poetry and the parallels between his poetic cosmology and the world view of the Dogon people, as Marcel Griaule related it in his book *Dieu d'eau* (1948). Cailler realized, of course, that by 1948 Césaire's own reference points—however he arrived at them—were already well established. He had already published two major collections of poetry and the *Notebook*. Her con-clusion on this point is, however, fascinating and symptomatic:

> In the Judeo-Christian tradition it is said that "In the be-ginning was the Word, and the Word was with God, and

the Word was God." At first glance the Logos of St. John
and African *Nommo* are identical, one and the same drop
of water. But in St. John we are reminded that it is in-
cumbent upon man to proclaim and testify to the divine
word. On the contrary, the freedom, the total autonomy
of *Nommo* and its power of permanent creation know no
limits . . .[7]

If one restricted oneself to a thematic reading of Cailler's conclusion, then it would be a simple matter to assimilate Césaire's
poetic discourse to such a spiritual principle. Surely he invites us
to do so. If, on the other hand, one focuses sharply on the literary
means used to achieve his effects, then Césaire's prophetic utterance is revealed as being anything but totally autonomous. His
prophetic voice is heir to a cultural tradition, to be sure; but the
literary tradition from which it springs is French and European.
When Césaire adopts an apocalyptic posture in his poetry, it is
the narrative sequence of Revelation that dominates his automatic
poem. The fact that he frequently reverses the values assigned
to events and symbols in the Christian Revelation in no way less-
ens his dependence on it as a necessary intertext.

"The Sun's Knife-Stab" exemplifies what Césaire had in mind
when he recommended, in his epistle to René Depestre, that the
black Caribbean poet should *marronner* the forms and values of
European literature. The analysis of the precise nature and function of automatism in this one poem from the original edition of
Beheaded Sun demonstrates that Césaire's practice of automatic
writing was consubstantial with his concept of negritude in the
forties and that it added to automatic writing a dimension that
does not necessarily appear in the work of the European surrealists. If, as Riffaterre and Jenny have argued, the comprehension of the European surrealists' automatism effect depends
on the recognition of the narrative sequence in its hidden intertext, then the comprehension of Césaire's automatism effect requires the further recognition of a synchretic intention. This
definition, which I have arrived at inductively, can be applied as
a test to other poems written in the same style. Those that meet
the first test but not the second—for instance, "When in the Heat
of the Day Naked Monks Descend the Himalayas" ("A l'heure
où dans la chaleur les moines nus descendent de l'Himalaya")—

can be judged derivative copies of the European style. Those poems that, like "The Sun's Knife-Stab," meet both tests can be considered to belong to the automatism of negritude as Césaire was in the process of elaborating it throughout the forties.

A Political Pseudoprophecy

The uniqueness of "The Sun's Knife-Stab" is even more apparent when compared with another poem in the same collection. "Tornado" shares with it the thematic emphasis on a natural cataclysm serving to purify a corrupt city. Both poems likewise declare a prophetic intention. In all stylistic respects, however, they are as different as they can be. "Tornado," from which Césaire merely omitted ten lines and one brief expression in editing it for *Cadastre,* develops a broadly satirical pattern that was even more flagrant in the text of *Beheaded Sun.* Most notably, "Tornado" is in no way related to the formal characteristics of the automatism effect. It displays few surrealist associative metaphors, and reading it requires no familiarity with modern poetry. It is, in short, a highly accessible poem with an obvious political thrust:

> The time it took for
>   the senator to notice the tornado
>   sitting
>   in his plate
>   [on his great sugar beet butt
>   and the sausage rounds of his thighs
>   viciously crossed]
> and the tornado was in the air rampaging through Kansas
>   City

> Le temps que
>   le sénateur s'aperçut que la tornade était assise
>   dans son assiette
>   sur ses grosses fesses de betterave
>   et les rondelles de saucisson de ses cuisses
>   vicieusement croisées
> et la tornade était dans l'air fourrageant dans Kansas-City[8]

In quite programmatic fashion the tornado creates "a brother-hood of black and white blotches tossed / about as cadavers on the hide of a horse shot down in full stride" ("une fraternité de taches blanches et noires répandues / en cadavres sur la peau d'un cheval abattu en plein galop"). The anticlericalism of the poem mingles with antiracism in the lines:

> and over everything the tornado performed a dainty laying
> on of hands its beautiful white clergyman's hands
> Time for God to realize
> > he's had a bit too much with those last
> > hundred glasses of torturer's blood

> et la tornade fit sur tout une jolie imposition de mains de
> ses belles mains blanches d'ecclésiastique
> Le temps pour Dieu de s'apercevoir
> > qu'il avait bu de trop cent verres de sang de
> > bourreau

The representatives of official religion and morality are of course hypocritical lechers:

> The time it took for
> > the pastor to notice the tornado in the blue
> > eyes of the sheriff's wife

> Le temps que
> > le pasteur aperçut la tornade dans l'oeil
> > bleu de la femme du shériff

And in a passage that Césaire prudishly cut from the new edition, commercial sex comes in for its share of raillery (the English translation is from p. 48 of the Kraus Reprint edition):

> the time it took for the tornado to bust out laughing in the
> sex of a whore.

> le temps pour la tornade de s'esclaffer de rire dans le sexe
> d'une putain

The element of prophecy is introduced in conclusion by way of a negation of all traditional religious prophecy:

> And the tornado which had swallowed its herd of roofs and chimneys like a swarm of frogs breathed out a dinning thought the prophets had never foretold

> Et la tornade qui avait avalé comme un vol de grenouilles son troupeau de toitures et de cheminées respira bruyamment une pensée que les prophètes n'avaient jamais su deviner

It is evident from the passages quoted that this poem is related to prophecy only insofar as Marxism has a politically prophetic function. "Tornado" is a political satire of a particularly simple, one-dimensional type. It declares its allegiance to the anti-Yankee posture of the Marxist left toward the beginning of the Cold War. Thematically it is akin to Sartre's antiracist play *The Respectful Prostitute* (1946), except that Sartre does give his whore a positive, albeit melodramatic, function. Stylistically it is related as well to much of Bertolt Brecht's poetry of socialist realism. Hannah Arendt's judgment of Brecht's style in "The Burial of the Agitator in A Zinc Coffin" or in "The Jew, a Misfortune for the People" is directly applicable to Césaire's effort in "Tornado": "Every time Brecht wanted to create a direct political effect he fumbled. He could never break through the boundaries within which a poet is constrained, despite all his political-aesthetic argumentation."[9]

For the same reasons, I think, "Tornado" is not good poetry, although Césaire has written good poems with a political thrust. The question to be raised here is: Why did Césaire retain "Tornado" in *Cadastre* and in his collected works, whereas "The Sun's Knife-Stab" has long since disappeared from the authorized canon? Any attempt to answer the question will necessarily be speculative, but the chapter on "Politics and Poetics" does provide some grounds for reasonable conjecture. *Cadastre* was published in the early sixties, when the African independence movements were beginning to show results. Césaire has often mentioned his desire at that time to express himself in a more accessible way so as to be read by, or otherwise communicate with, a wider audience. This desire is said to have led to his decision to write for the theater, and throughout the sixties it appeared that Césaire had abandoned poetry. *The Tragedy of King Christophe (La Tragédie du roi Christophe)* is a poetic play at the same time that it is very theatrical. *A Season in the Congo (Une Saison au Congo)* is a very political play and, perhaps for that very reason, has had a smaller following in Europe and North America. During the sixties Césaire became more of a political leader, if not a politician, with responsibility for an autonomous party that was seriously at odds with the local communists, his former patrons. All of these are ideological considerations that probably weighed in Césaire's editing of *Beheaded Sun*. In too many cases the decisions taken were not felicitous. I have intentionally juxtaposed a pseudoprophecy of no real depth, "Tornado," with the richly resonant "The Sun's Knife-Stab" in order to demonstrate that the political man was not always a good critic of the poet. This analysis of Césaire's editing of *Beheaded Sun* is intended to counter the widespread conviction that Césaire's surrealist practice in poetry was some sort of youthful aberration cured by age and maturity. The question of Césaire's surrealism cannot finally be separated from the broader question of his political and ideological evolution. An eventual critical edition of *Beheaded Sun* could go far toward accounting, in a way this study cannot pretend to do, for the multiplicity of voices and styles present in this collection from the first.

Visions of Mutilation

An overview of the original edition of *Beheaded Sun* suggests the outline of a spiritual quest; in this regard it prolongs *Miraculous Weapons*. But the second collection is much more insistent in its effort to establish a bestiary and a network of animistic forces to support the speaker. The nature of the monster in "The Sun's Knife-Stab" testifies to this intention. A thematic anti-Catholicism becomes troublesome at times, and Césaire excised from the text of *Cadastre* some of the poems in which it could not otherwise be muted or transformed. In the forties Césaire's bitterness against the representatives of the Catholic church was prompted and reinforced by their ultraconservative position in supporting first the repressive regime of Admiral Robert in Martinique during the war and then the return to colonial domination during the postwar period. In a poem like "Tornado" the operative assumption is that Protestant moralism is a feature of the North American version of neocolonialist, racist oppression. In many of these poems—"When in the Heat of the Day Naked Monks Descend the Himalayas" is a prime example—a certain gratuitousness pervades the imagery, and the poem never advances beyond a reiterative binary opposition. Césaire chose wisely in such cases when he removed these poems from the new edition of *Beheaded Sun*.

"Lynch I," the third poem in the original edition of the collection, is interesting because it was a successful poem of a type already used in *Miraculous Weapons*, yet it too was omitted from the revised edition. "Lynch I" calls to mind Césaire's early admiration for Lautréamont while setting the tone for a significant part of the original *Beheaded Sun*. Its basic structure is quite simple. An ironic version of spring's awakening is expressed in the question: "Why does spring go for my throat? what does it want of me?" ("Pourquoi le printemps me prend-il à la gorge? que me veut-il?")[10] There follow three affirmations that set the narrative against the images of malevolent violence attributed to spring. Without any transition *lynch* appears in the poem as the subject of a long series, or litany, of *métaphores filées*, in which, by metonymy, *lynch* condenses the violence inherent in *spring* at the outset. The last of the associative metaphors is extended into one of those epiphanic transformations discussed in the chapter on *Miraculous Weapons*. A detailed examination of the poem's development further reveals important aspects of the persona of the speaker in *Beheaded Sun*.

In "Lynch I" Césaire's poetic style so thoroughly avoids any thematic statement about the horrors of lynch law that no immediately apparent connection exists. The speaker at first objectifies lynching through metaphors of violence that continue the initial motif of spring as an enemy:

> Lynch is six o'clock in the evening in the mud of bayous
> it's a black handkerchief waving from the mainmast of a
> pirate ship it's the point of strangulation of the carmine
> fingernail of an interjection . . .

> Le lynch c'est six heures du soir dans la boue des bayous
> c'est le mouchoir noir agité au haut du mât d'un bateau
> pirate c'est le point de strangulation de l'ongle au carmin
> d'une interjection.

But a principle of fascination is at work within the poem. The same sentence concludes on a different note: "It's the pampa it's the queen's ballet it's the sagacity of science it's the unforgettable coitus" ("c'est la pampa c'est le ballet de la reine c'est la sagacité de la science c'est le coït inoubliable"). A transitional interjection follows immediately—"O lynch mercury salts and antinomy!" ("O lynch sel mercure et antimoine!")—after which a long sentence gradually draws the speaker into a strange identification with the monstrous act itself:

> Lynch is the blue smile of a dragon enemy of angels lynch
> is an orchid too beautiful to bear fruit lynch is an entry
> into matter[11] lynch is the hand of the wind bloodying a
> forest whose trees are galls that brandish in their hands the
> living torch of their castrated phallus . . .

> Le lynch est le sourire bleu d'un dragon ennemi des anges
> le lynch est une orchidée trop belle pour porter de fruits
> le lynch est une entrée en matière le lynch c'est la main du
> vent ensanglantant une forêt dont les arbres sont des galles
> qui brandissent dans leur main le flambeau de leur phallus
> châtré . . .

The succession of metaphors becomes deliriously involved in itself, oblivious, it would seem, to the contradiction of "living torch . . . castrated phallus." Note too the intertextual resonance of "a dragon enemy of angels," which, as in several other poems in *Beheaded Sun*, establishes the context of an apocalyptic revelation that cuts across and through the entire collection.

At this juncture the reader must readjust his expectation. Already at the outset spring was represented as a one-eyed creature. The final sentence of the poem reconciles the speaker with lynch, which through reiteration has taken on a kind of personification: "O lynch loveable companion beautiful spurted eye" ("O lynch aimable compagnon bel oeil giclé"). The central image has been transformed into one of castration or phallic mutilation. Such satellite images as "the unforgettable coitus" or the "too beautiful orchid" begin to gravitate around the physiological reaction of the hanged man: spontaneous ejaculation coinciding with death. But just as in one version of the legend of the mandrake plant the root grows from the sperm of a hanged man, so in Césaire's poem the islands will be reborn, whole and beautiful, from the speaker's sacrifice. The conclusion is sufficiently startling that it should be reproduced without cuts:

> O lynch loveable companion beautiful spurted eye broad mouth mute save that a jolt spill upon it the delirium of a snot, lightning, weave well on your loom a continent that will burst into islands an oracle that will slide in contortions in scolopendra a moon that will install on the breach the sulfurous peacock that will arise in the summary loophole of my assassinated hearing.

> O lynch aimable compagnon bel oeil giclé large bouche muette hormis qu'un branle y répand le délire d'une morve tisse bien, éclair, sur ton métier un continent qui éclate en îles un oracle qui glisse en contorsion en scolopendre une lune qui installe sur la brèche le paon de soufre qui se lève dans la meurtrière sommaire de mon ouïe assassinée.

The strangeness of the poem will not be explained away. Exegesis succeeds only in justifying this curious poetic proposition metaphorically. The intertextuality of Revelation further confers on the poem that verisimilitude that a coherent reading requires. It is also important to recognize in "Lynch I" the direction or general movement of Césaire's poetry throughout the forties. This poem, for all its startling effects, is also paradigmatic in the same way that "The Sun's Knife-Stab" is. In the face of awful, horrible threats Césaire's poetic persona does not typically set out to vanquish the enemy. Neither does he passively submit. He transmutes the deadly, mutilating malevolence (here a social evil represented as a natural force) but at the cost of his own life. As in "And the Dogs Were Silent," a heroic figure sacrifices himself for a future, better world.[12] The transmutation of evil into good is conceived as a spiritual, even a mystical operation. To speak of a Christ-figure here would be to betray Césaire. Certainly he envisioned the heroic figure of negritude in terms of a sacrificial offering; but the Christian example is the one he felt most obliged to resist. Indeed, the representation of the lynched man (in the place of the Crucified One) with its attendant imagery of gross sexuality would scarcely seem fitting to the Christian. In fact, once the parallels have been pointed out, it appears that the Christian is most likely to recoil from what he perceives as blasphemous. Perhaps what Césaire objected to in this poem, seen in retrospect, was the possible imputation of blasphemy. Not that Césaire would have been especially impressed by the reaction of the church. More likely he chose to condemn this poem, along with several others, precisely because blasphemy proclaims its own dependence on its object. In this regard one might reasonably but paradoxically conclude that "Lynch I" is a culturally Catholic poem.

The homology within the poem of one-eyed creature, phallic mutilation, and mystical recreation amply justifies and explains the title of the collection. The violence of *Beheaded Sun* is posited on the necessity of a ritual self-sacrifice as the ultimate realization of Césaire's personal solar myth. This aspect of the sun god places Césaire at a considerable remove from the macho phallocrat he is sometimes presented as being. The male principle in Césaire's world may finally sow the seed of renewal, but it is a sublimated, sacrificial triumph that bears little resemblance to vulgar machismo. The manifestations of the sun must pass through an agonistic, tragic action in order to attain wholeness, purity, and creative potency. In short, Césaire's message in many of the best poems in *Beheaded Sun* is largely eschatological. The hero, the god, must die that the community may live; but the entire natural world is subject to the same cycle of death and rebirth in this poetry. Cataclysmic events announce not the new Jerusalem but the new Africa. The mutilation of the hero leads ultimately to an apocalyptic vision.[13]

The *topos* of monstrosity, which Bernadette Cailler has treated in some detail, was quite pronounced in the original edition of *Beheaded Sun*. Her analysis, which relies more on anthropological texts and does not consider the biblical Revelation, can nonetheless be read as a useful complement to my own commentary on "The Sun's Knife-Stab." Cailler sees a dialectic of monster and antimonster as the underlying structure of these poems, whereas I have chosen to show the Césairean Antichrist in opposition to the Christian savior. The differences in our findings are largely attributable to our respective lines of approach. Hers has the advantage of indicating a pervasive binary structure that recurs in many of Césaire's poems, whether or not the *topos* of monstrosity is present: "On the side of the monster are the centipede, the dog, the crow, the hyena; on the side of the anti-monster are the bird, the spring, the tree, the firefly, the dawn, the thoroughbred."[14] On the other hand, the structuralist approach taken by Cailler can lead to a static rigidity that distorts the dynamics of a given poem. In "The Sun's Knife-Stab," for instance, the canine aspect of the first vision is clearly monstrous but mutable, and in my view it is the mutability of the dog's monstrosity that is primary, fundamental. The genius of Césaire's visionary poetry is to present monstrosity not as a metaphysical given but as a construct, the result of society's conditioning of our understanding. His use of the automatism effect justifies itself if it can recondition the reader's understanding to see in this monster a future antimonster. In his best poems of this type Césaire has transcended rigid opposition in the direction of future change conceived as the result of a better understanding of human reality in conditions of social oppression. Cailler is aware of the problem raised by Césaire's apparent binary oppositions and is quick to reject the facile interpretation that all white = ugly = monstrous and that all black = beautiful = antimonstrous: "The reversal of symbols and values in Césaire's work, when it occurs, if it is a negation of the 'Western' world view, is not a miraculous resurgence of an African cultural vision" (p. 128). Pointing out that this kind of dichotomy is itself the product of white racism, Cailler cites to excellent advantage Victor Turner's study of the symbolism of colors in Ndembu ritual (*The Forest of Symbols,* Cornell, 1967), concluding that beneath the contradictions of the phenomenal world may reside the fundamental unity of the real. This conclusion is entirely in keeping with Césaire's conception of the mythic dimension of human experience from the time of *Miraculous Weapons* through the publication of the original *Beheaded Sun.*

To Africa

Poems with an African motif make up a small part of the 1961 edition of *Beheaded Sun;* in the 1948 edition they were less important still in the overall design. Moreover, with a few exceptions, the African poems continued to express an imaginary and intensely subjective vision. "To Africa" ("A l'Afrique") is a fascinating poem to examine in its three versions, since it reveals as well as any the direction of the changes in Césaire's poetics from 1946 to 1961. "To Africa" was first printed in the Parisian magazine of wartime and postwar poetry, *Poésie 46,* for June–July 1946. It is contemporaneous with the poems of *Miraculous Weapons,* having been written at a time when black Africa was still as thoroughly colonized as Martinique itself. The text of the 1946 printing is in many respects close to the one printed in the original *Beheaded Sun.* A few telling changes are worthy of mention, however. In the magazine printing of "To Africa" the poem opened with a strophe of twenty lines of dense associative metaphors highly charged with surrealist eroticism and visionary synthesis. The strophe did not in fact have much to do with the rest of the text, and by 1948 Césaire had dropped it from *Beheaded Sun.* But in 1971 it turned up, with no indication of its prior existence, as a new poem in the revised edition of *Miraculous Weapons.* Freshly entitled "Prophecy," the poem had been laid out so that each syntactic repetition ("là où" / "là où" or "*d'avoir* injurié . . ." / "*d'avoir* gémi") constituted a separate line. Otherwise the only changes are the addition of an adjective, *prophetic* ("prophétiques"), and the exclusion of the coordinating conjunction *but* ("mais"). The result is a good poem entirely in keeping with the tenor of *Miraculous Weapons,* in which a contemplative speaker bears witness to a surreal transformation of his Caribbean seascape:

> and I watch it melting into britannic isles into islets
> into torn up rocks melting little by little into the sea
> lucid with air
> where bathe prophetic
> my mug
> my revolt
> my name

> et je la regarde en îles britanniques en îlots en rochers
> déchiquetés se fondre peu à peu dans la mer lucide de l'air
> où baignent prophétiques
> ma gueule
> ma révolte
> mon nom.[15]

By removing this introductory strophe not only from the poem "To Africa" but also to a collection where its Caribbean resonance was more appropriate, Césaire profoundly modified the reader's sense of both texts.

The three extant versions of "To Africa" bear the same dedication to Wifredo Lam. It is a small indication, to be sure, but by no means an insignificant one that the African poem should be dedicated to a fellow Caribbean artist and a fellow surrealist, the Afro-Chinese Cuban painter whom Césaire had met in Martinique during the war. The dedication, like the text of the poem, orients the reader toward the imaginary synchretic Africa of Lam's and Césaire's art in 1946. The only authentically African element in the poem is the single word *daba* in the phrase "Peasant strike the soil with the *daba*" ("Paysan frappe le sol de ta daba"), which punctuates the poem at irregular intervals. Within the total context this lexical item represents little more than a thematic intention.

Once Césaire had removed the extraneous first strophe, the poem "To Africa" was readily identifiable as belonging to the apocalyptic or eschatological type so common in *Beheaded Sun*. It has a loosely narrative structure evoking the final trials of a civilization. Its four plagues correspond in their narrative structure to the seven plagues of Revelation 16, and the two blasphemous strophes of the 1946–1948 text correspond closely to Revelation 16:5–9 (from p. 74 of the Kraus Reprint edition):

> and I shit upon those who do not understand that it is not
>   beautiful
> to praise the eternal and to celebrate thy name o Most High
> for thou hast neither the shining strength of the water buf-
>   falo nor the mathematical science of the ibis nor the
>   patience of the black

and the dung that thou rollest with less dexterity than the
scarab yields in luxury to the words knotted beneath my
tongue

et j'emmerde ceux qui ne comprennent pas qu'il n'est pas
beau
de louer l'éternel et de célébrer ton nom ô Très-Haut
car tu n'as ni la force luisante du buffle ni la science mathé-
matique de l'ibis ni la patience du nègre
et la bouse de vache que tu roules avec moins d'adresse
que le
scarabée le cède en luxe aux mots noués sous ma langue

This is the Césairean antithesis of the passage in Revelation 16:9
that reads:

And men were scorched with great heat, and blasphemed
the name of God, which hath power over these plagues: and
they repented not to give him glory.

In Césaire's poem (p. 73 of the Kraus Reprint) as in Revelation
the analogous narrative sequence occurs during the fourth plague:
"On the fourth day the vegetation wilted / and all turned bitter
from the agave to the acacia" ("le quatrième jour la végétation
se fana / et tout tourna à l'aigre de l'agave à l'acacia").
    Furthermore, the speaker in "To Africa" adopts the same ag-
gressively subjective attitude as the Antichrist figure in "The Sun's
Knife-Stab":

Strike peasant strike
there are born in the sky windows that are my spurted eyes

Frappe paysan frappe
il naît au ciel des fenêtres qui sont mes yeux giclés

Some crude and vulgar blasphemy was excised from "To
Africa" when it was reprinted in *Cadastre,* but this modification
should not be seen as simply a concession to taste. Two other im-

portant elements of the poem were either removed completely
or minimized. The first of these, the surrealist eroticism of the
1946–1948 text, is not unique to this poem. As I have mentioned
earlier, Césaire modified many other poems in the collection so
as to lessen their surrealist impact in this regard. One typical
modification of this type in "To Africa" will suffice to make the
point. Where in the original text (Kraus Reprint, p. 73) one
read:

> . . . I await with a vulnerary expectation a countryside to be
> born at the ears of my companion and to grow green
> on her sex
> the belly of my companion is the thunderbolt of fine
> weather
> the thighs of my companion play at being trees fallen along
> her step

> j'attends d'une attente vulnéraire une campagne qui naîtra
> aux oreilles de ma compagne et verdira à son sexe
> le ventre de ma compagne c'est le coup de tonnerre du beau
> temps
> les cuisses de ma compagne jouent les arbres tombés
> le long de sa démarche

This is not good poetry and doubtless deserves its oblivion. However, rather than improve it with a more satisfying effort in the
same vein, Césaire in 1961 replaced the strophe with a shorter one
of resounding socialist sentiment, while adhering to the established rhythms of the existing poem (from *Cadastre,* Seuil edition,
p. 40):

> Famine and groundswell of yourself
> Heap where gambles with a salvation the anger of the
> future
> strike Anger

> Famine et de toi-même houle
> ramas où se risque d'un salut la colère du futur
> frappe Colère

Granting that this is poetically an improvement, one cannot ignore that it is also, and perhaps primarily, a reorienting of the poem toward more direct ideological statement.

The second element, which Césaire removed entirely, is the chaotic use of verb tense and other temporal signifiers that characterize the 1946–1948 text. The apocalyptic narrative had, so to speak, been expressed in terms of a nowhere-nowhen (Kraus Reprint, p. 72):

> I remember the rare plague that will take place in the year
>   3000
> there had been no harbinger star
>
> . . . . .
>
> on the first day the birds will die
> on the second day the fish washed ashore
>
> je me souviens de la fameuse peste qui aura lieu en l'an 3000
> il n'y avait pas eu d'étoile annoncière
>
> . . . . .
>
> le premier jour les oiseaux mourront
> le second jour les poissons échouèrent

M. a M. Ngal is, to my knowledge, the only critic to have pointed out the importance of this grammatical chaos: "There is but one tense / time for the poet: a tense / time that is called eschatological, the mythical dimension of time. The characteristic of this conception is to abolish the notion of history, since the poet moves in an eschatological eternal present: the ancestor-heroes lived once and for all the perfect model of the tense / time of every Black in the world."[16] By 1961 Césaire had abandoned this mythic model of human experience, and his revised text of "To Africa" carefully restored to history what had previously been ascribed to myth. The future tense was replaced by the historical past of the preterite and the adverbial expression "in the year 3000" discreetly disappeared into the poet's desk drawer.

Readers of the 1961 edition of *Cadastre* might mistake the poem "Ode to Guinea" ("Ode à la Guinée") for one of those Césaire wrote to celebrate the emergence of a new African nation. Guinea became independent in 1958, and Césaire did in fact celebrate its

independence in the poem "Salute to Guinea" ("Salut à la
Guinée") in *Ferrements* (1960) and in an article on "The Political
Thought of Sékou Touré," which appeared both in *Présence Africaine* and as the preface of Sékou Touré's *Expérience guinéenne et
unité africaine* (1959, 1961). "Ode to Guinea" dates from the immediate postwar period, however, and has nothing whatever to do
with the as yet nonexistent political entity that was still a colony
of France. The title has special significance. In the Caribbean
Creole tongues, and particularly in Haitian, "Guinée" is a mythical
land, the heaven to which the souls of black folk will depart after
leaving their earthly bondage. Francis Huxley glosses the term
succinctly: "Guinea, or Africa: land of origin, or the loa, of
souls."[17] This is the meaning the land of Guinea has in Césaire's
poem: the mythical homeland, the Africa to which Césaire returns
through an act of profound imagination, of poetic disalienation,
but at the cost of blocking out the real present.

The name Guinea is used toward the middle of the poem, (pp.
102–103 in the Kraus Reprint edition) for its incantatory power,
as Césaire evokes its associations for him in the natural world[18]:

> I SALUTE YOU
> Guinea whose rains smash from the gritty heights
> of volcanoes a sacrifice of cows for a thousand hungers
> and thirsts of unnatural children
> Guinea wood and plant beautiful mad and climbing
> rubbed stone where never flies a female spark
> . . . . .
> Guinea with your cry with your hand with your patience
> there always fall to us arbitrary lands
> and when killed toward Ophir they shall have me ever mute
> from my teeth from my skin be made
> a ferocious fetish guardian of the evil eye

> JE TE SALUE
> Guinée dont les pluies fracassent du haut grumeleux
> des volcans un sacrifice de vaches pour mille faims
> et soifs d'enfants dénaturés
> Guinée bois et plante belle folle et grimpante
> pierre frottée dont jamais ne jaillit une lumière femelle
> . . . . .

> Guinée de ton cri de ta main de ta patience
> il nous reste toujours des terres arbitraires
> et quand tué vers Ophir ils m'auront jamais muet
> de mes dents de ma peau que l'on fasse
> un fétiche féroce gardien du mauvais oeil

The text edited for *Cadastre* contained none of the incantatory evocations of plants, whereas the original edition contained some sixteen lines governed by this imagery. The appeal to Guinea as the blacks' final resting place was, however, reproduced without modification, as was the invocation to surrealist woman as the core metaphor of an eroticized nature. Césaire may have felt obliged to keep this part of the strophe intact because it contained both the single word connecting the poem to the geography of West Africa, *Fouta-Djallon,* and the metaphor that had provided the title of the collection *Cadastre* (Kraus Reprint, p. 101):

> and by the woman with the ill known cadastre
> . . . . .
> and by the woman's fire in which I seek the path of ferns
>   and of the Fouta Djallon

> et par la femme au cadastre mal connu
> . . . . .
> et par le feu de la femme où je cherche le chemin des
>   fougères et du Fouta-Djallon

Quite manifestly in this context the mountain range of northern Guinea, the Fouta Djallon, is to be conjured up by the same poetic magic as the ferns through the mediation of surrealist woman, man's key to the lost natural world and to the lost Africa as well. The Guinea of the "Ode to Guinea" is seen, on examination, to be the same type of poetic creation as the Africa of "To Africa."

Thus far the investigation of Césaire's Africanism in the 1948 *Beheaded Sun* has revealed a poetic exploration of that Africa of the heart discussed earlier, with surrealist devices serving as the privileged means of expression, very much in the manner of *Miraculous Weapons* although without the relatively tight structure of that collection. One might reasonably expect that a very different poetics would obtain in a poem published first in an organ of the

Communist party. This was the case of "Since Akkad Since Elam
Since Sumer" ("Depuis Akkad depuis Elam depuis Sumer"),
which appeared in the magazine *Action* for 25 April 1947. The
poem is frequently mentioned for its forceful expression of the
subjugation of blacks from the empires of the ancient Near East
to the present day (Kraus Reprint, p. 67):

> I have borne the parasol I have borne the explosives I have
> worn the iron collar and as on the shores of the Nile you
> see in the soft silt the precise foot of the ibis I have left ev-
> erywhere on the banks on the mountains on the shores the
> grigri of my cancan feet. Since Akkad. Since Elam. Since
> Sumer.

> J'ai porté le parasol j'ai porté l'explosif j'ai porté le carcan
> et comme sur les rives du Nil on voit dans la vase molle le
> pied juste de l'ibis j'ai laissé partout sur les berges sur les
> montagnes sur les rivages le grigri de mes pieds à cancans.
> Depuis Akkad. Depuis Elam. Depuis Sumer.

These are not the familiar strains of socialist realism, however,
and one may surmise that Aragon, using his ideological balance
scale, found these lines to tilt excessively in the direction of
personal expression. As elsewhere in *Beheaded Sun*, Césaire's
speaker expresses a very lyrical, personal experience, even when
he claims to speak for his race. Nonetheless there was a sufficiently
clear element of social protest in this poem for it to be translated
as a representative piece in the magazine *Black Orpheus* published in Ibadan, Nigeria, in January 1958.

When Césaire edited the poem for *Cadastre*, he cut out the
entire passage translated above, with the exception of the first and
last lines quoted. He also removed the adjective *supernaturally*
and four other lines. But even in the shortened version of 1961
the poem contains an element that throws into question the sup-
posedly historical reference of the refrain "Since Elam. Since
Akkad. Since Sumer." It is the invocation of the unnamed "Master
of the three roads," who is called upon four times in the definitive
text and five times in the original version of the poem. The speaker
addresses this mysterious master directly, and in the final long
passage he utters a supplication (p. 67):

Master of the three roads. Master of the three channels may it please you that for once—the first time since Akkad since Elam since Sumer—. . . I may move forward through the dead leaves with my little sorcerer step

Maître des trois chemins. Maître des trois rigoles plaise que pour une fois—la première depuis Akkad depuis Elam depuis Sumer—. . . j'avance à travers les feuilles mortes de mon petit pas sorcier

Who is this Master? Césaire does not say, but his poem does suggest, with its peculiar use of repetitive invocation, the spiritual or religious aura of a prayer. Identification of this Master will help to clarify an important part of the poem's imagery.

Elsewhere in the poetry there are discreet traces of Césaire's interest in voodoo, and in his play *A Tempest* the Yoruba *orisha* Eshu is made to appear, creating havoc among Shakespeare's neoclassical divinities. Eshu is one of the two names given to the loa who, in voodoo and in Brazilian macumba, opens the paths or lifts the barriers between the world of men and the world of spirits.[19] Césaire's poem is, on a literal level, about the many roads on which blacks have walked as laborers, as slaves; but understanding the invocation to Eshu opens up another dimension, that of energy or force, African principles that have survived in the New World and with which Césaire seeks to regain contact.

Alfred Métraux's study of Haitian Voodoo, *Le Vaudou haïtien,* bears out this hypothesis in all important particulars and adds this information: Legba, as Eshu is called in Haiti, is the patron of sorcerers ("my little sorcerer step") and "many magical formulas generally begin with the words: 'By power, Master-Crossroads' " (p. 89). Métraux points out that every voodoo ceremony must begin with the invocation of Legba, without whom it is impossible to communicate with Guinea. He reproduces (p. 88) both in Creole and in French one of these chants, which is invariably performed to the accompaniment of drums. An English version would give:

Atibon-Legba, open the barrier for me, Agoé!
Papa-Legba open the barrier for me
For me to pass over

When I return, I will salute the loa
Voodoo Legba, open the barrier for me
For me to return;
When I return, I will thank the loa, Abobo.

Atibon-Legba, ouvre-moi la barrière, agoé!
Papa-Legba ouvre-moi la barrière
Pour que je passe
Lorsque je retournerai, je saluerai les loa
Vaudou Legba, ouvre-moi la barrière
Pour que je rentre;
Lorsque je retournerai, je remercierai les loa, Abobo.

Seen in this light, the poem displays a high degree of tension between ancient history bordering on legend and the mythic realm
of contemporary black experience in the Caribbean opened up to
Césaire by voodoo. The refrain of the title sets up a dialogue in
the poem with the invocation of the "Master of three roads," who
is finally asked for help so that the speaker "may move forward
. . . with [his] little sorcerer feet." As one's experience of this poem
deepens, it recedes ever farther from the clear day of historical
writing to rejoin other poems in *Beheaded Sun* that, in different
ways, attempted to recreate the aura of a living, spiritual presence
that the poet could finally identify with Africa.

One's overall impression on comparing the editions of *Beheaded Sun* is that at the time when real change was taking place
in the colonized world, at the end of the fifties and the beginning
of the sixties, the anarchistic posture of many of the original texts
seemed to the poet out of place and inopportune. No longer was
it enough for a logocentric poet to promise a Rimbaldian change
in mankind; the Marxian injunction to first change the world took
precedence.

8

Lost Body

And yet what have you left from ancient times

. . . . .

Closed wizard's book forgotten words
I question my mute past
                    Césaire, "Song of Wandering"

Et pourtant que te reste-t-il du temps ancien

. . . . .

grimoire fermé mots oubliés
j'interroge mon passé muet
                              "Dit d'errance"

*L*OST BODY *(Corps perdu)* is surely the least known of
Césaire's four major collections of poetry, an unhappy fact in
light of the consistently high quality of its ten poems. There
are several reasons for this anomaly, but the determining one
concerns the conditions under which it was originally published.
The Editions Fragrance in 1950 produced a de luxe edition
of the collection richly illustrated by Picasso. When one considers the number of engravings—thirty-two—in proportion to the
number of poems, one must conclude that Picasso was the principal artist in the project. Of course Picasso in 1950 was the best-
known living artist in the world. Beside him Césaire was a complete unknown, at least in those circles for which this elegant
object was manufactured. The total press run was limited to 207
copies, with twelve additional copies issued *hors commerce,* signed
by Picasso and Césaire. The economics of art determined the
rarity of the volume in order to insure, in the first instance, the
investment value of Picasso's engravings. The collection was mar-
keted in 1950 for seventy thousand francs. At the rate of exchange
then current it cost bibliophiles and Picasso collectors the equivalent of $200.90—all in all a profitable venture for those two un-
likely members of the French Communist party.[1]

It ought not to surprise anyone that the original edition of *Corps perdu* went quite unnoticed in the literary world or that, as a collection, it has occupied no special place in assessments of Césaire's poetry. *Lost Body* has been available to the general reader of French only since 1961, when it was published in a revised definitive edition as the final quarter of the volume entitled *Cadastre,* where it has been overshadowed by the much more extensive collection *Beheaded Sun.* Even recent scholarly studies of Césaire's poetry refer to such poems as "Lost Body" as belonging to *Cadastre* (1961), although it underwent only minor modifications by Césaire after 1950.[2]

Overall the collection *Lost Body* has seen fewer changes of any sort than Césaire's other two early collections or the *Notebook.* The ten original poems seem to have been written especially for the joint project with Picasso since, unlike many of the poems of *Miraculous Weapons* and *Beheaded Sun,* they did not appear first in magazines over a period of several months or years. There is consequently a greater unity of style and inspiration to be found here than in any other collection by Césaire. This feature is particularly significant because *Lost Body* reveals important but often subtle changes between 1945 and 1950 in Césaire's conception of poetry, its potential, and its limitations. The obstacles encountered by the political man begin to make themselves felt in several major poems in this collection. Those selected for extended commentary testify to one or another aspect of Césaire's poetics during this transitional period.

In the Beginning Was the Word

The 1950 and 1961 editions of *Lost Body* both opened with the poem "Word" ("Mot"), which evokes the poet's incantatory, magical activity in creating the poem.[3] The poet's activity is solitary and his material is the slightest possible; he manipulates the physical reality of the word:

Within me

from myself
to myself
outside every constellation

clenched in my hands
only the infrequent hiccup of a last delirious spasm
throb word

                    Parmi moi
de moi-même
à moi-même
hors toute constellation
en mes mains serré seulement
le rare hoquet d'un ultime spasme délirant
vibre mot[4]

The emphasis on the first-person singular pronoun and possessive adjective suggests the individualism that characterizes European lyric poetry, but differences begin to make themselves felt very early on. Césaire's insistence on the imperative verbal form *vibre* to denote the word's special function already gives a particular inflection to the phonemic structure of the poem. As vibration, sound wave, its pure materiality also rejoins spiritual or mystical notions of the truth of words. Paraphrasing Jahn and Tempels, M. a M. Ngal writes of the African concept of words that "the transformations that come about in the world—generation, conception—are due to the efficacy of the word [*parole*] . . . And when an object is considered, the magician who names it confers upon it its 'unique and singular' value."[5] Ngal was commenting on the section of the *Notebook* beginning at "Words?" He could just as well have applied this thought to the poem "Word," since here Césaire deals directly and straightforwardly with the poet's relationship to his words and to a word: *nègre*.

Among the modifications that this view of poetry involves for readers in the European tradition is an ability to consider the poetic text as a verbal score, the poem in the fullest sense being a reading or a performance. Césaire would wrench us out of our habits regarding the poem as a verbal icon. In a poem like "Word" a truly somatic effect is sought; word and rhythm, all the expressive elements in the poem, exist to produce for the reader modifications that affect the body as well as the mind. Such a total poetics is of course not exclusively African, nor is it by any means unknown in European poetry. But it has been an

undercurrent rather than the mainstream, and it takes an occasional maverick such as Stanley Burnshaw or Roger Shattuck to
remind us of its importance.[6]

In "Word" the vibrating, pulsating reverberation is conceived
as a means of escape: "I should make it outside the labyrinth /
word throb longer and wider" ("j'aurai chance hors du labyrinthe / plus long plus large vibre"). It may be that this magical
operation constitutes "a last delirious spasm" ("un ultime spasme
délirant"). At all events, the metaphors in the second strophe tell
of the poet's, or the speaker's, martyrdom. He sees himself pierced
with arrows tipped with curare, a black St. Sebastian assassinated
by Caribs: "And may all their arrows / and their bitterest curare
nail me / to the beautiful center stake of the cool cool stars" ("et
que me clouent toutes les flèches / et leur curare le plus amer / au
beau poteau-mitan des très fraîches étoiles"). The *poteau-mitan*,
or center stake of the voodoo *houmfor* (temple), links the spirit
world with our own; down it the *loa* descend to possess their servants. But Césaire presents a poet-priest, magus, or *houngan*,
whose intercession requires that he become the scapegoat of the
community. This is no African motif; it is uniquely Césairean,
another manifestation of the agonistic hero who recurs throughout
Césaire's work.

The next strophe, of three lines, was set off from the rest of
the text in the original edition:

> throb
> throb the very essence of darkness
> on the wing and full-throated from so much dying.[7]

> vibre
> vibre essence même de l'ombre
> en aile en gosier c'est à force de périr

The dying (*périr* in the original) is left quite ambiguous in the
text. Historically the referent must be *nègres*, as yet unnamed in
the poem; metaphorically it is a reiteration of the speaker's sacrifice in the preceding strophe.

The originality of this part of Césaire's poem can be seen to
better advantage if one reads it intertextually with a well-known
section of Paul Valéry's *Graveyard by the Sea (Le Cimetière*

marin). In the twenty-first stanza Valéry exploited two of the paradoxes of the pre-Socratic philosopher Zeno of Elea. The first of these is the paradox of the arrow which, to arrive at its goal, must first traverse half the distance, then half of the half, and so on ad infinitum. In Valéry's poem, as in Césaire's, the speaker is pierced, killed by the vibrating arrow. Even if one considers the death to be a conceit, Valéry did nonetheless evoke a spiritual and physical birth of consciousness arising out of the arrow's initial vibration:

> Zeno! Cruel Zeno! Zeno of Elea!
> And have you pinned me down with your barbed arrow
> Vibrating, flying and which cannot fly!
> The sound engenders me, the arrow kills!

> Zénon! Cruel Zénon! Zénon d'Elée!
> M'as-tu percé de cette flèche ailée
> Qui vibre, vole, et qui ne vole pas!
> Le son m'enfante et la flèche me tue![8]

If we take this encounter of two very different poets to be sheer coincidence, credulity is strained by the number of identical or very similar elements or effects: Valéry (cette *flèche, ailée,* m'as-tu *percé,* Qui *vibre, vole,* et qui ne *vole* pas!), Césaire (toutes les *flèches,* en *aile,* me *clouent, vibre . . . vibre . . . vibre*). More probable in my view is the likelihood that Césaire, who in *Tropiques* guarded against imitation of this consummate European poet, cannibalized a stanza of *Le Cimetière marin,* transforming it into his personal signature at the same time that he used it for its African potential. This hypothesis is entirely in keeping with Césaire's recommendation, in his epistle to René Depestre, to *marronner* European writers. A privileged metaphor in *Le Cimetière marin*—which for Césaire's generation was the pinnacle of French formalist accomplishment in poetry—thus becomes an intertext within an excellent poem of a quite different type. It also stands as an example of the anxiety of influence, which Harold Bloom has discussed at length. Indeed, my understanding of Césaire's poetics, in which negritude involves a dialectical struggle with modernism, can be seen as an ethnic variation on Bloom's theory.

Valéry's poem is concerned with life and death as they impinge on the individual consciousness. Césaire's "Word" shares with Valéry's *Graveyard by the Sea* certain aspects of dramatic monologue; in "Word" the arrows nailing the speaker to the center stake of the temple dramatize or realize a metaphor. In every other respect, however, the poems diverge. "Word" dramatizes the transformation of the vile word *nigger* into the proud word *black*. Since *nègre* must serve both significations, an act of African word magic is invoked to account for the astonishing and unexpected transformation:

> throb
> throb the very essence of darkness
> on the wing and full-throated from so much dying
> the word nigger
> expelled fully armed from the pangs
> of a poisonous flower
> the word nigger
>
> vibre
> vibre essence même de l'ombre
> en aile en gosier c'est à force de périr
> le mot nègre
> sorti tout armé du hurlement
> d'une fleur vénéneuse
> le mot nègre

The remainder of the poem becomes a litany of the sufferings that constitute the crucible in which has been formed the positive value of the word *nègre*. Mothers and children have suffered. Flesh has been seared. The words *sun* and *night* are appropriately transformed by surrealist metaphors that lead up to the final movement (*Poèmes*, p. 269):

> the word nigger
>   hardened don't you know
> with the summer thunder
>   expropriated
>   by [incredulous freedoms]

> le mot nègre
>> dru savez-vous
> du tonnerre d'un été
>> que s'arrogent
>>> des libertés incrédules

Finally the reader recognizes that the value of the word *nègre* does not derive directly from the act of the poet or the magus. He merely dramatizes or sets the stage for the real suffering of a collectivity that has given value to this word through its living and its dying. Césaire's speaker is rather more modest than has sometimes been said. Yes, he reveals a truth, and in that respect his poetry presents itself as necessary. But he knows full well that he has not created that truth. The poet of "Word" fulfills a priestly function in accord with Césaire's wish expressed in 1959: "In our present circumstances, the greatest ambition of our literature must be to aim to become *sacred literature,* our art, *sacred art.*"[9] If this statement appears very seldom in discussions of Césaire's poetics, it must be because there has been such reluctance to discuss his profoundly religious sensibility. Césaire has reinforced this attitude in many texts, verse and prose, which attack the collusion between organized religion and colonialism. But when he was questioned by Jacqueline Sieger on the significance of islands in his poetry, he answered with a paraphrase of Pascal: "A phrase of Pascal's illustrates my feeling rather well, *although I am not religious:* 'Imagine men abandoned on an island who are waiting for death.' "[10] The concessive clause "I am not religious" says more than it means, as my earlier quotation from Césaire's "The Responsibility of the Cultivated Man" (Rome, 1959) suggests unambiguously.

To my mind the tendency to invoke archetypal explanations of Césaire's imagery arises out of an embarrassment over treating poetry and religion together in an open fashion. The problem is part of the larger modernist dilemma in aesthetics. Questions that had formerly been assumed to belong to religious discourse have taken refuge in the arts. A new range of experience and of expression has been opened up for creative artists, but critical discourse has often suffered from critics' unwillingness to deal analytically with the problems attendant on the aesthetic masking of a religious sensibility. That branch of criticism that seeks fundamental truths in the archetypes proposed by Carl Jung, Gaston Bachelard, or Gilbert Durand wishes to avoid facing the awkward problem of dealing with the disappearance of a transcendent divinity. The use made of Durand's fascinating book *Les Structures anthropologiques de l'imaginaire* (Paris: Bordas, 1969) is a case in point. As though its appeal to anthropology were not sufficient, at least one effort has been made to convince the skeptical by affirming peremptorily that recent biological research (as reported by a topologist!) proves the scientific validity of his archetypes. This is the sort of critical posture that through an appeal to a presumably objective truth, usually advanced under the guarantee of anthropology or biology, forecloses discussion of Césaire's poetry at the very point where it may have something valuable to impart.

One of the features of the collection *Lost Body* that distinguishes it on the one hand from the apocalyptic texts of *Beheaded Sun* and on the other from the praise poems of *Shackles (Ferrements)* is precisely the pain experienced by Césaire in moving from the basically religious attitude toward mythopoesis in his earlier poetry toward a more straightforward, socially committed poetry. The entire collection is strained to the breaking point by this contradiction between the felt need for an intensely inner-directed discourse and the conviction that poetry must somehow speak openly to and for blacks throughout the world. On one level the images of tearing and cutting that are everywhere in the poem "Song of Wandering" must be understood in this perspective.

The reader notices as well that, in the main, the rhythmic features of this collection are less prominent than in *Miraculous Weapons*. "Word," for instance, is far less dependent on insistent rhythms than is that other poem on a word, "Batouque." This aspect of the gradual but difficult modification of Césaire's poetics toward the end of the forties can be shown by taking a second look at "Batouque."

Ambiguous Rhythms

In the early forties Césaire believed firmly that the poetic word was a "rupestral design in the stuff of sound" as he put it in "Poetry and Cognition." To read "Batouque" satisfactorily is to participate physically in the powerful percussion designed to beat down "man's resistance at that point of most basic humanity, the nervous system," to quote from *Tropiques* no. 2 the poet's own appreciation of the Harlem Renaissance movement. All commentators on the poem "Batouque" agree that its rhythmic effects are primary, fundamental to the poem's structure. Beyond that point, however, there exists the most basic disagreement as to the nature and the origin of the rhythms each reader finds in the poem. Finally, the problem exists because Césaire's poem does not come to us like a blues song or a Louis Armstrong piece with a musical score. Although we may all agree that a poem such as "Batouque" is made to be performed, there is no reasonably objective way to decide who the best performers are or—and the question is aesthetically a different one—what constitutes an appropriate performance.

An analogous problem was handled with great tact by Jahn in his commentary on the role of rhythms in Senghor's poetry. Keeping in mind that Senghor had remained in touch with his own Serer tribal traditions in music and oral literature, one cannot but be impressed by the contradictory impressions received by apparently qualified listeners. Lilyan Kesteloot gave an enthusiastic appreciation of a reading of Senghor's poem "Chaka" by a student at the Congolese University of Lovanium around 1960. She found the tom-tom accompaniment illuminating: "It was astonishingly successful, and the whole of Leopoldville was talking about the 'Senghor recital.' Clear proof that this writer's poetry loses its apparent tonelessness when it is recited as it should be."[11] At the other end of the scale, Ezekiel Mphahlele declared in Berlin in 1964: "There have even been attempts to read Senghor's poetry to the accompaniment of drums—poetry in French. I have heard this and I frankly must say I felt it was phoney. Because the rhythm of drums is just not the rhythm of French poetry."[12] Mphahlele's position is that rhythm is so thoroughly culture bound—tied to the linguistic vehicle of a culture—that it cannot conceivably be translated into the language of another culture. The very notion of a neo-African poetry is condemned by such a position. Jahn prudently concluded that an informed discussion of this question would have to await a competent comparison of Senghor's "poetical rhythms to the rhythms of his specific musical background" (p. 263).

Elsewhere in this study I have argued rather pointedly for reconsideration of the European modernist attitude, which Césaire, by his own admission, adapted to his own ends in the forties. I have pushed this paradoxical aspect of Césaire's situation to the extent of agreeing with Bastide and Hubert on the Europeanness of Césaire's poetry. But there is a limit to this line of argument beyond which it turns rapidly to absurdity—just the opposite absurdity from that embodied in the statement by Mphahlele. Certainly in the area of rhythm as in the area of syntax Césaire worked to fashion poetry in French that would not give an impression of French poetry written by a white man. Quoting from his interview with Jacqueline Sieger: "Moreover, in my opinion, the word, though it be of capital importance, does not have the importance of rhythm. You are right to speak of breathlessness: I wanted to introduce into French an element which is foreign to it. Rhythm is an essential quality of blacks. I believe, without having premeditated it, that it [non-French rhythm] occurs constantly in my poems. Africans have made an observation that pleases me: mine are among the rare poems, it seems, which are easily performed on a tom-tom" (p. 65).

The assumption made by Césaire—and it is not an obvious one at all—is that his non-French rhythms are African, whence the importance of the anecdote. For Jahn rhythmic innovation in Césaire was of secondary importance at best.

M. a M. Ngal approaches the problem carefully at first, cautioning his reader against the appeal to atavistic traits made frequently by Senghor. He proposes that Césaire's rhythms are more probably analogous to those of jazz, but his examples contain very little analysis and make no real connection with jazz rhythms. The level of discourse can be measured by this conclusion, from his *Aimé Césaire,* which follows a rapid comparison of Eluard's "Curfew" ("Couvre-feu") with a passage from Césaire's *Notebook:* "The Black-African genius is made up of dynamism, of rhythm, contrary to the European genius" (p. 134). Ngal's argument is ultimately circular; it affirms in conclusion its own first premise, thus begging the question. In Bernadette Cailler's analysis of "Batouque," just at the point where the question of specific rhythmic patterns becomes pressing, she digresses on the function of the concept of *mana* in Malinowski's writings on the Trobriand Islanders. When she returns to "Batouque," rhythm has been set aside in favor of the symbolic charge of the deep structures to which the rhythms presumably refer us. The reader who hopes to find anything substantial that might connect any of Césaire's poems to precise African or Afro-American rhythms will encounter promises and suggestions enough but no demonstration or even much sound argument.

The most promising development in this important but neglected area of Césaire's poetry is currently to be found in the performances of his texts by the Martinican actor and theatrical director Yvan Labejof. For him, Césaire's rhythms are neither European nor African but Creole; that is, they introduce into French constructions peculiarities of the Creole idiom, which is the mother tongue of all black Martinicans. In his published comments on staging "And the Dogs Were Silent" Labejof cites several examples of repetitions ("*O roi debout, O roi debout*" or the choric use of "*beaucoup beaucoup*"). This is, according to him, "the rhythm of the *bel-air,* that traditional dance of the cane cutters and so many others. These passages will have to be scanned with onomatopoeias recited by a chorus; this would be simply to develop the intention of the text, because if Césaire repeats, he knows what he's doing."[13] Labejof gives concrete examples of Creole syntax in the play, adding a useful comment on what he sees as the proper method for reciting Césaire's poetry: "You have to punctuate the text [,] never modulate it. Césaire must always be recited pow, pow, pow; never give him musical purring. I heard an interpretation of the 'Dogs' on the radio just that way, done by Sylvia Monfort and other French actors; it was very beautiful, but it was cello music, it wasn't Césaire" (p. 155).

I have heard Labejof perform some of Césaire's texts, both lyric and dramatic; as Kesteloot noted in the case of a Senghor recital, it was very impressive. One had the sense that Césaire's lines were meant to be hammered out to a tom-tom accompaniment. In conversation Labejof revealed that he prepares his performances with the assistance of Césaire, who listens to the program and makes occasional suggestions. It may eventually be possible to present for analysis and discussion the rhythmic notation used by Labejof and by his drummers. At that time it should also be possible to take the question of Césaire's rhythms beyond the point where it is currently stuck. It would be a mistake, however, to believe that what can be learned from such an analysis

will hold for all of Césaire's poetry. It is already obvious that
Labejof's strictures against ever modulating Césaire's poetry are
too exclusive. Césaire has written poems that can be described
entirely in terms of traditional French rhythmic units. They may
not be the favorites of some of Césaire's admirers, but they do
exist, and it is permissible to make a case for Césaire's recourse
to French prosodic conventions in such instances. After listening
to Labejof and his group perform a particularly powerful speech
by Lumumba in act 1, scene 6 of *A Season in the Congo,* during
which I had made some rudimentary notes on the drumbeats
used in the accompaniment, I went back to Césaire's poem to
verify what can be said to be there, in the text. The heavily accented, punctuated, or stressed diction used by Labejof is certainly
supported by the text. However, pending proper examination of
the notation used, I do not find grounds for deriving a precise
tom-tom accompaniment from the text.

From the standpoint of aesthetics the performance of Césaire's
poems by Yvan Labejof—or for that matter by Sylvia Monfort—
is a question of staging and interpretation. Certain rhythms, a
powerfully accented diction in certain poems, sometimes a Creole
syntax can be said to be inherent in the text. Other aspects re-
lating to performance are closer in nature to critical statements.
They may be appropriate; they will be more or less satisfying;
seldom can they be said to be necessary.

In "Word" the recurring line "the word nigger" ("le mot
nègre") seven times punctuates the middle section of the poem,
providing periodic stops. In this sense it is a rhythmic device as
well as a reiteration of the theme word of the title; given the affective connotations of *nègre,* it heightens the sense of emotional in-
volvement with the poem at each recurrence. However, unlike the
sequences of *batouque de* . . . in "Batouque," it does not set out
to imitate a frenzied state of possession. One can immediately
identify a theme in "Word." This is never the case in "Batouque,"
a poem in which the rhythm is the medium is the message. "Word"
appeals to the intellect, describing the vibrant nature of the word
as well as invoking it. "Batouque" makes a direct appeal to the
nervous system, and in that respect one can say that it is a primi-
tivist piece. "Word" builds on the truth of the primitive word
toward a recognizable metaphoric structure that is lacking in
"Batouque."

The Poet as Demiurge

"Lost Body," the poem that gave its title to the collection, has always been firmly anchored in the center of *Corps perdu*.[14] It is by all accounts one of Césaire's most powerful poems and lends itself exceptionally well to oral recitation. "Lost Body" represents the finest example of Césaire's demiurgic manner. The poem is very pure in its development of a mental and spiritual attitude that achieves an explosive climax in affirming its rights and its power over the natural world. After 1950 Césaire was never again to create such a wholly confident incarnation of the hero of negritude. In this regard the poem is located at the watershed that slopes in one direction toward the origins of negritude and in the other toward the modifications necessitated by a hostile political and economic situation.

The overture, lines 1–7, is postively volcanic in its effects; the opening line, "Moi qui Krakatoa" ("I who Krakatoa"), bursts upon the air, mimicking the violent eruption suggested by the name Krakatoa. This brief line establishes the identification of self *(moi)* with volcanic activity and thus provides a plausible thematic justification for the litany of *moi qui* constructions that begin the next six lines as well. The term *overture* applies to these seven lines because they are set apart in several ways from the dialectical evolution of the hero that constitutes a represented action and occupies the remainder of the poem. Syntactically the overture is entirely relative and subordinate to the first movement of the action. The litany of *moi qui* constructions is grammatically subordinated to the *je* (I), subject of the principal clause, which begins line 8.[15] The sensation of eruption or explosion that the overture communicates is at least as much a matter of phonemic combinations as of metaphors, which are rather loosely tied together by a savage or primitive motif. In order to grasp Césaire's true accomplishment in "Lost Body" one must first have a sense of its musical mode of composition. This is not to say, however, that one need be expert in either French phonetics or French poetry to appreciate the poem. Conversations with English-speaking students of poetry who had heard a reading of "Corps perdu" in French suggest that the poem has a powerful and appropriate effect quite apart from its meaning in the usual semantic or syntactic sense.

I shall attempt to render something of the physical and auditory nature of the poem by means of a phonemic analysis of a phonetic transcription of the text. The analysis assumes that modern French poetry has evolved a reasonably consistent tradition of expressive phonemes used, in appropriate combinations, to suggest certain feelings and emotional responses. Since there is considerable misunderstanding and skepticism on this subject, I should point out that my hypothesis does not involve the extreme theses of Maurice Grammont, Henri Morier, or Otto Jespersen. I use the statistical findings of Pierre Guiraud's general study of modern French poetry.[16] As a linguist, Guiraud accepts the axiom of modern linguistic science according to which the signs of language are unmotivated. However, his work on Valéry also demonstrates that French poetry at least since symbolism has self-consciously exploited the potential of phonemes for their expressive value. The example of Valéry's practice is apposite to an analysis of Césaire's poem, because Valéry was for Césaire both the consummate poet of high modernism and, like Saint-John Perse, one of those Europeans to be *marronnés*.

Lines 1–7 of "Lost Body" have a combined total of fifty syllables. This overture reveals an extremely unusual combination of phonemes. There is a 56 percent frequency of occlusive consonants—[k] [g] [t] [d] [p] [b]—whereas the norm for modern French poetry (1880–1920) studied by Guiraud is 38.2 percent. More spectacular is the fact that the guttural or velar occlusives [k] and [g] alone account for 32 percent of consonant phonemes in the overture. These are precisely the phonemes most avoided by modern French poets and by Valéry especially. Guiraud points out the marked "degutturalization" of Valéry's poetry overall. As "Lost Body" will shortly reveal, Césaire is in his overture exploiting the un-French and harshly expressive tendency of these sounds to a strategic end.

The exceptional combination of consonants in lines 1–7 is articulated with vowels belonging to an equally restricted group, which I take to be the mark of an expressive intention. The vowels [a], [i], and [u], which Léandre Bergeron finds to be potentially "explosive," "piercing," and "sharp but rather somber," respectively, based on their physical, acoustical characteristics, together constitute 64 percent of the vowels in the overture, a manifestly dominant tone.[17] In conjunction with the prominent gutturals and dominant occlusive consonants, these vowels create a mood that is aggressive, volatile, explosive, quite apart from attributions of meaning to individual words and lines. I would suggest furthermore that any effort to attribute a meaning or even a direction counter to the suggestion of the phonemic play in the overture could be dismissed as erroneous. "Lost Body" is to that extent composed on a phonemic structure that can be taken as primary. In other words, in this poem Césaire has given a conscious and artful form to his early conviction that poetry is the "rupestral design in the stuff of sound." The acoustical material of poetry is nowhere more basic and more audibly perceptible than in his "Corps perdu."

What I have called the first movement of the poem, beginning at the line (from p. 118 of the Snyder-Upson translation) "I would like to be more and more humble and more lowly" ("je voudrais être de plus en plus humble et plus bas"), is characterized for the ear by a modulation of a quite musical type. Both pitch and tone change in a way that a sensitive hearer can scarcely fail to perceive as expressive and indeed as meaningful. First of all, one notices the almost total absence of the harsh sounds—[k] [g]—that had so strongly inflected the overture. From a frequency of 32 percent they drop to 1.8 percent of the total consonants in the fifty-four syllables of lines 8–11. On the other hand, the "soft, weak" consonant [v], as Bergeron describes it, has a frequency of 13 percent, compared to 2 percent in the overture. Overall, the spirants [s] [ʒ] [z] [v], all of which soften the consonantal texture of the movement, represent 33 percent of the total as opposed to a mere 8 percent of the consonants in the overture. They are further reinforced by the liquidity of the lateral consonant [l] (13 percent) and by a 20 percent frequency of [r], which, in almost half the syllables where it occurs, softens the occlusives [d], [t], and [g] with which it is articulated.

This reversal of direction in pitch and tone is identical and even more clearly defined in the vowels of lines 8–11. The dominant vowels are the nasals, which approximate 13 percent, a bit lower than the norm in modern French poetry generally; [ɛ], identical in frequency to the nasals; [y], 11 percent; and—for Césaire—an extraordinarily high frequency of the mute e [ə], 14.8 percent. Taken together these vowels represent 51 percent of the total in lines 8–11, whereas they form but 16 percent of the vowels in the overture. The mute and the open e and the nasals communicate a physical opening up, a relaxation of muscular effort throughout the first movement, promising an abrupt change in attitude on the part of the speaker. At the same time the lines are perceptibly longer, so that a rhythmic modulation reinforces the acoustic or phonemic modulation. From the sharply staccato lines of the overture (noticeably absent is the mute e, which brings air, space, and a more relaxed tempo) Césaire has proceeded to a more varied tempo. (In the overture the first six lines are all choppy, with five to seven syllables per line; in the part of the first movement under consideration the line lengths are thirteen, ten, seven, and fourteen syllables, respectively.) The more relaxed pace both signals an abrupt, presumably significant change and announces the conditions characteristic of modern lyric in French.

A rapid review of the phonemic structures of lines 1–11 of "Lost Body" reveals the striking distinction of two different tempi, which correspond to two equally distinct textures in the acoustical material of the poem. This distinction is further borne out by the syntactic subordination of the overture to the first movement, where the speaker initially utters the lyrical *je* (I). (The *moi* of the overture constitutes something more on the order of an exclamation or ejaculation. At all events, grammatically the self is first an object, *moi*, before it becomes the subject, *je*, of its own utterance.) One can locate the Africanization of the poem acoustically in the overture in the guise of a highly original departure from the norms of phonemic usage in modern French poetry. Once this originality has been forcefully established in lines 1–7, however, the poem returns immediately to an approximation of those same French norms. Indeed, if one were to complete the phonemic analysis of the entire poem along these lines, one would find that Césaire's departure from the norm is in the same range as Valéry's (with the exception of the overture), which is to say that it is of the degree that we normally attribute to the individual style or signature of any modern French poet. The overture is also characterized by a lexical Africanization (*Zambèze, cannibale*) and by a suggestion of primitivism: *bêle* ("bleat"), *frénétique* ("frantic"), *rhombé* ("rhombic"). But even here one finds two inconsistencies. *Krakatoa* was, I am certain, chosen for its expressiveness, whereas the name of any African volcano would have been preferable from a thematic standpoint. Likewise *laïlape* (laelaps) is taken not from African or Martinican folklore but from Greek mythology, where it attributes canine features to the howling wind of the storm.

In "Lost Body" Césaire has created a poem in which sound, mood, and metaphor suggest each other reciprocally. The metaphoric structure is posited on a root metaphor of telluric creativity, which subtends the gradual emergence of a heroic figure whose final action in ordering the islands to exist is prefigured in the overture by nature itself. There are three distinct movements in the poem. The first, lines 8–27, moves through three subdivisions: lines 8–15, 16–20, and 21–27. In general the first movement presents a speaker who declares his need to reenter the earth (lines 8–11, the phonemic structure of which is discussed above) and who imagines (lines 12–15) a beneficent original chaos in which the phenomenal world is obliterated (*RENCONTRE BIEN TOTALE*), where stars and hopes, petals of the flamboyant tree and undersea retreats are indistinguishable (lines 16–20), where finally (lines 21–27) he imagines a marvelous synesthetic bath in which life is palpable energy and odors are succoring hands passing through his porous body, which has been opened to all forms of experience.

The second movement again modulates in tone, mood, and metaphor. At first (lines 28–31) there is a hesitation between rest *(repos)* and activity, between a definitive rooting of the speaker's being *(racines ancreuses,* "anchoring roots") and his need to affirm himself *(ma terrible crête,* "my terrible cockscomb"). This artfully balanced section is typified by a blending of the two types of consonants that Césaire had carefully separated in lines 1–7 and 8–11; it gives way in turn to the forceful affirmation of self (lines 32–35, *Poèmes,* p. 278):

> Things I sound I sound
> me the burden bearer I am root bearer
> and I weigh and I force and I arcane
>   I omphale

> Choses je sonde je sonde
> moi le porte-faix je suis porte-racines
> et je pèse et je force et j'arcane
>   j'omphale

The rooted self now claims to root being through a series of actions. *Arcane* and *omphale* are both nouns used as active verbs, the first alluding to the object of the alchemists' quest, the second to Omphale, queen of Lydia in Greek mythology. The suggestion that this action is sexual and phallic was much stronger in the original text of "Corps perdu," where these two lines were intercalated between lines 34 and 35:

> I spit I unwind myself
> I penetrate I omphale I omphale
>
> je crache je me déroule
> je pénètre j'omphale j'omphale

From this momentary climax the poem again modulates (lines 36–43), this time to images of lassitude, ancient secrets, gnomic utterance, concluding the second movement with the introduction of "your cold face of unkempt laughter" ("ta froide face de rire défait") next to "my fresh and unstable muzzle" ("mon museau instable et frais").

The third movement (pp. 120–121 in the Snyder-Upson translation) begins on a melancholy note:

> [The wind alas I shall hear it still]
> nigger nigger nigger from the depths
> of the timeless sky
>
> Le vent hélas je l'entendrai encore
> nègre nègre nègre depuis le fond
> du ciel immémorial

This theme of social and racial oppression is briefly reinforced (lines 49–50) by images of runaway slaves ("notre poursuite toujours marronne") being tracked by horses and dogs. Then, very abruptly in line 51, articulated only by the word *but,* the hero arises, strong, violent in his righteous anger, to "splatter the sky" ("j'éclabousserai le ciel") with his shout, commanding the islands to come into their own, to exist.

This close reading of the text reveals a sharp distinction between the socially oriented imagery of the final movement and the tendency toward oracular utterance in the first and second movements. What might appear to be a serious flaw in tone and diction has actually been carefully prepared on other levels, phonemic and metaphoric. It may already be apparent from my presentation of the first and second movements that they create a mood and a coherent imagery of a regressive quest, a return to the original chaos of the maternal waters, to the rooting of the umbilicus, a weighing of whether to stay or to leave the rejuvenating medium, and a sexualized scene in which rebirth is actually presented as carnal union, a penetrating outward toward the world of things, people, and problems. On this level the speaker has prepared for his social responsibility by turning inward, by renewing himself spiritually in terms with which literature has experimented more or less self-consciously since the dissemination of the writings of Freud and Jung.

On another level Césaire has used specific mythological allusions to organize his version of the myth of the rebirth of the hero. The one relatively unambiguous clue left in the poem since 1961 is the name Omphale, which can of course be justified on phonemic grounds as conducive to a representation of the female principle. (It has all the physical characteristics that are lacking in Krakatoa; therefore their union implies true wholeness.) Omphale in Greek mythology purchased Hercules as a nameless slave. During his period of service to Omphale Hercules was obliged to wear female garments and to spin wool at the feet of his mistress. In the original text of "Lost Body" Césaire had added after line 11, which first expresses the desire to return to Tellus Mater, "to lose myself fall / into the living grain of a well-opened earth" ("me perdre tomber / dans la vivante semoule d'une terre bien ouverte"), the comparison "like a black woman" ("comme une femme noire"). Combining the original juxtaposition of the regressive self with a black woman and the suggestion that the speaker may be acting out the episode of Hercules' enslavement, one arrives at this polysemic reading of the metaphor:

(psychological axis):	I / Hercules →	[lose myself] →	well-opened earth / black woman
(mythological axis):	I / Hercules →	[fall] →	like a black woman / well-opened earth

Both readings are borne out by the speaker's action in the second movement. On the mythological axis he forces and penetrates Omphale who, according to one version of the story, married Hercules on account of his prowess. On the psychological axis the self must regress to the point where it joins with that original Oneness described by Nietzsche in *The Birth of Tragedy*. Only then can it be reborn as the truly heroic self.

This reading finds throughout the poem a double motif: the hidden allusions to Hercules' period of slavery and his service to Omphale articulate with the social and ethnic consciousness that emerges in the third movement. At the same time the regressive psychological quest, which strikes the reader more immediately through the senses in the first and second movements, makes possible the birth of a black hero whose triumphant voice in the third movement displaces the sweeter tones of the earlier movements.

In revising the text of "Corps perdu" for *Cadastre* Césaire chose to cut out of the poem those lines that reinforce the hypothesis of a Greek mythological reading. By so doing he strengthened its African resonance; that is, he weakened an original European resonance. He also wagered that the phonemic and metaphorical-psychological structures in the poem were already sufficiently strong to support it without the additional strength of Hercules. The Hercules-Omphale axis was secondary to begin with, and the poem may finally be a better poem—though less of a virtuoso piece—without it.

Osiris and the Phoenix

Throughout Césaire's poetry one finds an insistence on the human body in its intimate, carnal aspect, as erotic agent and object, as aggressor and victim of aggression. These concerns are often found within poems in the form of related images, strophes functioning within a larger context, or as thematic echoes. In "Song of Wandering" ("Dit d'errance") they provide a coherent vehicle for the theme of the black diaspora, the intimate, individual note that confers a sense of authenticity and poignancy on the poet's expression of a collective disaster. The vision of mutilation in the poem "Lynch I" is set in the context of a narrative with manifest mythic overtones in "Song of Wandering." It is, in yet another guise, the agonistic scenario that had received full treatment in *And the Dogs Were Silent* but that, in most of Césaire's lyrical and automatic pieces, can be apprehended only fleetingly, in the interstices of the poem as it were.

"Song of Wandering" relies on a more direct form of expression than the automatic texts of *Beheaded Sun,* and it has consequently been the object of rather more good commentary. References in this poem and others to the death and rebirth of the phoenix suggested to Lilyan Kesteloot that the fabulous bird that is reborn from its own ashes may be a privileged symbol for Aimé Césaire.[18] She also associated the images of rebirth in Césaire with their apparent opposite: the very numerous, often predominant images of aggressive action by the poet's surrogate speakers. This suggestion served as a starting point for Keith Walker's study, *La Cohésion poétique de l'oeuvre césairienne,* which traces image clusters throughout Césaire's poetry in a systematic Bachelardian fashion. Walker concludes, somewhat programmatically, that "this situation of the phoenix reborn from its ashes and of the black Prometheus whose liver is reborn of courage, dramatizes the hope that we all keep in the depths of our selves, and which permits us to go on living. . ."[19] Aliko Songolo has likewise stressed Césaire's "phenicism," giving it still more prominence than does Walker.[20] The tendency of all three commentators to see in this aspect of Césaire's imagery the essentially triumphant affirmation of self and the affirmation of blackness or Africanism as a positive cultural value has led them to emphasize the triumph and to depreciate or overlook the attendant sacrifice. In those of Césaire's poems that develop dialectically toward a motif of heroic rebirth one invariably encounters a negative moment or downward pull toward the infernal regions that must entail death so that the hero may be born anew and pure. In "Lost Body" the regressive quest of the future hero, or alternatively Hercules' period of slavery, serves the same function. As pseudomytheme it represents the necessary sanctification of the hero, who is then reborn to glorious deeds. Walker cites without commentary (p. 67) the line in "At the Floodgates of the Void" ("Aux écluses du vide") in which the speaker waits to be dubbed "knight of a Plutonian order." This sacrificial action has its own dynamics; if the metaphoric vehicle changes from poem to poem, the mythic scenario does not. It is doubtless the reductionist nature of Bachelardian image analysis that has kept otherwise good observers from making this connection. Walker notes pertinently that, in what he calls Césaire's bestiary of despair, "the circular flight and the waiting of crows and vultures" corresponds to "the beatific flights of the phoenix and the eagle" (p. 113); but a Bachelardian inventory does not take one very much closer to the tragic nature of Cesaire's heroes. A reading of "Song of Wandering" will show that in his later poetry Césaire has not always concluded on the triumphant note.

A very clearly defined opposition of image clusters does indeed inform the poem. At the outset images of mutilation set the tone: *déchiré, mutilé, coupé* ("torn," "mutilated," "cut up") are all attributes of "myself" or of the metonymic substitute for *en moi*, as in the two lines that close the first strophe: "the cut up fruit of the moon always away / toward the contour to be invented of the other half" ("le fruit coupé de la lune toujours en allée / vers le contour à inventer de l'autre moitié"). The ideal of wholeness, the metaphoric opposite of present mutilation, is discreetly present as that "other half" still to be invented. If the opening strophe is lacerated and torn in its dominant image patterns, it strains toward wholeness in both rhythm and meter. Every line but one ends in the identical masculine rhyme in *é*, so that the past participles that express mutilation simultaneously bring a strong sense of stability in their phonemic structure. The rhythms of the first strophe, and of the poem as a whole, are likewise stable and tend toward regularity and recurrence:[21]

(1) Tout ce qui / / jamais / fut déchiré   3 / / 2 / 4
     (everything which has ever been torn)

(2) en moi / s'est déchiré   2 / 4
     (has been torn in me)

(3) tout ce qui / / jamais / fut mutilé   3 / / 2 / 4
     (everything which has ever been mutilated)

(4) en moi / s'est mutilé   2 / 4
     (has been mutilated in me)

(5) au milieu / de l'assiette / / de son souffle / dénudé   3 / 3 / / 3 + / 3
     (in the middle of the plate stripped of its breath)

(6) le fruit coupé / de la lune / toujours en allée   4 / 3 / 5
      (the quartered fruit of the moon forever moving)

(7) vers le contour / à inventer / de l'autre moitié   4 / 4 / 4+
      (toward the projected contour of the other side)

In scanning the first strophe one is constantly drawn to the basic
rhythm of the French twelve-syllable alexandrine. Lines 5–7 approximate it very closely; line 5 has the caesura of the classical
quaternary alexandrine with but one extra syllable (easily swallowed) in the third rhythmic group; lines 6 and 7 scan like
Romantic ternary alexandrines. Lines 2 and 4 are readily identifiable as hemistichs, or one-half of the classical alexandrine. In
lines 1 and 3, after the three-syllable attack, the line settles com-
fortably into a hemistich with precisely the same internal structure (2 / 4) that governs lines 2 and 4, which thus appear to echo
1 and 3. Overall the momentary imbalance or instability suggested by the uncomfortable nine-syllable rhythm of lines 1 and
3 is more than compensated for by the very stable hemistichs
that follow and then give way to approximate alexandrines. To
a French ear this type of prosody suggests a very orderly construct,
which a careful reading must take into account.[22]
    The second and third strophes constitute a question and a
tentative answer:

         3   5   4   (12)
      Et pourtant / que te reste-t-il / du temps ancien
      (And yet / what have you left / from ancient times)

The question is couched in the form of an irregular alexandrine,
but the five-line response is the only strophe in the poem to be
composed on an odd-numbered scheme, which in French is used
typically to suggest doubt, hesitation, melancholy, or some kind
of instability (pp. 134–135, Snyder-Upson):

         3   3   3   (9)
      à peine / peut-être / certain sens
      (little more perhaps than a certain tendency)

```
   3          3          3          3              (12)
dans la pluie / de la nuit / / de chauvir / ou trembler
(to prick up my ears or to tremble in the night rain)


   4              4          3                      (11)
et quand d'aucuns / chantent Noël / revenu
(and to dream of stars)


   3          2                                     (5)
de songer / aux astres
(gone astray)


   3                                                (3)
égarés
(while others sing the return of Christmas)
```

The effect of this strophe is not unlike that of the melancholy Verlaine in his use of the *vers impair,* or uneven line, in "Chanson d'automne." Tristan Corbière also comes to mind. The important difference is that these five lines are set off, typographically as well as prosodically, from the remainder of the poem, which is dominated by the octosyllabic line of narrative poetry in French, with occasional paired decasyllabic lines for balance and/or thematic statement, and a few alexandrines essentially to begin or end a movement.

Césaire introduced a sense of melancholy into his versification, I believe, so as to afford a physical, rhythmic correlative to the doubt that he expressed metaphorically in this poem (*Poèmes,* p. 286):

> closed wizard's book forgotten words
> I question my mute past
>
> grimoire fermé mots oubliés
> j'interroge mon passé muet
>   .   .   .
>
> toward an Ophir without an Albuquerque
> shall we ever stretch out our arms?

vers une Ophir sans Albuquerque
tendrons-nous toujours les bras?

. . .

I invented a secret cult
my sun is the one that ever is awaited

J'ai inventé un cult secret
mon soleil est celui que toujours on attend

"Song of Wandering" supports the reading of the last two lines as a slightly veiled reference to the heroic version of negritude disseminated by the solar cult of *Miraculous Weapons* and of an important part of the original *Beheaded Sun*. The poet of "Song of Wandering" declares himself a "doleful sibyl" ("moi sybille flébilant") whose wizard's book is shut tight, whose past is mute. The effort to dredge up the legendary past of black peoples is reduced to a weary and unanswered question concerning the fabulous land of Ophir before its territory was discovered, charted, and colonized by Albuquerque.

In between the disillusioned reference to Ophir and the two very Rimbaldian lines on Césaire's secret cult, or personal solar myth, one reads this five-line strophe (*Poèmes,* p. 286):

Of old o torn one
She piece by bit
reassembled her dismembered one
and the fourteen pieces
took their triumphant place in the rays of the evening

jadis ô déchiré
Elle pièce par morceau
rassembla son dépecé
et les quatorze morceaux
s'assirent triomphants dans les rayons du soir

The "torn one" of the first line is the poet's alter ego, the speaker of the first strophe. "She" had been named in the original edition of 1950; the name Isis in the text directed the reader to an

Egyptian version of the myth of the god who was torn asunder
and then resurrected in glory by the loving agency of his mother-
sister-wife. The "dismembered one," then, was originally Osiris,
but Césaire later preferred the less specific reference. He may well
have known the history of this divine couple given by the French
Hellenist Paul Foucart, according to whom national cultural differences, but not meaning, differentiated the Eleusinian couple
Dionysos-Demeter from the earlier Egyptian couple Osiris-Isis.
At all events, the context obliges one to see in this strophe both
a *mise en abyme* of the speaker's present situation and another
myth of the agonistic tragic sacrifice that has run through
Césaire's poetry like a golden thread since the days of *Tropiques*.

Directly following the three lines on the secret cult of the sun
(*Poèmes*, p. 286), which I read as an expression of bittersweet
irony concerning Césaire's earlier confidence in the efficacy of
poetry, the poem opens onto a litany of the feminine body that
heals the islands' wounds (as Isis makes Osiris whole, as a woman
is the speaker's other half, and so on):

> Feminine body island turned about
> feminine body well rigged out
> feminine body foam-born
> feminine body island found anew   .   .   .

> Corps féminin île retournée
> corps féminin bien nolisé
> corps féminin écume-né
> corps féminin île retrouvée   .   .   .

At this juncture it is obvious that the thematics of dismember-
ment are universal in the poem: the islands themselves are "mal-
joined," "disjointed" fragments of a great continent, now lost.
The dialectic of the agonistic hero still functions in the poem,
mirroring the destiny of Osiris: to bring a promise of wholeness
to the speaker and to his islands. But the old confidence is gone.
To be sure, the same strophe alludes to the phoenix (*Poèmes*, p.
287):

> feminine body palm tree gait
> coifed by the sun with a nest

where the phoenix dies and is born
we are souls of good birth
noctural bodies of lively lineage
faithful trees gushing wine
I a doleful sybil.

corps féminin marche de palmier
par le soleil d'un nid coiffé
où le phénix meurt et renaît
nous sommes âmes de bon parage
corps nocturnes vifs de lignage
arbres fidèles vin jaillissant
moi sybille flébilant.

Osiris, phoenix, Dionysos, or the Rebel of *And the Dogs Were Silent:* they are so many incarnations of the Césairean hero of negritude. But in "Song of Wandering" the prophet has lost faith in his prophecy. The sybil renders oracles because it is her lot. The final strophe leaves little room for dispute over the pessimistic, melancholy tone the poem has taken:

slow rustic diamond-broker prince
might I be the toy of a nigromancer?

lent rustique prince diamantaire
serais-je jouet de nigromance?

And finally, the last line of the poem calls into question the paradisaical visions formerly conjured up by Césaire's own poetry:

I fell the trees of Paradise

j'abats les arbres du Paradis

The dynamics of the metaphors in this poem cannot in themselves account for the newness of "Song of Wandering" in 1950. Neither the phoenix nor Osiris can be taken at face value. They exist within the poem as part of a very subtle play of tone, mood, and prosodic convention. I began this reading of "Song of Wandering" with a glance at Césaire's use of formal techniques available to all modern poets writing in French. Without wishing to stress the point beyond what has actually been demonstrated, I submit that in this poem Césaire wrote in a tradition that is very familiar to readers of French poetry. At times Apollinaire is only an image or a rhythmic foot away.[23] This is not to suggest even remotely that Césaire might somehow be a derivative poet. He has mastered the modern idiom as few poets in metropolitan France have done. He has meditated on a tradition, deepening and extending it by bringing to it his own individual stamp and style. There may be still another reason for Césaire's reliance on very French and European techniques in this particular poem. If, as my reading indicates, this poem marks a turning point in Césaire's poetics, a questioning of his earlier triumphant assurance then it is curiously appropriate that his poetic reflection be set in a form with its own venerable tradition. The word *dit* in the title "Dit d'errance" recalls the poetic form that in medieval times was a long poem of contemporary observation and reflection. This tradition goes back some six hundred years, and I believe Césaire was self-consciously situating himself within it. If one looks at the poem in this light, as the meeting place of a specific modern sensibility and an ancient tradition, then the poem begins to speak differently. It says that for the poet who can no longer be certain of his message the writing of poetry is itself a consolation. It is also true that "Song of Wandering" has always had the final word in the collection *Lost Body*. Other poems have had their position and their text modified; this one remains essentially unchanged except for the removal of several lines that did not contribute directly to the general movement of the poem.

In the final analysis the title of the collection *Corps perdu* has a profoundly ambiguous resonance. In the title poem the body must be lost in order to be reborn: a symbolic death followed by a rebirth. I have chosen the English translation "Lost Body" over Snyder and Upson's "Disembodied" because the latter term does not maintain the positive side of the ambiguity. But in "Song of Wandering" the dispossessed, disembodied, mutilated islands of the black diaspora are not reintegrated. The black Osiris, the phoenix are present only as nostalgic reminiscences contained in a now closed wizard's book. Poetry will not make the revolution. The literary hero of negritude will not suffice to make the islands, or the speaker, whole. In his final collection of poetry, *Shackles*, Césaire was to include several poems that further develop these implications. The elegiac poems of *Shackles* throw into sharper relief the transitional features of "Song of Wandering," showing it to be an early example of an incipient crisis.

9

The Three Voices of *Shackles*

"The Cannibal has settled down . . ."
L'Express, 19 May 1960

THE COLLECTION *Ferrements (Shackles)* is poetically the most diverse in Césaire's oeuvre. It is the product of a crisis in his art, the last volume of poetry he published before turning to the theater. *Shackles* lends itself to a more direct reading than the earlier collections, yet its inspiration is anything but simple. The title is a play on words: *ferrements* are shackles, the slave's irons; but the title is also homophonic with "Ferment," the title of a poem in which the speaker is a punished Prometheus. At times the reader feels abruptly wrenched from one mood to another, as though Césaire were intent on driving home the uneasy tension in life between hope and despair.

The forty-eight poems of *Ferrements* appear to have been composed throughout the decade of the fifties.[1] Only eight had been published previously in magazines, the earliest in 1955. The collection represents the changing moods and styles of a poet whose social and political situation required serious modification of his original poetics. The chapter on *Lost Body* revealed only a hint of the changes that were to affect Césaire's poetry from the mid-fifties onward. It is in *Shackles* that one sees the result of the new poetics outlined in chapter 6. The stylistic diversity of the collection is such that it deserves more attention than it has received. There would appear to be considerable ideological overdetermination in the nearly monothematic treatments given to *Ferrements.* Some critics give the impression that poems dealing with history, with social and political subjects, relieve them from the obligation of paying attention to anything else. It is as though they felt that only one part of *Ferrements* represents the mature

Césaire, at long last emerged from surrealist experimentation to write clearly about contemporary life.

There are, however, three voices in *Shackles*, only one of which is raised in unambiguous praise for the end of colonialism in Africa south of the Sahara. This is the virile voice that salutes Guinea, independent of France in 1958 ("Salut à la Guinée"); the Third World, emerging into a difficult but nonetheless promising independent existence toward the end of the decade ("Pour saluer le Tiers Monde"); and the continent of Africa itself—Mother Africa ("Afrique"). These are good poems deserving of the praise they have received, but they represent only one voice in a polyphonic collection.

The intertextual poetics discussed at length in the chapter on *Beheaded Sun* by no means disappeared from *Shackles*, as both Lilyan Kesteloot and Bernadette Cailler have in different ways suggested.[2] The poem "Beautiful Spurted Blood" ("Beau Sang giclé") is brief, condensed, and hauntingly enigmatic. It is not necessary to recognize or to know the story of Yé, the peasant who killed the enchanted bird, in order to appreciate the intense feelings of dispersal and loss that are contained in the eight lines of the poem (p. 170). It is enough to follow the movement from mutilation—"trophy head lacerated members / deadly dart beautiful spurted blood / lost warblings ravished riverbanks . . ." ("tête trophée membres lacérés / dard assassin beau sang giclé / ramages perdus rivages ravis . . .")—through a pitying recollection of the past—"childhood childhood too stirred up tale" ("enfances enfances conte trop remué")—to a revenge that is wished for but not actual—"Dawn bites its chain ferocious to be born / o belated assassin / the bird once plumed more beautifully than the past / demands the account of its dispersed feathers" ("L'aube sur sa chaîne mord féroce à naître / ô assassin attardé / l'oiseau aux plumes jadis plus belles que le passé / exige le compte de ses plumes dispersées"). Here are the elements of the myth of the mutilated hero as they appear in *Beheaded Sun* and *Lost Body*, but they have been transferred, via the folkloric intertext, to the entire suffering people for whom Césaire would be the spokesman.

This is a significant modification in itself, of course. In "Beautiful Spurted Blood" Césaire does envisage an eventual collective assumption of revolutionary destiny by a people, whereas in his earlier collections the dominant voice had been that of the sacrificial hero. But folklore is not history, and the revolution posited in this poem is merely another aesthetic consolation for present suffering, sustaining the soul for a better future. Given the importance Césaire attributed to Afro-Caribbean folklore for the renewal of culture in Martinique during the war years, it is puzzling that his poetry made so little use of motifs like the story of Yé. For every Creole intertext in his poetry there are ten that derive from the European tradition, predominantly from biblical or classical mythological literature. This puzzle is of the same nature as Césaire's avoidance of Creole language as a literary vehicle. It testifies to the extraordinary degree of his own and his generation's assimilation of French and European culture, which he must draw upon and transform in the very effort to free himself from it. During the 1979 meeting of the American Association of Teachers of French in Martinique there were several interesting attempts to circumscribe this question. The most telling was made by a young Martinican linguist, Jean Bernabé, who holds that it is only the Martinicans now coming of age who can use Creole as a vehicle for culture through social change.[3] His discussion of Creole as being historically and sociologically the language of servitude and therefore a mark of humiliation goes far toward explaining Césaire's attitude toward his mother tongue.

A question that needs to be answered biographically and critically concerns Césaire's supposed speech impediment as a young man. According to Ngal, Césaire stuttered until he visited Haiti in 1944. There he found a people who shared much of his own history but who were independent and had evolved a living, dynamic Creole culture. Upon encountering an unself-conscious awareness of being Creole, Césaire ceased to stutter and has since become a formidable orator in French. The anecdote has never been verified, however, and it may be apocryphal, as Thomas Hale thinks. Ngal's biographical argument would have it that since Césaire found his natural medium of communication depreciated, excluded from the civilized exchange of the dominant culture, in order to master French as thoroughly as he has done he had to simultaneously internalize the humiliated image of his mother tongue. This hypothesis would account for the stuttering that disappeared when Césaire discovered that Creole need not be in the subservient position assigned to it in the Caribbean islands still in French hands. Whether or not the behavioral problem was ever as serious as Ngal has claimed, the psychic damage that had been done could not be undone so easily. This collective cultural wound may well be the root cause of the theme of personal mutilation in Césaire's work and of his rallying to the modernist agonism of Nietzsche's *The Birth of Tragedy*. Even in the short poem "Beautiful Spurted Blood" the Creole story of Yé is associated with the recollection of childhood as a time of suffering and humiliation, not of healing comfort. Similarly we can understand more readily the personal and collective need of black Martinican intellectuals of Césaire's generation to take refuge in a largely imaginary Mother Africa, since access to their real maternal culture—the Creole culture—was blocked by the very project that made of them "French" intellectuals. The resulting tension between sensibility and intellect, ethnicity and high culture, runs very deep in Césaire. These are contradictions that cannot be resolved in any individual's lifetime, certainly not when the colonial institutions that produced them remain essentially intact. All of these features of Césaire's poetry recur obsessively and insistently within one group of poems in *Shackles*. One should consider them in their relation to the original Césairean project of negritude before examining the two-stage metamorphosis that they undergo in this last major collection of poetry.

"Ferment" is the paradigm case in *Shackles* of the type of poem that offers an exemplary sufferer as hero. Césaire has chosen to represent his speaker in the guise of one of European culture's great symbolic figures: Prometheus (*Poèmes*, p. 176):

Ferment
Seducing from the feast of my liver o Sun
your birdlike reticence, rolling, flayed.
The harsh struggle taught us our wiles,
biting the clay, stamping the ground
marking the sweating land
with the blazon of our backs, with the tree of our shoulders
bleeding, bleeding
convulsion of dawn extrication of eagles.

                        Ferment
        Séduisant du festin de mon foie ô Soleil
        ta réticence d'oiseau, écorché, roulant.
        L'âpre lutte nous enseigna nos ruses,
        mordant l'argile, pétrissant le sol
        marquant la terre suante
        du blason du dos, de l'arbre de nos épaules
        sanglant, sanglant
        soubresaut d'aube démêlé d'aigles.

The eagle is assimilated to the sun in this poem, providing a metaphoric vehicle. The tenor of the metaphor, however, bears no
direct or necessary relation to the Prometheus myth. The new
thought that begins at line 3 could just as well have developed
in the direction of the familiar figure of Br'er Rabbit, who in
Martinican folklore incarnates the wily behavior acquired in
servitude just as he does in the tales of Uncle Remus. The four
lines beginning at l.3 might, in short, have been the focus of a
poem centered on a hero drawn from popular culture. Instead
of that Césaire has given us another compelling version of a more
private obsessive world, which projects its psychological and sociological structures outside time and history to lodge them in
Greek mythological figures taken as universal types.[4] This time
the intertext is practically self-evident: the *Prometheus Bound*
of Aeschylus is a standard reference point of the Western tradition. More specifically, Césaire's poem is the elaboration of the
lines of Hermes' speech that foretell the nature and extent of Prometheus' bondage. The first and final images of Césaire's poem
play, in a now familiar surrealist manner, on the following lines:

        ... a tedious length of time you must fulfil
        before you see the light again, returning.
        Then Zeus's winged hound, the eagle red,
        shall tear great shreds of flesh from you, a feaster
        coming unbidden, every day; your liver
        bloodied to blackness will be his repast.[5]

In Aeschylus the return of the devouring eagle corresponds to the
return of the sun; Césaire has simply conflated the two terms of
the narrative into a richer metaphor in his first and second lines.

Prometheus Bound serves as both an intertext and a framing device for Césaire's "Ferment." As I have indicated, Césaire was in possession of the elements to make a poem of another type entirely. The fact that he did not do so reveals the true nature of his poetic genius and, from a contemporary Antillean point of view, perhaps its limitations as well. Césaire's Prometheus will not struggle to free himself from the unjust laws of the new prince, whom Aeschylus himself portrays as a tyrannical usurper and destroyer of the old customs. *Prometheus Bound* could have offered the model of an adaptation in which a Promethean hero enlisted the aid of an already sympathetic Hephaestus to launch a revolution and topple Zeus from power. This option Césaire refused as well. His conclusion differs markedly from the way in which Aeschylus' Prometheus is to be freed (p. 243):

> And of this pain do not expect an end
> until some God shall show himself successor
> to take your tortures for himself and willing
> go down to lightless Hades and the shadows
> of Tartarus' depths.

The sacrificial substitution introduced by Aeschylus is religious in nature and, as such, not inconsistent with the sacrificial nature of the Césairean hero. But the manner of achieving closure is fundamentally different in Césaire. His final line, "convulsion of dawn extrication of eagles" ("soubresaut d'aube démêlé d'aigles") is a fine example of Césaire's use of the exploding-fixed type of closure. Just as the sun and the eagle were identified as the torturer in lines 1 and 2, so here the two elements of the image are juxtaposed with no apparent logical or syntactic link. This is, once again, an invocation of the surrealist concept of the marvelous; in Césaire's poem it is an epiphany that frees the hero of negritude from his shackles.

The same hermeneutic principle that confers its special meaning on the poem is at work in the title. Shackles—"fetters" in the Grene translation—are predominant in the opening scene of *Prometheus Bound*. By exploiting the homophony of *ferrements* and *ferments* Césaire has served two ends. It is a miraculous weapon that transforms Prometheus' punishment into a mental ferment promising a new dawn or age. At the same time, the reader of

"Ferment" cannot but be reminded that the first poem in the collection offers as a consolation to the perdurable shackles of enslavement the bond of love between a man and a woman. In "Shackles" love does not, as a more orthodox surrealism would have it, conquer all; love is a palliative for an enslavement in which only the forms have changed (*Poèmes*, p. 143):

> like before
> slaves stowed with heavy hearts
> just the same my dear just the same we scud along
> hardly a little less heartsick at the pitching
>
> comme jadis
> esclaves arrimés de coeurs lourds
> tout de même ma chère tout de même nous cinglons
> à peine un peu moins écoeurés aux tangages

By the very homophony of their titles these two poems represent the two poles between which the first voice of *Shackles* moves. It is evident that in describing two poles one does not posit two fundamentally different states but rather two faces of the same unbearable reality that permits no easy solution.

A brief, schematic look at eight poems of this type that Kestel-oot included in her joint study with Barthélemy Kotchy suggests the nature of this pendular swing. She noted that in all eight poems, including "Ferment," a self is represented as suffering victim while another self—sometimes qualified as "mine" as well—acts as torturer. Their struggle takes place in a closed space: island, cell, tower, pit. The conclusion she characterizes as a leap *(sursaut)*, seeing a necessarily positive social and psychological connotation in a line such as "convulsion of dawn extrication of eagles." Her conclusion involves some manipulation of the image, which is glossed in Kesteloot and Kotchy as "the devouring eagles are mixed with *dawn*, i.e. [become] bearers of renewal, of youth, of a new age" (p. 105). While the description of the situation presented metaphorically in the poem is unexceptionable, the absence of a sense of tragic vision causes some distortion in her conclusion, which is correct in a sense but for the wrong reason. In other words, the optimistic conclusion Kesteloot forces from the poem does not fit its metaphoric structure or the nature of its intertextual play. The third common element in her reading of the eight poems is the recognition that they are all set in a *champ clos,* the lists used for medieval judgment by combat. The atmosphere of close confinement, combined with a violent action wherein the self is sometimes pitted against itself, provides a modernist, psychological version of the conditions requisite to tragic action. The lines of opposition are drawn, and the situation has already hardened into intransigent positions from which only suffering, violence, and death can result. The modernist device that Césaire regularly employs, thus aligning himself with the Nietzschean precept, is to present the hero as a future redeemer whose tragic action will be efficacious only on the condition that he be sacrificed in the present.

To pursue the Nietzschean analogy to its logical conclusion, it becomes apparent that the Prometheus of "Ferment" is a Dionysian figure. This observation bears upon the manner in which Césaire has interpreted or cannibalized Prometheus, the dominant culture hero of contemporary, technological Western civilization. By transforming the punished, suffering Prometheus into a Nietzschean tragic hero, what Césaire has done is to present Prometheus—stealer of fire, symbolic hero of Western individualism—in terms of his opposite, Dionysos, who symbolizes the tendency toward unity, peace, and harmony. In *Eros and Civilization* (part 2, chapter 8) Herbert Marcuse made the point that modern cultural representations of Narcissus, Orpheus, and Dionysos are utopian efforts to find an alternative reality principle, one not based on repression of instinct. This was precisely Césaire's project in refining the concept of negritude in his outline of a poetics in "Poetry and Cognition." The poem "Ferment," when seen in this light, is one more example of what Césaire intended by the proposal to *marronner,* or to escape European literature by cannibalizing it: his Prometheus is, from the standpoint of the dominant culture, a countertype. The unexpected encounter of Marcuse and Aeschylus in this poem leads inevitably to the conclusion that, even to a significant extent in *Ferrements,* Césaire practiced a radical poetics. Thus, Césairean negritude aimed at the creation of a counterculture *avant la lettre.*

The problem these poems have presented to readers of *Shackles* is that they do not fit the image of the collection as exhorting "the Martinican people to take cognizance of their situation and to

create for themselves a future in which they will no longer be the
puppet of tourists or the instruments of wealthy plantation owners. The political message permits no equivocation . . ."[6] The
author of these lines, who had in mind only the second of Césaire's
three voices in *Shackles,* has little to say about the style of the
first voice. Césaire's surrealist style corresponds to a particular
sense of how a black Martinican intellectual experiences his alienation—economic and psychological—within a neocolonial system that he does not see as likely to change. There is an obvious
and important contradiction here between the violence of this
poetic style and the absence of historical subjects in poems of this
type.[7] Faced with this painful prospect, Césaire did not write
revolutionary poetry between 1939 and the mid-fifties. Instead
he took the same road to the absolute as the European surrealists,
concentrating on techniques for survival of the individual mind or
soul. He projected into the poetry of this long first stage a
disintegrated ego that typically regresses from social norms in
order to find a stable position that is not threatened by exterior
reality. The violence that frequently precedes the renewal of the
self should not be confused with a socially revolutionary activity.
It is the violence of repressive desublimation, to use Marcuse's
felicitous term. The goal of this project is not social in the usual
sense; it is meant to sustain the wounded self, which an unjust,
oppressive social and racial system has alienated from itself. The
true goal of Césaire's surrealist voice is to create lyrical structures,
in many cases pseudomyths, that will enable educated blacks to
endure until some real social change may be possible.

   In those poems of this period in which Césaire represented a
heroic figure the hero was not conceived in primarily social terms.
He was not a revolutionary in any political sense. His quest was
spiritual rather than political. This judgment holds for the heroic
speaker of the *Notebook* as much as for the Rebel of *And the Dogs
Were Silent.* The speaker in the *Notebook* had to pass through a
painful self-examination and a metamorphosis before emerging
as a leader. This spiritual project was frequently expressed as
apocalyptical discourse in *Beheaded Sun. Lost Body* combined a
demiurgic creativity with a spiritual concept of the efficacy of the
poetic word. Césaire's accomplishments in this style are, as I have
argued, among the most considerable of any postsymbolic poet.
The unfortunate misunderstanding that continues to surround

this group of his poems, which constitutes the bulk of his production in the lyric, derives from systematic misreading or from efforts to find in it features that are not there, which amounts to the same thing. The surrealist voice of Césaire's negritude did not address directly the social and political questions of the day. For that purpose he employed an incomparable prose—in the *Discourse on Colonialism* and in the *Letter to Maurice Thorez*—in which he excelled in manipulating a wide range of rhetorical devices, a feat that study of his political texts will one day show to full advantage.

Songs of Combat and Praise

The end of the decade of the fifties saw an irreversible movement toward the independence of colonized black Africa. In 1960 the momentum increased with the birth of new republics in Ghana (a member of the Commonwealth since 1957), and Zaïre. Since the adoption of the constitution of the Fifth Republic in 1958, the way was open to qualified independence within the French Community for numerous other West African states, including Senegal (with L. S. Senghor as president), Ivory Coast, Chad, Gabon, and Congo (Brazzaville). Césaire's collection *Ferrements* was published in the early months of 1960, coinciding perfectly with the height of the movement toward independence. The reputation of his last major collection of poetry has been linked in the public mind with this historic juncture. But even those who have been most eager to establish Césaire in the position of cofounder of neo-African literature usually agree with Kesteloot that "a great part of Césaire's success in the black world is still owing to the aggressivity of his earliest works," and most especially to the *Notebook*.[8] A French historian of colonialism, Henri Brunschwig, likewise wrote of the *Notebook* in 1963 that "On rereading this poem today one discovers the kernel of all the themes of the doctrine that the Africans progressively elaborated."[9] The truth is that from 1960 onward Césaire the poet had little more to say to a free Africa, which was entering an era of needs and requirements no longer served by the inspiration that had nourished his lyrical writing for two decades.

Césaire drew his great strength as a poet from the possibility of positing an ethos of revolt on the unity of African values as he was able to either know or imagine it to have been prior to the European colonization of the continent. As I have shown, Césaire's spiritual home was a partly imaginary, partly idealized Africa whose unity he could maintain intellectually only as long as Africa was still subject to Europe and unable to speak in its own great variety of voices. Even insofar as one can refer to the historical aspect of Césaire's Africa, it too existed largely in the past. The present, up until the end of the fifties, united black Africa and the Caribbean islands in a similar colonial status, which made it possible for a black poet writing in Fort-de-France or Paris to be read with equal impact by the African elite of Dakar, Conakry, Abidjan, Yaoundé, or Leopoldville. After 1960 Césaire was read even more widely in many parts of Africa south of the Sahara; the *Notebook* sold hundreds of thousands of copies, according to information supplied to Thomas Hale by Présence Africaine. However, Césaire's ethos of revolt had to be perceived in a new light. In a word, Patrice Lumumba or Sékou Touré stepped beyond any need they may have had for Césaire's brand of negritude the day they found themselves responsible for the mineral wealth of Katanga or for the sale of their nation's agricultural products. This analysis of the value of *Shackles* for an unfettered Africa weighs heavily on the side of the possible social impact of contemporary poetry. In that respect it is only a partial analysis. It does, however, illustrate a problem that recurs frequently in writing on Césaire. Almost without exception, commentators have insisted on the unity of inspiration in Césaire's poetry and his theater, which is explained as essentially an effort to reach a wider audience. Césaire has himself contributed to the dissemination of this view. Yet there is demonstrably a crisis in Césaire's work, and one can follow its development within the pages of *Shackles* in the evolution of its three voices. The crisis was brought about by the challenge to Césaire's ethos of revolt inherent in the emergence of a new Africa, no longer unified in a static, partially mythic past but suddenly bursting with pent-up energies and contradictions that were the legacy of European rule. It is no accident that Césaire's powerful lyricism suddenly went silent after 1960, with but occasional pieces appearing after that date (seventeen are collected under the title *Noria* in the *Oeuvres complètes*, and some of those were first published prior to 1960).

The image of *Shackles* that has been most widely circulated is that of the poetry of decolonization, of unshackling. Not only does this interpretation overlook the connotations of the poems discussed in the preceding section; it is also derived from a rather small part of the poems in the collection. At most some thirteen poems out of forty-eight can be read in this manner.[10] Roughly three-quarters of the poems in *Shackles* prolong the poetics of miraculous weapons that Césaire had been practicing for twenty years. When he said to Jacqueline Sieger in 1960 that "In my recent collections," by which he presumably meant *Ferrements* and *Cadastre,* which he was then revising, "the hermetic aspect has been significantly diminished,"[11] Césaire was describing a modification in the degree of difficulty of access to three-quarters of the pieces in *Shackles;* he could not have been referring to a difference in their nature as poems. "Ferment" is far more accessible than "The Sun's Knife-Stab in the Back of the Surprised Cities," but both poems are dependent on a particular kind of intertextuality and an identical type of closure.

If ease of access, readability, is not the central issue in *Shackles,* then what is? The distinguishing features of the second and third voices in *Shackles* are bound up with the nature of the speaker's represented self and his relationship to the real world of contemporary history and politics. A very small group of poems (see note 10), no more than seven in all, presents a stabilized ego that reaches out confidently to the emerging nations of black Africa, declaring its solidarity with their combat in the final stage of decolonization. The uniqueness of this posture in Césaire's poetry is most readily grasped by a comparison with those elements of his former poetics that do not appear in these poems: the alienated self that sought stability in regressive erotism; the refusal of history through the creation of a pseudomythology; intertextuality as a form of cannibalism of European culture. It is important to note that this psychological evolution corresponds to, and is surely supported by, a very special set of social and political conditions. As a member of the French legislature, Césaire had taken part in the debates that helped modify political opinion and eventually prepare the end of the French colonial empire. In this respect the events of 1958–1960 brought with them a momentary euphoria for the Martinican poet. Although the decolonization of Africa did nothing to change the neocolonial status of Martinique, it did permit Césaire to live vicariously the rebirth of Africa.

This is the context that accounts for Césaire's odd affirmation in October 1960: "I am an African poet!" The euphoria was short-lived, but while it lasted Césaire produced some poems that are among his most widely appreciated.

The nature of this new voice in Césaire's poetry rapidly becomes apparent when one compares the poems "Africa" and "Salute to Guinea" in *Shackles* to their counterparts "To Africa" and "Ode to Guinea" in *Beheaded Sun* (see chapter 7). "Salute to Guinea" ("Salut à la Guinée") is the fifth poem in *Shackles*, coming after four pieces belonging to Césaire's earlier poetics. Its place in the collection is presumably intended to introduce early on, and for a contrapuntal effect with the first piece, "Shackles," the image of independent Africa. This poem is in fact unique in *Shackles*. It is the only one written to commemorate an individual state. It is written from the standpoint of an intensely admiring observer who sends greetings and a lyrical wish for the preservation of (p. 147) "this rolling / of fragile freedom" ("ce roulis / de liberté fragile").

Guinea became an independent republic in 1958 by refusing the constitution of the Fifth Republic, which contained a provision for reorganizing the former colonies of French West Africa into an economic community along the lines of the British Commonwealth. In Césaire's eyes the decision by Sékou Touré, first president of the Republic of Guinea, to reject this neocolonial version of assimilationism represented a heroic gesture and a model for the new Africa. His article of December 1959, "The Political Thought of Sékou Touré," is eloquent on this subject. There is a large measure of Césaire's own ideals in the interpretation he gave of Guinea's version of African socialism: "The process of legislation is slow, patient, as though it were a matter of germination in hard ground. This is so because their law is never the result of a 'fiat,' be it that of a man or that of an assembly, but the result of an infinite number of painstaking deliberations in the most distant bush country, in the most out of the way village and the result of successive approximations which the Guinean National Assembly merely sanctions definitively and which the signature of Sékou Touré ratifies."[12]

This is the beautiful utopian ideal of a prophet who has turned from eschatology (the style of *Beheaded Sun*) to the prediction of the African millennium. In a gloss on a page by Sékou Touré,

Césaire revealed to what extent he continued to believe in a dialectical process of history that is more Hegelian than Marxist:
"After the 'moment' of precolonial Africa, the moment of 'immediate truth,' and the colonial 'moment,' the moment of a mutilated African consciousness, independence inaugurates a third
dialectical 'moment,' which must correspond to a reconciliation
of the spirit with its own consciousness and with the reconquest
of plentitude" (p. 67). Thus, the socialist state that Césaire envisaged for Guinea in 1959 is characterized above all else by the
fullness of being, the realization of something like the Hegelian
Idea in a contemporary African nation. I shall not comment on
the political implications of this prophecy, except to note that this
is the stuff of which good lyric poetry is made. A few months
earlier at the Rome conference of black writers and artists Césaire
had insisted that not just any decolonization would do for Africa,
and he had concluded that "the greatest ambition of our literature must be to aim to become *sacred literature,* our art, *sacred
art*" (see chapter 8, note 9). One understands how, in this quasi-
ecstatic frame of mind, Césaire was able for a brief moment to
overcome his own profound sense of subjection, mutilation, and
depersonalization as a colonized man. The songs of combat and
of praise in *Shackles* themselves result from a new act of imagination, the imminent rebirth of a free Africa was experienced by
Césaire as an intensely spiritual event. The result in his poetry is
a temporary, and necessarily fleeting, grasp of that fullness of
being that modern man can imagine only as the psychological
wholeness that eludes him in his normal state. Césaire projected
that wholeness into a few poems that stand out by their difference.
In view of their healing virtue they may be considered paeans;
rather than poems to propitiate the healing god, these are songs
of praise by a poet who already feels himself healed. With respect
to its generic type one may entertain the hypothesis that Césaire
wished to approximate in a European language that form of traditional African praise poetry that is related to the lyric. It is
customary to use this type of praise poetry in rites of passage.
Was not the birth of the Republic of Guinea the result of a rite
of passage in which the nation is collectively reborn to a new
status? Césaire's article on Sékou Touré is compatible with this
view.

"Salute to Guinea" (p. 147) is organized around a lyrical evo-

cation of the new nation's geography, its physical being. It begins by naming towns and a river that have undoubtedly been selected for their special euphony; they denote places but they
connote a lyrical mood: "Dalaba Pita Labé Mali Timbé / puis-
santes falaises ["powerful cliffs"] / Tinkisso Tinkisso." A phonemic analysis of this opening would show a systematic exploitation
by Césaire of the softer consonants [l] [m] [s] [z] in conjunction
with the vowels [a] and [i] to create a very affirmative yet delicate
texture (see chapter 8). These are in fact the dual themes that the
poem subsequently pursues: self-affirmation and gentleness. "Tinkisso Tinkisso" is a sonorous, delicate refrain, which is echoed
immediately in the next line, "eaux belles" ("beautiful waters")
and taken up again in the interjection "Guinée oh / te garde ton
allure" ("Oh Guinea / may you maintain your stylish pace").

One of Césaire's privileged images, the volcano, figures prominently but its role has been appropriately transformed. In this
song of praise its "primordial fire" stands guard over "this most
rare treasure." From a destructive instrument of apocalyptic ven-
geance the volcano has been transformed into a symbol of paternal strength. The sea is personified as the mother of the new
nation, and a prayer is addressed to her:

> caress and suckling with mother's milk
> the new form and cradle
> oh cradle
>   with a maternal meander
> this sand
>   this rolling
>   of fragile freedom
>
> caresse et l'allaitant du lait premier
> la forme nouvelle et berce
> oh berce
>   d'un maternel méandre
> ce sable
>   ce roulis
>   de liberté fragile[13]

Both great natural forces are called on to protect the initiate
from the dangers inherent in its perilous journey to a new mode

of being. The reader is gradually made aware that this is a praise song of a particular type, the one used for the naming of a new-born. Césaire in "Salute to Guinea" has compensated for his exclusion from the independence of Africa by assuming the privileged position of the celebrant who recites the praise song.

"Africa" ("Afrique") is in several ways more typical of Césaire's combative voice in *Shackles*, but it shares with "Salute to Guinea" the sense of wholeness and confidence on the part of the speaker. Like all the other poems in this group, with the single exception of "Salute to Guinea," it was inspired by the final phase of the African independence movement. The poem expresses confidence in the eventual, indeed the imminent, success of decolonization and in sum exhorts the continent as a whole to persevere to the end. "Africa" contains all the elements that were to become serious threats to Césaire's poetics once the struggle for a free Africa had in large measure been won. Africa is represented as one and indivisible in its colonial status, a formerly glorious spiritual mother reduced to the humiliation of prostitution by her conquerors (*Poèmes*, p. 199):

> your solar tiara forced around your neck by rifle butts
> they transformed it into an iron collar; your clairvoyance
> they put out its eyes; prostituted your modest face;
> muzzled, screaming that it was guttural,
> your voice, which spoke in the silence of shadows

> ta tiare solaire à coups de crosse enfoncée jusqu'au cou
> ils l'ont transformée en carcan; ta voyance
> ils l'ont crevée aux yeux; prostitué ta face pudique;
> emmuselé, hurlant qu'elle était gutturale,
> ta voix, qui parlait dans le silence des ombres

The middle section, devoted to the exhortation to combat, is remarkably unimpressive. Competent poetry, but not memorable. In fact Césaire seems to be struggling here to avoid the commonplace, and he does not always succeed:

> Africa,
> tremble not the battle is new,
> the living wave of your blood elaborates without faltering

a season constant; the night is now in the depths of
swamps
the formidable unstable back of a sleepless star . . .

Afrique,
ne tremble pas le combat est nouveau,
le flot vif de ton sang élabore sans faillir
constante une saison; la nuit c'est aujord'hui au fond des
mares
le formidable dos instable d'un astre mal endormi . . .

Without excessive irony, and bearing in mind Césaire's objections
to Aragon a few years earlier, I would suggest that Aragon at his
best was more convincing in this style. Césaire's syntactic inver-
sions ("constante une saison"), which were a mainstay of his
earlier poetic voice, ring false here, and the images become almost banal. One begins to miss the mysterious power of his surrealist metaphors and the positive challenge of earlier poems.

The final movement improves markedly in quality. Césaire has
found a familiar posture, one in perfect accord with his own
poetic genius. At the same time the conclusion of "Africa" is
symptomatic of the difficulty Césaire was to encounter as a poet
shortly after publication of *Shackles*. The outcome of the battle,
the future of the new Africa, he envisages as a splendid rebirth of
the past (*Poèmes*, p. 199):

Africa the forgotten days which ever make their way
in recurved shells in the doubt of a gaze
will flash forth on the public face amongst happy ruins

Afrique les jours oubliés qui cheminent toujours
aux coquilles recourbées dans les doutes du regard
jailliront à la face publique parmi d'heureuses ruines

Or again (*Poèmes*, p. 200):

the hidden things will climb again the slope of dormant
music . . .

les choses cachées remonteront la pente des musiques
endormies . . .

These and similar images relate Césaire's faith in the efficacy of the presumed collective unconscious of "Africa." On the eve of the entry onto the international stages of extremely diverse African states, the songs of combat in *Shackles* confused the harsh exigencies of contemporary history with the soothing comforts of myths that had been wrought for the purpose of surviving colonialism.

The Elegiac Voice

The crisis in Césaire's art precipitated by the African independence movement was to become permanent, even as it stimulated new creative activity. As African nations began to evolve, each in its own direction, the lack of political change in Martinique made itself painfully felt. What was the proper role of a poet from Martinique whose writings had been read by many in Africa and in the Americas as prophetic of the political revolution to come? The revolutionary sixties came and went. Aimé Césaire turned from lyrical prophecy to a theatrical form in which he grappled with the consequences of political and social revolution in black nations.

His first play written for the stage, *The Tragedy of King Christophe* (1963–1964), treats the problem of leadership in a postcolonial black nation by focusing on Henri Christophe, emperor of Haiti from 1811 to 1820. This attempt to treat the current problems of African nations obliquely, using the larger-than-life figure of Henri Christophe as a symbol, has met with considerable success wherever it has been staged: in Paris (May and September 1965); Dakar, Senegal (April 1966); Montreal (1967); and later in Yugoslavia and at Milan's Piccolo Teatro. Martinicans saw *The Tragedy of King Christophe* at home only in 1976, in a production by the Théâtre National du Sénégal, which accompanied an official visit to Fort-de-France by that country's president, L. S. Senghor.

A Season in the Congo has gone through three versions (1966, 1967, 1973). It is Césaire's only theatrical plunge into contemporary events. The independence of the former Belgian Congo came about in 1960 in an atmosphere of political chaos, tribal competition, and eventually, warfare, European intervention, and the ineffectual presence of representatives of the United Nations. Out of this confusion Césaire decanted a drama in which Patrice Lumumba bears a striking resemblance to the Rebel of *And the Dogs Were Silent,* with the important modification that the tragic hero is surrounded by an extraordinary array of lively characters and crowd scenes that testify to an unusual talent for epic theater.[14] For reasons that have never been entirely clear this play has not received the critical acclaim of its predecessor. The very existence of *A Season in the Congo* cries out for a similar play set in the Caribbean. At this writing Césaire gives no sign of ever producing it.[15]

Césaire's only creative effort since 1960 to treat the situation of Caribbean societies is his play *Une Tempête* (1968–1969), which is subtitled "Adaptation of Shakespeare's *The Tempest* for a Black Theater." I have written elsewhere that Césaire's play is in part a critical reflection on the value system of Western humanism using Shakespeare's play as a paradigm.[16] Even in *A Tempest* creativity cannot be separated from a critical activity, and the Caribbean society Césaire presents in the play is a schema in which characters and plot outline come from Shakespeare but personal interrelations are posited on an amalgam of Marxian analysis and Adlerian psychology. In various ways he introduced into *A Tempest* his familiar type of Africanism, the most notable being the creation of a new character, the Yoruba god Eshu. Shakespeare's Ariel is designated as a mulatto and Caliban as a black by Césaire, who thus injects class along with race as a problem in his play. The conclusion is identical with the one Césaire proposed as a goal for an independent Guinea in 1959: Caliban (colonized man) must negate the value system of the colonialist (exploitation, repression, enslavement) in order eventually to achieve a new synthesis in freedom. Prospero states the case in *A Tempest,* although in cruel jest:

> It's definitely a topsy-turvy world. Now we've seen everything: Calaban a dialectician![17]

On the positive side, the play makes the valuable point that the white world needs to learn from the experience of the nonwhite world. On the negative side, *A Tempest* can be seen as one more example of Césaire's apparent inability to treat directly the social and political dilemma of blacks in a white-dominated society. Consider the reservations expressed on this point in an otherwise sympathetic and even admiring article by a black scholar from the Caribbean, Frederick Ivor Case: "In writing these allegorical plays, did Césaire hope to transcend the stifling context of the Antilles to universalize the drama of Blacks? Must one conclude that there are no lessons to be learned from the Antillean tragedy? Why has Aimé Césaire never written a play about Antillean reality? Why this escape to other shores and other periods, when Blacks in his native island are often victims of the colonialists' bullets?"[18]

M. a M. Ngal, whose long article on Césaire's theater Case knew, saw the same recurring characters and the same tragic plot. Yet his assessment is firmly on the positive side, insisting that "One has [in this theater] the harshest criticism that has been leveled against the new African regimes. The danger that threatens them is that they may create in reality a 'Christophe' who would be but the negation of themselves. It can be avoided only by transcending the contradiction, the false contradiction, through the authentic play [*jeu*] of their own existence."[19] The African scholar adopts a position of cultural conservatism with an existentialist overtone: "the authentic play of their own existence." For him Césaire's theater is a model. The Caribbean scholar adopts a Marxian analysis that finds Césaire's theater seriously flawed because it avoids the concrete realities of his situation as a Martinican. Nearly everything written on Césaire to date gravitates toward one or the other of these two poles.

I would suggest that the direction Césaire took in his theater during the sixties is a direct outgrowth of the crisis one discovers in *Shackles*. He turned to the public art form of theater because, in a sense, he had to. Only a creative mode that permits the objectification of conflict outside oneself offered Césaire any real possibilities after 1960. What he accomplished was an admirable projection onto a larger, collective scale of the conflict that he could no longer synthesize as before in the persona of a lyrical, represented self. His Henri Christophe and Lumumba are both tragic figures who continue in their different ways the timeless, cosmic drama of the Rebel in *And the Dogs Were Silent*. One can understand the political argument that Césaire should have turned his great talent to what he knew best—to the society that remains his own, that he represents politically, and that he has always wanted to change. It can be argued, however, that Césaire is not free to accomplish the very task for which he would appear to be best suited.

During the fifties, before he decided on the theater as the only genre capable of treating new developments in the black world, a different tone appeared in Césaire's poetry. Poems dealing with Caribbean and American subjects took on an elegiac quality. They became more reflective, less explosive, and established a more conventional aesthetic distance between the speaker and the sacrifice of human life that he relates. The elegiac voice is not completely absent from Césaire's earlier collections, but it is rare, and it has gone quite unnoticed. In *Lost Body* the beautiful "Song of Wandering" is as pure an example of the elegiac spirit as one can find in contemporary French poetry. It is a lamentation on the sufferings of black people throughout the diaspora.[20]

The poems in *Shackles* that I would locate within a somewhat loosely defined elegiac tradition are "Statue of Lafcadio Hearn" ("Statue de Lafcadio Hearn"), "Cenotaph of Paul Eluard" ("Tombeau de Paul Eluard"), "Memorial to Louis Delgrès" ("Mémorial de Louis Delgrès"), "To the Memory of a Black Union Man" ("A la mémoire d'un syndicaliste noir"), "On the State of the Union" ("Sur l'état de l'Union"), and "In Truth" ("En vérité"). The four middle titles in this list are grouped together in *Shackles* immediately preceding a group of four songs of combat: "Africa" ("Afrique"), "Out of Foreign Days" ("Hors des jours étrangers"), "Salute to the Third World" ("Pour saluer le Tiers Monde"), and "Indivisible." This is to say that, whereas Césaire appears to have made a distinction between the two voices by grouping the poems in this fashion, it would be improper to infer that he stressed the elegiac voice in conclusion. Were it not for the fact that the final poem, "In Truth," is elegiac while holding the door open on the future ("un enfant entrouvrira la porte"), one could affirm quite confidently that Césaire intended to end the collection on a strongly optimistic note. As it is, one must take into consideration the evident counterpoint of the organization of the last dozen poems. There can be no doubt that there was a conscious intention to create a modulation of voices within the collection, emphasizing the presence of Césaire's earlier poetics in the first three-quarters of *Shackles* and setting up a dialogue between the elegies and the songs of combat in the last quarter of the collection.

To conclude this study of Aimé Césaire's poetry with a consideration of his elegiac voice involves a decision that takes the
reader outside the collection entitled *Shackles*. The elegiac poems
were published in *Présence Africaine* between 1955 and 1959,
for the most part; the songs of combat and of praise, "Salute to
Guinea" and "Salute to the Third World," appeared in the same
magazine in mid-1959. With one exception—Césaire's placing
"Salute to Guinea" toward the beginning—this is also the relative
order of their distribution in *Shackles*. The internal logic of the
collection suggests a mental and moral evolution from surrealist
revolt to elegiac reflection to an enthusiastic salute to Africa and
the Third World. One cannot in fact be certain that this is not
the reading Césaire himself intended or meant to suggest by his
distribution of the poems. However, as analyses of the poems
"Ferment" and "Beautiful Spurted Blood" have already shown,
fundamental ambiguity and doubt exist with regard to the possibility of facing the dilemma of Martinique in any direct way.
The taboo against using Creole, which Césaire had internalized
and made a part of himself, extends to any confrontation of a
poetic nature with the depressing realities of his own society.
There is a psychological dynamic at work in Césaire's elegiac
voice that permits a comparison of this aspect of his later poetry
with his play *A Tempest*, written a decade later.

The stabilization of the represented self in Césaire's poems
"Salute to Guinea," "Africa," or "Salute to the Third World"
can be seen as logically intermediary between the psychologically
regressive strategy of his surrealist poetics and the formal mediation between speaker and world afforded by the elegiac voice. In
his elegiac poems Césaire adopts a position of retrenchment in
the face of a neocolonialist system so firmly established in the
overseas departments of France—the Départements d'Outre-
Mer, including Martinique—that their abolition through revolution cannot even be envisaged. A better understanding of this
development in Césaire's poetry will go part way toward bridging
the gap that has been presumed to exist between the politics he
has practiced as leader of the Parti Progressiste Martiniquais
(founded in 1958) and the aura of revolution that continues to
surround *Shackles*. In his elegiac poems, as in *A Tempest*, the
promise of revolution has been deferred. The project of a satisfactory reintegration of the self in a just and free society is con-

sequently held in abeyance: by the mediation of structures derived from Shakespeare and treated critically in the play and by the aesthetic distance of the elegiac voice in poems treating Caribbean and American subjects in *Shackles*. If there is a continuity to be found between Césaire's poetry and his plays, it will be located in the elegiac poems.

The "Memorial to Louis Delgrès" is devoted to a black Martinican hero of the revolution that failed: in 1802 he held Fort Saint-Charles in Guadeloupe for three days against a far superior force commanded by General Richepanse and seconded by the Antilleans Gobert and Pelage, who had joined the repression. It is the longest poem in the collection. "Memorial to Louis Delgrès" is generally considered to be didactic. Kesteloot put it well in her 1962 study of Césaire: "The poet hopes that in the long run these examples of overmen will give Martinicans a taste for simply being men. This is the humble work of raising statues to the heroes of the past instead of exalting the valiance of his people in the present" (p. 73). She had in mind the several poems memorializing dead heroes in *Shackles*, but this otherwise good appreciation of political education through cultural example does not ask the crucial question: Why does Césaire resort to such a long-term strategy? To answer in terms of political realities—which Césaire's adversaries would be sure to call expediency or worse—invites the very criticism Case has made of Césaire's theater. A more literary answer will reveal the nature of the continuity in Césaire's work at the same time that it illuminates the connection between his poetics and his politics.

"Memorial to Louis Delgrès" contains a double epigraph: the second, from J.-J. Dessalines's proclamation to the Haitians on 28 April 1804, celebrates the "magnanimous warrior"; the first, from the 1870 Larousse encyclopedia, outlines a mythic scenario: "Without any illusions as to the certain outcome of a struggle that he had accepted, but not provoked, [Delgrès] distinguished himself by his chivalrous courage. He was seen sitting in a cannon port, his violin in hand, defying the bullets of General Richepanse, the commander of the odious expedition, and like a modern Tyrtaeus, playing his instrument to inspire his soldiers" (*Poèmes*, p. 189). The allusion to Tyrtaeus, seen as a *mise en abyme*, connects the poet of seventh-century Sparta, who wrote elegies to stimulate soldiers on the battlefield, with both the Martinican hero Delgrès and the poet Césaire, whose elegy memorializes him. The connection Tyrtaeus–Delgrès–Césaire also makes a claim for the eventual efficaciousness of the elegiac poem. The purpose of the second epigraph now becomes clear. Delgrès died defending freedom and justice. (He blew himself to bits along with the fort rather than surrender.) His revolution may have failed, but Dessalines was successful in Haiti; moreover, he recognized and proclaimed the heroism of Delgrès. By subtle implication Césaire's poem places him in the very position of Delgrès. In both form and overt message the "Memorial to Louis Delgrès" declares that poetry may not make the revolution but it can condition the soul of a people to endure. Although both the independence of the French overseas departments and the poet's true glory are presented as belonging to a time that has not yet come, the poem invokes historical example to ensure that both will come to pass. The historical subject guarantees a high degree of continuity in Césaire's poetic vision in that it incarnates in a real hero of the Caribbean world the drama of the agonistic hero that Césaire had previously treated as an atemporal, mythic *topos*. Myth and history come together happily in the "Memorial to Louis Delgrès"; in that sense Césaire's elegiac voice permits a new synthesis of the ideal and the actual. The few poems he has written in this vein are similar in their didactic intention to the movement to promote the study of black history in the United States. Indeed, at the same time that he was writing this poem he was preparing his essay on black history in the Caribbean, *Toussaint Louverture* (1961). Chapter 16, "The Masks are Dropped," relates the sequence of events leading up to Richepanse's victory at Matouba, identifying personally and politically the dramatis personae of the poem.[21] Four pages of rather dry, matter-of-fact prose in the essay provide the only preparation necessary to grasp all the historical references in the poem, which is as different from it in mood and spirit as Archilocus is from Herodotus. In a more formal perspective, Césaire in "Memorial to Louis Delgrès" has created an original blend of the two earliest forms of elegy: the martial (insofar as the poem relates a glorious *fait d'armes* and inspires by example) and the lamentation for a dead hero.

The next poem in the collection is "To the Memory of a Black Union Man." Its most significant originality lies in the choice of subject: a contemporary trade unionist symbolic of the struggle for dignity of the working class. He is representative in his anonymity, ennobled in the tradition of elegiac poetry. This is by no stretch of the critical imagination popular poetry, despite the ostensible subject. In the first strophe a formal tradition may be said to dictate the use of the preterite and a certain allusiveness, but the syntax is more Mallarméan than that of Mallarmé's own *Tombeaux* (his elegies for Poe, Baudelaire, and Verlaine):

> Lest a hurricane wane lest the rock lurch
> for him breast that was sure
> whose fiery clarion in shadow and chance
> rustic diminished not

> Qu'une tempête ne décline que le roc ne titube
> pour celui poitrail qui fut sûr
> dont le clairon de feu dans l'ombre et le hasard
> rustique ne décrut[22]

This is the language of Mallarmé's sonnets, which no ordinary Martinican trade unionist could be expected to read. In this poem the mutual implication of poetics and politics is once again inescapable. It would be plausible to argue that in the "Memorial to Louis Delgrès" Césaire circumvented the iron law according to which his creative representation of Caribbean reality must be filtered through a modernist poetics. But that would be inaccurate. Louis Delgrès and his struggle exist in a historical past, as the essay on *Toussaint Louverture* demonstrates. His is not an actual or present reality. The reality that stimulated the reflection that resulted in the elegy "To the Memory of a Black Union Man" was painfully close to the poet.

Thomas Hale questioned Césaire on the subject of this poem in 1972 and learned that it had been written to commemorate the death of a compatriot from Basse Pointe, Martinique, which was the birthplace of Delgrès and of Césaire himself. Albert Cretinoir died (from natural causes) on 17 December 1952. At that time Césaire was still, like Cretinoir, a member of the Communist party.[23] He chose to treat this hometown comrade as a symbol in his funeral elegy. The poetic result is extraordinary. If, as Hale says, "the funeral is for Martinicans only," how many Martinicans constitute the intended public of the first strophe?

I feel that in "To the Memory of a Black Union Man," as in the other elegies in *Shackles*, the coefficient of modernist indirection rises in proportion to the proximity of the subject to Césaire's own lived experience. Put somewhat differently, the Creoleness of the subject is marked by its opposite, the most hypersophisticated version of modernism, in this case a Mallarméan syntax. Only the dominant European high culture (modernism) authenticates for Césaire the creative treatment of a Creole subject (negritude close to home).

Hale gives a sensitive reading of the middle and end of the poem, which are significantly less allusive than the first strophe. Césaire used the expression *maître marronneur* (literally "master marooner") in praising his dead comrade. *Marooner* in this Afro-Caribbean context is to be taken as applying to the leader who showed other slaves the way to freedom (for instance, the maroons of Jamaica): "The 'Maître marronneur' becomes, in what appears as a combination of the two words, 'montreur' [guide], another image for the sun. The combination of solar and telluric warmth in the last stanza suggests the possibility of hope, rebirth, and regeneration in the face of death, and it is this sense of rebirth, sweeping the Black diaspora in the years to come, which answers, implicitly, the prayers of the poet" (p. 116). The danger in this reading is that it may lead to the conclusion that Césaire's Martinican elegies testify to the same hope—and in the same way—as do his poems in praise of free Africa. They do not. The highly formalized discourse of Césaire's elegiac voice does express hope, of course, but there is nothing direct or certain about it. The reader of "To the Memory of a Black Union Man" should not take away from his reading a sense that freedom for Martinicans, in Césaire's view, is just around the corner.

Examination of the other Martinican elegies would lead to the same conclusions and would prolong the demonstration needlessly. Keeping in mind the thesis that contemporary Martinican reality required for Césaire a concomitant poetic distancing, it will be useful to take a second look at a poem that I, like previous critics, placed provisionally among the songs of combat. "Out of Foreign Days" is a much simpler poem in its diction and rhythm. The syntax is relatively direct and does not exceed the norm for paratactic construction in twentieth-century poetry. The theme is plainly the liberation of the poet's own (*mon peuple*) from foreign domination. So simple is all of this that it has led one recent commentator to gloss it as a message to "the Martinican people to take cognizance of their situation and to create for themselves a future in which they will no longer be the puppet of tourists or the instruments of wealthy plantation owners" (see note 6). No doubt that is Césaire's sincerest wish. However, it is inaccurate to conclude from this poem alone that "the political message permits no equivocation." Unfortunately equivocation, or at the very least temporization, is precisely what the poem is about. Here are the strophes in question (*Poèmes,* p. 201):

> when
> when therefore will you cease to be the dark plaything
> in the carnival of others
> or in the fields of others
> the antiquated scarecrow
>
> til when tomorrow my people
> the mercenaries in flight
> the holiday finally over
>
> quand
> quand donc cesseras-tu d'être le jouet sombre
> au carnaval des autres
> ou dans les champs d'autrui
> l'épouvantail désuet
>
> demain
> à quand demain mon peuple
> la déroute mercenaire
> finie la fête

The plaintive, questioning *when* recurs like a refrain, establishing a haunting, melancholic tone of lamentation. There is in fact no exhortation in the poem, nor is there a single, unambiguous image to suggest the millennium. Even the discreet symbol of socialism in the line following those quoted—"but the redness of the east with the heart of the *balisier*" ("mais la rougeur de l'est au coeur de balisier")[24]—is plumped down in the middle of the poem, set off from the strophes so that one cannot be at all sure of its revolutionary function. Due attention to the interrogative form of the poem leads one to conclude that Césaire feels obliged to defer into an indefinite future, *mañana*, the day of liberation (p. 202): "tomorrow higher softer broader" ("demain plus haut plus doux plus large"). The combined effect of tone and interrogative construction draws this poem into the orbit of Césaire's Martinican elegies. Its distinguishing feature, its refreshing simplicity, merely permits the poetic voice to distance itself in a different way from the ugliness of the Martinican reality that intrudes only with the utmost discretion.

Early in 1976 Aimé Césaire gave unexpected support to a reading of his poetry that stresses the elegiac result of his lifelong utopian ideal. In his official greeting to L. S. Senghor at the city hall of Fort-de-France on 13 February he attributed to Senghor a concern that I have found to be characteristic of his own later poetry in *Shackles:*

> What have we to do with childhood? What have we to do with the idyll or the elegy?
> The mockers are wrong, for the reconquest of the realm of childhood is not the elegy that they think it is . . .
> Ask the utopians, the believers in the golden age, the madmen of hope . . . It is they whom you find first of all, pioneers of the great upheavals and the great rearrangements of the world.
> Take heed! By establishing a contradiction between the present, on the one hand, and the realm of childhood, on the other, you condemn yourself to looking for a solution which cannot be, despite your sense of moderation, other than *the revolution,* because there is no other transcendence of the contradiction that you sense between existence as it is and the marvelous in life, glimpsed for a moment.[25]

Political revolution is presented as an unacceptable alternative. The revolutionary leap into an uncertain future having once been put aside, the only solution Césaire sees for the contradiction between the marvelous vision of childhood and the ugliness of the real world, a contradiction that is to be negated, avoided, or masked, is the poetic flight to an altitude where the two begin to blend harmoniously. In Aimé Césaire's poetics the last word is elegiac.

Epilogue: Negritude at Forty-Five

THE NEGRITUDE MOVEMENT was conceived in 1934, was born in 1939 after a long gestation, and experienced its youthful triumphs in the forties. The fifties were a period of reflection and searching. For Aimé Césaire the value of the term itself became questionable during the sixties. In mid-1979 he addressed the opening session of the annual convention of the American Association of Teachers of French at Trois-Ilets, Martinique, on "Martinique As She Really Is" ("La Martinique telle qu'elle est"). At no time did he utter the word *negritude,* and the casual listener could conclude that the movement existed entirely in the past. The intellectual coordinates Césaire provided in that speech, however, point toward another conclusion.

Who are the main thinkers and writers considered by Césaire in 1979 to have provided his generation with the building blocks of a Martinican culture? Nietzsche and Adler (for their understanding of European will to power and aggression), Georges Sorel (for his concept of a necessary, dynamic social myth), Spengler, Proudhon, and Bakunin, as well as "the great German ethnographer, who influenced Senghor and myself so deeply, Frobenius."[1] Césaire specifically and carefully noted his opposition to Marx on the fundamental question of the primacy of centralized power and authority. The political position that emerges is a revolutionary radical socialism, with some special Césairean overtones. Césaire posited a basic Martinican or Antillean philosophy that derives largely from Father Placide Tempels's book on Bantu philosophy. The only recent thinker cited by Césaire was André Glucksmann, whose questionable notion of the genetic role of violence in Europe he mentioned approvingly. Against the innately violent nature of European thought Césaire set an idyllic vision of "the black world whose philosophy is founded upon an essential will to integration, to reconciliation, to harmony, that is to say, to a just insertion of man in society and in the cosmos through the operational virtue of justice, on the one hand, and of religion on the other" (p. 185). To my question concerning the central position he continued to ascribe to Frobenius, Spengler, and Nietzsche forty years after the formulation of the ideal of negritude, Césaire replied: "I have remained faithful to certain ideas . . . Without being beholden to any school, I choose within world culture what can help me."[2]

The point of most striking fidelity to his early conception of negritude was made by Césaire in his vision of the future of Martinique and the French West Indies. The special particularism of negritude continues to govern and direct his view of political and social change. Quoting Sorel on the importance of a visionary myth for a given society, Césaire specified that by myth he meant "a dynamic plan, a catalyst for the aspirations of a people, and a prefiguration of the future, precisely because it is capable of mobilizing the emotional energy of the collectivity."[3] The romantic irrationalism of this appeal to collective emotion is patent, and it is constitutive of that quality in his writing that is sometimes called African. Césaire was especially helpful on this sticky issue when he took pains to chart once again its coordinates in modern European thought.

Césaire's speech to the AATF concluded with a remarkable tripartite dialectic of Martinican history, which he divides into three periods representing three myths that in his view stand in dialectical relation to one another: 1635–1848 (the period of slavery), the myth of universal freedom leading to emancipation; 1848–1948 (the period of continued colonialism and racial discrimination), the myth of full citizenship within France leading to the transformation of the colony—he said "the country"—into an overseas department of France; 1948– (an end to neo-colonialism?), the myth of a Martinican Martinique, the vehicle of Martinican nationhood. Césaire's only suggestion as to an effective means for bringing a Martinican Martinique into being was the necessity of a galvanizing and saving collective leap ("un sursaut collectif"), which could inaugurate the new era.

Politically this vision may appear ineffectual or simply mystifying. That would not make it any less significant or relevant, as a glance at the recent history of Quebec should demonstrate. Its implications for Césaire's poetry and poetics are likewise important. His longer poems testify to a tripartite dialectical composition, and many shorter ones develop an element of the dialectic that takes on a fuller meaning with respect to the whole myth or the whole collection. The homology between poetic imagination and social vision is quite remarkable. The galvanizing and saving collective leap that Césaire envisions for his country is the social equivalent of the typically surrealist exploding-fixed poetic closure. It is the immanent, desacralized equivalent of a miraculous event. To the end the political man draws his quality of charismatic leadership from the old arsenal of miraculous weapons.

Notes
Index

Notes

Prologue. Being Black and Being French

1. M. a M. Ngal, *Aimé Césaire: un homme à la recherche d'une patrie* (Dakar-Abidjan: Nouvelles Editions Africaines, 1975), p. 258, note 21. I am indebted to Ngal, whose biographical research is the most extensive to date. I have supplemented or corrected it with material drawn from Maryse Condé, Susan Frutkin, and Thomas A. Hale, whose work is credited in the notes wherever appropriate.

2. Information concerning Césaire's mother's role in this aspect of his upbringing is curiously lacking, although in 1979 she was still living in Fort-de-France. Hale described her to me in conversation (21 March 1980) as a dignified woman who exercises a certain authority on those around her. Her family origins appear to have been simpler than the Césaires', whose aspirations seem to have been the dominant element in the household.

3. V. S. Naipaul, *The Middle Passage* (London: Andre Deutsch, 1962), p. 197.

4. Maryse Condé, *"Cahier d'un retour au pays natal": Césaire, analyse critique* (Paris: Hatier, 1978), p. 6.

5. Susan Frutkin, *Aimé Césaire: Black between Worlds* (Coral Gables, Fla.: Center for Advanced International Studies, University of Miami, 1973), p. 8. The figures are for 1935.

6. "An Interview with Aimé Césaire" in his *Discourse on Colonialism* (New York-London: Monthly Review Press, 1972), p. 69.

7. For the political ramifications of Senghor's version of negritude, see his *Les Fondements de l'africanité ou négritude et arabité* (Paris: Présence Africaine, n.d.), passim. A sympathetic presentation of Senghor's position can be found in Sylvia W. Bâ, "The Future of Negritude: The 'Civilization of the Universal,' " chapter 6 of her *The Concept of Negritude in the Poetry of Léopold Sédar Senghor* (Princeton: Princeton University Press, 1973), especially pp. 176–177.

8. I have adopted the title and the text of the new translation by Clayton Eshleman and Annette Smith, as published in *Montemora*, no. 6 (1979). It is scheduled to replace the Goll-Abel-Snyder translation in the Présence Africaine edition.

9. This anecdote, related by J.-B Barrère to Ngal but not used in his book, was made available to me by Professor Barrère, who kindly supplied a photocopy of his original letter to Ngal. The anecdote dates from the period when the ras, Haile Selassie, was very much in vogue in Europe and the Americas, at the time of the subjugation of Ethiopia by Mussolini.

10. Some doubt has been expressed as to the existence of this edition. There is a copy in the Bibliothèque Nationale in Paris. The *Catalogue général des livres imprimés, 1960–1969,* 1st ser., vol. 4, p. 728 gives a complete bibliographical description.

11. André Breton, "A Great Negro Poet / Un Grand Poète noir," in Aimé Césaire, *Memorandum on My Martinique,* trans. Ivan Goll and Lionel Abel (New York: Brentano's, 1947), unpaginated.

12. Jean-Paul Sartre, "Orphée noir," in *Anthologie de la nouvelle poésie nègre et malgache de langue française,* ed. L. S. Senghor (Paris: Presses Universitaires de France, 1948), p. xiv.

1. Césaire's Negritude in Perspective

1. Quoted in G. R. Coulthard, *Race and Colour in Caribbean Literature* (London: Oxford University Press, 1962), pp. 30–31.

2. The French text is that of the original magazine publication of "Cahier d'un retour au pays natal," *Volontés* (Paris), no. 20 (August 1939), 42. My comments on the 1939 printing have been based on comparison with all subsequent editions of the poem. The English translation is by Clayton Eshleman and Annette Smith, "Notebook of a Return to the Native Land," *Montemora,* no. 6 (1979), 9–37. It is used here with the permission of the translators, *Montemora,* and the copyright holder, Présence Africaine.

3. Coulthard, *Race and Colour,* p. 34.

4. Nicolás Guillén, "Ballad of My Two Grandfathers," trans. and ed. G. R. Coulthard, *Caribbean Literature: An Anthology* (London: University of London Press, 1966), p. 112.

5. Lydia Cabrera, "Contes nègres de Cuba," trans. Francis de Miomandre, *Cahiers du Sud* 21 (1934), 12–22. The three tales were "La Vase de l'Almendares," "Le Cheval d'Hicotea," and "Noguma."

6. "An Interview with Aimé Césaire" can be found in the North American edition of the *Discourse on Colonialism,* published in New York by the Monthly Review Press in 1972. It is one of the most important interviews Césaire has given.

7. Ghislain Gouraige, *La Diaspora d'Haiti et l'Afrique* (Ottawa: Naaman, 1974), p. 75.

8. *Cahier d'un retour au pays natal* (Paris: Bordas, 1947), p. 41. My thanks to Professor Gerard Pigeon, who provided a photocopy of this edition, which has become quite rare. He and T. A. Hale have noted the important differences between this edition and the 1947 bilingual edition published somewhat earlier by Brentano's. See the *Cahiers césairiens,* no. 3 (Spring 1977), 17 n 3.

9. Jacques Roumain, "Sales Nègres," in *La Montagne ensorcelée* (Paris: Editeurs Français Réunis, 1972), pp. 246–247. My translation.

10. Césaire's address on culture and colonization in 1956 testified to a detailed and sympathetic reading of *The Decline of the West:* "Culture et Colonisation" in his *Oeuvres complètes,* vol. 3, *Oeuvre historique et politique* (Fort-de-France: Désormeaux, 1976), p. 442.

11. Cited in Lilyan Kesteloot, *Les Ecrivains noirs de langue française: naissance d'une littérature,* 2nd ed. (Brussels: Université Libre de Bruxelles, 1965), p. 30. Here and elsewhere translations from the French are my own unless otherwise indicated. Kesteloot's pioneering study has been ably translated by Ellen C. Kennedy as *Black Writers in French: A Literary History of Negritude* (Philadelphia: Temple University Press, 1974), p. 20.

12. Arthur P. Davis, *From the Dark Tower* (Washington, D.C.: Howard University Press, 1974), pp. 40, 42.

13. L. S. Senghor, "La Poésie négro-américaine," in *Liberté,* vol. 1, *Négritude et Humanisme* (Paris: Editions du Seuil, 1964), p. 116.

14. Quoted by Robert H. Brisbane, *The Black Vanguard* (Valley Forge, Pa.: Judson Press, 1970), p. 85.

15. Aimé Césaire, "Introduction à la poésie nègre américaine," *Tropiques,* no. 2 (July 1941), 37.

16. Jahnheinz Jahn, *Muntu: An Outline of the New African Culture* (New York: Grove Press, 1961), p. 140.

17. Jahn devotes an interesting chapter of *Muntu* to the concept of the universal force of all life, the "universe of forces," called *Ntu* in the Kinyaruanda tongue (p. 114).

18. Bernard Fonlon, "The Kampala Conference," in *Negritude: Essays and Studies,* ed. Albert H. Berrien and Richard A. Long (Hampton, Va.: Hampton Institute Press, 1967), p. 108.

19. Samuel W. Allen, "Négritude and Its Relevance to the American Negro Writer," in *The American Negro Writer and His Roots* (New York: American Society of African Culture, 1960), p. 20.

20. The four books in question are *Les Noirs de l'Afrique* (Payot, 1922), *L'Ame nègre* (Payot, 1922), *Les Civilisations négro-africaines* (Stock, 1925), and *Les Nègres* (Rieder, 1927), all published in Paris.

21. Maurice Delafosse, *The Negroes of Africa: History and Culture* (Washington, D.C.: Associated Publishers, 1931), p. 217. The American

edition is a collection of essays from Delafosse's several works on black Africa.

22. Delafosse, *The Negroes of Africa*, p. 248.

23. It is probable that Césaire attended the exhibit of African artifacts assembled by Leo Frobenius and displayed at the Musée d'Ethnographie du Trocodéro in November 1933. At that date he may already have read in the *Revue du monde noir*, no. 5, 1932, that Frobenius was a man "free from traditional routine and from prejudice against Africa. . . . Frobenius conjures up Africa from the night of ages, with its past traditions and culture." Two years later he may also have read in the French translation of Emma Cabire two African tales collected by Frobenius (*Cahiers du Sud*, November 1935). At all events, he was certainly primed for the revelation of Frobenius' *Histoire de la civilisation africaine* when it was published in 1936 by Gallimard.

24. "Entretien avec Aimé Césaire," *Tropiques*, 1 (Paris: Place, 1978), ix.

25. Frantz Fanon, "Le Colonisé en question," in *Pour la révolution africaine* (Paris: Maspéro, 1964), p. 31.

26. L. S. Senghor, "The Lessons of Leo Frobenius," in *Leo Frobenius, an Anthology*, ed. E. Haberland (Wiesbaden: Franz Steiner Verlag, 1973), p. vii.

27. "Un Poète politique: Aimé Césaire [propos recueillis par François Beloux]," *Le Magazine littéraire*, no. 34 (November 1969), p. 32.

28. Quoted in M. a M. Ngal's *Aimé Césaire*, p. 186.

29. Aimé Césaire, *Cahier d'un retour au pays natal* in his *Oeuvres complètes*, vol. 1, *Poèmes* (Fort-de-France: Désormeaux, 1976), p. 60. Eshleman-Smith translation, p. 23.

30. Guillaume Apollinaire, *Oeuvres poétiques* (Paris: Gallimard, 1965), p. 44.

31. Arthur Rimbaud, *Oeuvres* (Paris: Aux quais de Paris, [1958]), p. 148.

32. Aimé Césaire, *Les Armes miraculeuses* (Paris: Gallimard, 1946), p. 104.

33. Jonathan Ngaté, " 'Mauvais Sang' de Rimbaud et *Cahier d'un retour au pays natal* de Césaire: la poésie au service de la révolution," *Cahiers césairiens*, no. 3 (Spring 1977), 25–32.

34. Lilyan Kesteloot and Barthélemy Kotchy, *Aimé Césaire, l'homme et l'oeuvre* (Paris: Présence africaine, 1973), p. 231. The interview in *Afrique* was given to Jacqueline Sieger, "Entretien avec Aimé Césaire," *Afrique*, no. 5 (October 1961), 65. It was quoted by M. a M. Ngal in his *Aimé Césaire*, p. 143.

35. Lucien Attoun, "Aimé Césaire et le théâtre nègre," *Le Théâtre*, no. 1 (1970), 111–112.

36. Maryse Condé, "Négritude césairienne, négritude senghorienne," *Revue de littérature comparée* (July-December 1974), 409–419.

37. Stanislas S. K. Adotevi, *Négritude et négrologues* (Paris: Union Générale d'Editions, 1972), pp. 88–89.

38. Roberto Fernández Retamar's *Caliban: notas sobre la cultura de nuestra América* (México: Diógenes, 1971) can be taken as a quasi-official ideological statement, given the author's position as editor-in-chief of the Cuban government-run publishing house, Casa de las Américas.

39. Marta E. Sanchez, "Caliban: The New Latin-American Protagonist of *The Tempest,*" *Diacritics* 6, no. 1 (Spring 1976), 60.

40. See Arvin Murch, *Black Frenchmen, the Political Integration of the French Antilles* (Cambridge, Mass.: Schenkman Publishing Co., 1971), p. 103–105. Although he did not see in Angola and Mozambique the conditions for a split between revolutionary blacks and mulattos, Murch made some illuminating comparisons between the two Portuguese colonies and the French Antilles as regards the relative absence of true nationalism in the French overseas departments. His sociological study would have benefited from a sharper grasp of the foundations and the significance of the negritude movement.

41. The text quoted appeared in a UPI story originating in Christiansted, St. Croix, and printed in newspapers on 11 March 1978. My colleague Alfred MacAdam points out that Sebastianism in nineteenth-century Brazil had millennialist features similar to the Rastafarians'.

2. Césaire and Modernism

1. W. B. Yeats, quoted by Guy Davenport, "Pound and Frobenius," in *Motive and Method in the Cantos of Ezra Pound,* ed. Lewis Leary (New York: Columbia University Press, 1961), p. 35.

2. Armand Hoog, "Malraux, Möllberg, and Frobenius," in *Malraux,* ed. R. W. B. Lewis (Englewood Cliffs, N.J.: Prentice-Hall, 1965), p. 91.

3. Lemuel A. Johnson, *The Devil, the Gargoyle, and the Buffoon: The Negro as Metaphor in Western Literature* (Port Washington, N.Y.: Kennikat Press, 1971), p. 93.

4. Aimé Césaire, "Maintenir la poésie," *Tropiques,* nos. 8–9 (October 1943), 8 (italics mine).

5. Aimé Césaire, "Poésie et Connaissance," in Lilyan Kesteloot and Barthélemy Kotchy, *Aimé Césaire, l'homme et l'oeuvre* (Paris: Présence africaine, 1973), p. 124. I shall refer to this reprinting of the *Tropiques* text since it is readily available. In his use of *connaissance* Césaire does not differentiate among the possible meanings: cognition, understanding (German *Verstand*), or knowledge (usually rendered in French by

savoir). I have therefore been obliged to translate *connaissance* variously depending on the context.

6. Jahnheinz Jahn, *Muntu: An Outline of the New African Culture* (New York: Grove Press, 1961), p. 136.

7. Henri Bergson, cited in *Dictionnaire des idées contemporaines* (Paris: Editions Universitaires, 1966), p. 243.

8. Pierre Mabille, *Le Merveilleux* (Mexico City: Editions Quetzal, 1945), p. 40.

9. Kesteloot and Kotchy, *Aimé Césaire*, p. 21.

10. Letter quoted by Lilyan Kesteloot in her *Les Ecrivains noirs de langue française: naissance d'une littérature*, 2nd ed. (Brussels: Université Libre de Bruxelles, 1965), p. 238. Also in Ellen C. Kennedy, tr., *Black Writers in French: A Literary History of Negritude* (Philadelphia: Temple University Press, 1974), p. 262.

11. Aimé Césaire, "Corps perdu," in *Oeuvres complètes*, vol. 1, *Poèmes* (Fort-de-France: Désormeaux, 1976), p. 278.

12. D. H. Lawrence, *Fantasia of the Unconscious* (New York: A. & C. Boni, 1930), p. 279.

13. L. S. Senghor, "La Poésie négro-américaine," in *Liberté*, vol. 1, *Négritude et Humanisme* (Paris: Editions du Seuil, 1964), p. 115.

14. Aimé Césaire, "Isidore Ducasse comte de Lautréamont," *Tropiques*, nos. 6–7 (February 1943), 13.

15. Sigmund Freud, "Humour," *Collected Papers*, vol. 5 (London: Hogarth Press, 1950), pp. 218–219.

16. Details contained in a letter from J.-B. Barrère to M. a M. Ngal, 21 January 1967, quoted in *Aimé Césaire, un homme à la recherche d'une patrie* (Dakar-Abidjan: Nouvelles Editions Africaines, 1975), p. 199.

17. Aimé Césaire, in a conversation with M. a M. Ngal on 18 April 1967, in Ngal's *Aimé Césaire*, p. 258.

18. Césaire, in the same conversation with Ngal, quoted in *Aimé Césaire*, p. 40.

3. Poetry and Cultural Renewal: *Tropiques*

1. See Michel Leiris, "Le Problème d'une culture spécifiquement antillaise," in his *Contacts de civilisations en Martinique et en Guadeloupe* (Paris: UNESCO / Gallimard, 1955), pp. 106–108. In a satirical vein the brief note by Suzanne Césaire in *Tropiques* for January 1942, "Misère d'une poésie," remains unsurpassed.

2. Frantz Fanon, "Le Colonisé en question," in *Pour la révolution africaine* (Paris: François Maspéro, 1964), p. 31.

3. The use of Creole in Martinique and Guadeloupe has been the

object of strong social disapproval from those groups who have attempted to identify with the dominant white minority. The dynamics of this repression are discussed by Fanon in *Peau noire, masques blancs* (Paris: Seuil, 1952) and in the English translation of Charles L. Markmann, *Black Skin, White Masks* (New York: Grove Press, 1967).

4. "Entretien avec Aimé Césaire," in *Tropiques,* vol. 1 (Paris: J.-M. Place, 1978), pp. x-xiii. Reprint of the original edition, with a minimal critical apparatus; in two volumes.

5. "Entretien avec Aimé Césaire," p. vi.

6. Thomas A. Hale, *Aimé Césaire: His Literary and Political Writings with a Bio-Bibliography* (Ann Arbor: University Microfilms, 1974), pp. 68–69.

7. The sociological study of surrealism that this observation supposes has been only partially and inadequately treated. The reader may refer to the third chapter of Jules Monnerot's *La Poésie moderne et le sacré* (Paris: Gallimard, 1945), entitled "Sur la sociologie du Surréalisme." Also useful is Alfred Sauvy's "Sociologie du surréalisme," in *Le Surréalisme,* ed. Ferdinand Alquié (Paris and The Hague: Mouton, 1968), pp. 486–504.

8. In an eloquent statement defending eighteen Gaudeloupean nationalists being tried in 1968 on a charge of sedition before the Cour de Sûreté de l'Etat français, Césaire specifically upheld the notion of national consciousness. The French text was printed in an anonymously published volume, *Le Procès des Guadeloupéens* (n.p., 1969), pp. 293–301.

9. Is this not the sign of the elective affinity that induced Césaire, in this same issue of *Tropiques,* to publish several poems by Charles Péguy, including thirty strophes of his "Présentation de la Beauce à Notre Dame de Chartres?" In the *Notebook* Césaire's use of very repetitive devices to link the strophes may be a manifestation of the same affinity.

10. The text of *Tropiques* is the only version of "The Thoroughbreds" ("Les Pur-Sang") to give "Jour diurne / nuit nocturne" ("Diurnal day / nocturnal night"), which must be a misprint. The poem at this point calls for the identity of opposites present in "Nocturnal day / diurnal night" ("Jour nocturne / nuit diurne"), the version Césaire has given in all editions of *Miraculous Weapons.*

11. Jean-Paul Sartre, "Orphée noir," in *Anthologie de la nouvelle poésie nègre et malgache,* ed. L. S. Senghor (Paris: Presses Universitaires de France, 1948), p. xliii.

12. *Saisissement,* Frobenius' term in the French translation read by Césaire, can just as well mean "being grasped" as "grasp." It orients us toward the idealist climate of this concept of cultural morphology.

Change is imposed on civilization by a kind of oversoul (Frobenius at one point places *âme, soul,* in apposition to *Païdeuma.* Nonetheless *Tropiques* considered Frobenius to be something of a creative artist. The problematic situation of human freedom in such a scheme appears not to have troubled Césaire's group at this time, perhaps because Frobenius could be made to agree with Ménil's Hegelian and Freudian interpretation of Marx. This unresolved contradiction became an important part of Césaire's concept of myth as he incorporated it in *Miraculous Weapons.*

13. Robert Benayoun, *Erotique du surréalisme* (Paris: J. J. Pauvert, 1965), p. 53.

14. Benayoun, *Erotique du surréalisme,* p. 53. Concerning the relation between Freudian analysis and statements of this type, which are to be found in surrealist documents of all periods, see inter alia J.-L. Houdebine, "D'une lettre en souffrance (Freud / Breton, 1938)," *Promesse,* no. 32 (Spring 1972), 87–96. In brief, the Freud letter expressed his disagreement with the surrealists on the question of the relation between the manifest and latent content of dreams. Freud formally dissociated himself from the project of publishing a "collection of dreams" in which a meaning (archetypal or poetic) might be understood by the reader immediately, without the interpretation or the elaboration of the dream; Freud considered the analytic interpretation to be fundamental. Césaire's letter to Kesteloot, quoted above (chapter 2, note 10), places him solidly in the surrealist tradition of misinterpretation of psychoanalytic thought or, more to the point, in the Jungian rather than the Freudian camp.

15. See Xavière Gauthier, *Surréalisme et Sexualité* (Paris: Gallimard, 1971), p. 208 and passim.

16. Pierre Klossowski, cited by Gauthier, *Surréalisme et Sexualité,* p. 51.

17. Gauthier, *Surréalisme et Sexualité,* p. 190. Gauthier discusses the link between surrealist utopianism and genital sexuality on pages 36–37.

18. For this use of the terms *mode* and *movement* see Paul Ilie, *The Surrealist Mode in Spanish Literature* (Ann Arbor: University of Michigan Press, 1968), especially chapters 1 and 2. According to Ilie, a surrealist mode can be identified in Spanish literature in the absence of any articulate movement. Césaire can be said to have written in a surrealist mode before André Breton drew *Tropiques* into the surrealist movement. From my point of view the sociological position of M. Szabolcsi (note 22 below) is an important complement to Ilie in that it permits a far greater range of discriminations.

19. René Ménil, "Pour une lecture critique de *Tropiques,*" *Tropiques,* vol. 1 of the Place reprint, p. xxxiv.

20. André Masson, superscript text of the third drawing, in André Breton, *Martinique charmeuse de serpents* (Paris: J. J. Pauvert, 1972), p. 127. I quote from the Pauvert reedition, which groups Masson's drawings as back papers.

21. Aimé Césaire, *Les Armes miraculeuses* (Paris: Gallimard, 1946), p. 66.

22. Miklós Szabolcsi, "Avant-garde, Neo-avant-garde, Modernism: Questions and Suggestions," *New Literary History* 3, no. 1 (Autumn 1971), 49–70 and especially 62–63.

23. For a sympathetic treatment of this brand of psychiatry, see Gaston Ferdière, "Surréalisme et aliénation mentale," in *Le Surréalisme,* ed. F. Alquié, pp. 293–323.

24. Frantz Fanon, *Pour la révolution africaine,* p. 36.

25. Ménil, through his participation in *Légitime Défense,* had already contributed to attempts to conciliate Marxism and psychoanalysis during the thirties. The sad fate of such efforts has become a chapter in the history of the radical left both in Europe and in the Americas. From the standpoint of intellectual history the major shifts in the political position of surrealism in the thirties can be considered a part of this much broader social phenomenon.

26. André Breton, "Prolégomènes à un troisième manifeste du surréalisme ou non," in *Manifestes du surréalisme* (Paris: Gallimard, 1963), p. 164.

27. "Un Poète politique: Aimé Césaire," *Le Magazine littéraire,* no. 34 (November 1969), p. 32.

28. Aimé Césaire, "Hommage à Victor Schoelcher," *Tropiques,* no. 13–14 (1945), 230.

4. *Miraculous Weapons*

1. Etiemble, "Aimé Césaire et 'Tropiques,' " *L'Arche* (Algiers) 1, no. 4 (June-July 1944), 137–142.

2. Roger Bastide, "Variations sur la négritude," *Présence africaine,* no. 36 (1961), 16.

3. Lilyan Kesteloot and Barthélemy Kotchy, *Aimé Césaire, l'homme et l'oeuvre* (Paris: Présence africaine, 1973), p. 119.

4. Leo Frobenius, *Histoire de la civilisation africaine* (Paris: Gallimard, 1936), p. 31. My emphasis.

5. Aimé Césaire, "Entretien," *Tropiques,* vol. 1 (reprint 1978), xvii.

6. Harry Levin, "Some Meanings of Myth," in *Myth and Mythmaking,* ed. Henry A. Murray (Boston: Beacon Press, 1960), p. 105.

7. I reserve the form *erotism* for the more clinical, Freudian ap-

proach to sexuality; *eroticism* is used in the text with its usual range of meaning.

8. Aimé Césaire, "Batéké," *Les Armes miraculeuses* (Paris: Gallimard, 1946), p. 34. Citations of the original edition of the collection will be given separate notes. Parenthetical references in the text, except for *Chiens*, are to *Poèmes*, vol. I of Césaire's *Oeuvres complètes* (Fort-de-France: Désormeaux, 1976).

9. Césaire, *Les Armes miraculeuses* (1946), p. 64.

10. Césaire, *Les Armes miraculeuses* (1946), p. 99. Both speeches, the Lover's and the Rebel's, were cut from the definitive edition of 1970. The edition of the *Oeuvres complètes* removed the dramatic poem entirely from *Miraculous Weapons*.

11. The treachery of the "slippery smiles" can be compared to the net used to entrap another king in Aeschylus's *Agamemnon*. But Aeschylus develops his metaphor in such a way that only after the murder does it shift from the figurative to the literal sense: "That he might not escape nor beat aside his death, / as fishermen cast their huge circling nets, I spread / deadly abundance of rich robes, and caught him fast," says Clytaemestra in the translation by Richmond Lattimore in *The Complete Greek Tragedies, Aeschylus,* vol. 1, *Oresteia* (Chicago: University of Chicago Press, 1953), p. 80, ll. 1381–1383.

12. This was the position taken by the late Michel Benamou in his article "Demiurgic Imagery in Césaire's Theatre," *Présence africaine,* no. 93 (1975), 165–177.

13. Interview with Ghislaine de Préville published in *Club des lecteurs d'expression française,* no. 3 (November-December 1964), cited by M. a M. Ngal, *Aimé Césaire: un homme à la recherche d'une patrie* (Dakar-Abidjan: Nouvelles Editions Africaines, 1975), p. 181.

14. Friedrich Nietzsche, *The Birth of Tragedy and the Genealogy of Morals,* trans. Francis Golffing (Garden City: Doubleday, 1956), p. 60.

15. Wole Soyinka, *Myth, Literature and the African World* (Cambridge: Cambridge University Press, 1976), p. 141. Soyinka is professor of comparative literature at the University of Ife, Nigeria, and has been a frequent, vocal critic of negritude.

16. See especially Césaire's irritated reply to Lucien Attoun in his "Aimé Césaire et le théâtre nègre" in *Le Théâtre,* no. 1 (1970), 110–111.

17. Numerous other parallels exist, according to Soyinka, which draw the *Mysteries of Ogun* even closer to the atmosphere of the Mysteries of Eleusis as evoked by Nietzsche: "Dionysos' thyrsus is physically and functionally paralleled by the *opa Ogun* borne by the male devotees of Ogun . . . A long willowy pole, it is topped by a frond-bound lump of ore which strains the pole in wilful curves and keeps it vibrant . . . Through town and village, up the mountain to the

grove of Ogun this dance of the straining phallus-heads pocks the air above men and women revellers who are decked in palm fronds and bear palm branches in their hands . . . Most significant of all is the brotherhood of the palm and ivy. The mystery of the wine of the palm, bled straight from the tree and potent without further ministration, is a miracle of nature acquiring symbolic significance in the Mysteries of Ogun" (pp. 158–159). But none of these parallels are to be found in "And the Dogs Were Silent," which indicates something of the degree of selectivity Césaire used in adapting *The Birth of Tragedy* to his own ends.

18. For the relationship of Camus's play to the Nietzschean theory of tragedy see A. J. Arnold, "Camus' Dionysian Hero: 'Caligula' in 1938," *South Atlantic Bulletin* 38, no. 4 (November 1973), 45–53.

19. André Breton, *L'Amour fou* (Paris: Gallimard, 1937), p. 21.

20. Michel Benamou, "Entretien avec Aimé Césaire, Fort-de-France le 14 février 1973," *Cahiers césairiens*, no. 1 (Spring 1974), 5.

21. Aimé Césaire, "Liminaire," *Présence africaine*, no. 57 (1966), 3.

22. Roger Bastide, *Les Amériques noires* (Paris: Payot, 1967), p. 97. The Luso-Brazilian word *batuque* is also taken metonymically in Rio Grande do Sul, Brazil, to designate the Afro-Brazilian macumba sect, according to Serge Bramly in *Macumba, The Teachings of Maria-José, Mother of the Gods* (New York: Avon Books, 1979), p. 222. This usage is in keeping with the ecstatic state that Césaire's poem seeks to provoke rhythmically.

23. Bernadette A. M. Cailler, *Proposition poétique: une lecture de l'oeuvre d'Aimé Césaire* (Sherbrooke, Quebec: Naaman, 1976), p. 73.

24. G[eorges]-E[mmanuel] Clancier, "Orphée métis," *Cahiers du Sud,* nos. 378–379 (1964), 108.

25. Michael Riffaterre, "Semantic Incompatibilities in Automatic Writing," *About French Poetry from Dada to "Tel Quel," Text and Theory,* ed. Mary Ann Caws (Detroit: Wayne State University Press, 1974), p. 224.

5. The Epic of Negritude

1. Aimé Césaire, "Isidore Ducasse comte de Lautréamont," *Tropiques,* no. 6–7 (February 1943), 10.

2. Aimé Césaire, *Cahier d'un retour au pays natal* (Paris: Présence Africaine, 1971), p. 29. The English translation of *Notebook of a Return to the Native Land* used throughout is by Clayton Eshleman and Annette Smith, published in *Montemora,* no. 6 (1979), 9–37. It will eventually replace the Abel-Goll-Snyder translation in the next Présence

Africaine bilingual edition. Parenthetical page references are to the French text of the current bilingual edition. On those few occasions where I do not follow the *Montemora* version of Eshleman and Smith, brackets identify my substitutions.

3. Lautréamont, "Hymne au poulpe," *Tropiques,* no. 6–7, quoted by Césaire, p. 16; my English translation, as are all those not otherwise identified.

4. Lautréamont, "Hymne au pou," *Tropiques,* no. 6–7, 17.

5. The best biographical approach to this style is in Thomas A. Hale, "Structural Dynamics in a Third World Classic: Aimé Césaire's *Cahier d'un retour au pays natal,*" *Yale French Studies,* no. 53 (1976), 163–174.

6. St.-John Perse, *Eloges and Other Poems,* trans. Louise Varèse (New York: Pantheon, 1965), pp. 6–7. On the subject of their respective relations to Caribbean society, see "Saint-John Perse et Aimé Césaire" in Emile Yoyo's *Saint-John Perse et le conteur* (Paris: Bordas, 1971), pp. 71–84.

7. Perse, *Eloges,* pp. 10–13. The word *joy* was omitted in the Varèse translation.

8. Arthur Rimbaud, "Une Saison en enfer," in *Oeuvres* (Paris: Aux quais de Paris, 1958), p. 143.

9. See Anna Balakian, *The Literary Origins of Surrealism* (New York: New York University Press [1965]), especially chapter 4 on Lautréamont and Rimbaud.

10. Fyodor Dostoyevsky, *Letters from the Underworld,* trans C. J. Hogarth (London: J. M. Dent, 1957), pp. 38, 40.

11. Jahnheinz Jahn, *Muntu: An Outline of the New African Culture* (New York: Grove Press, 1961), p. 144.

12. Michel Benamou, "Sémiotique du *Cahier d'un retour au pays natal,*" *Cahiers césairiens,* no. 2 (Autumn 1975), 5.

13. Bernard Zadi Zaourou, *Césaire entre deux cultures* (Abidjan-Dakar: Nouvelles Editions Africaines, 1978), pp. 223–224. Like Jahn, Zadi Zaourou depreciates in the extreme the importance for Césaire of the European tradition, and specifically of surrealism.

14. André Breton and Paul Eluard, "Essai de simulation de la démence précoce," in Eluard, *Oeuvres complètes,* vol. 1 (Paris: Gallimard, 1968), p. 332. The notes to this Pléiade edition specify that the text cited was entirely the responsibility of Breton.

15. Man Ray and Paul Eluard, "Les Tours d'Eliane," in Eluard's *Oeuvres complètes,* vol. 1, pp. 654–655.

16. For a more detailed analysis of this question see my *"Cahier d'un retour au pays natal:* Reflections on the Translations into English," *Cahiers césairiens,* no. 3 (Spring 1977), 33–41.

17. Thomas A. Hale, *Aimé Césaire: His Literary and Political Writ-*

ings with a Bio-Bibliography (Ann Arbor: University Microfilms, 1974), p. 27.

18. At this point one must renounce attempts to translate *nègre* in "bon nègre" and "mauvais nègre" by an identical term in English. Césaire, Senghor, Damas, and their followers have successfully given a positive connotation to *nègre* in French. It is doubtful that a similar promotion awaits *nigger* in the English-speaking world at large. However, in the idiom of black Americans, "He's a bad nigger" comes remarkably close. Eshleman and Smith have captured this Afro-American flavor in their translation of "mes danses de mauvais nègre" as "you bad nigger dances!" (*Notebook*, p. 153).

19. The Eshleman-Smith translation ("in my firm embrace") in *Montemora* follows the French text used through the 1947 editions of the *Cahier*. In the 1956 and 1971 Présence Africaine editions a different reading of the last word appeared: *embrasement* ("conflagration") is consistent with the volcanic nature of the imagery and with the exploding-fixed metaphors that Césaire employed extensively in the late forties and early fifties. "In my firm conflagration" corresponds neatly to the final image of the poem, "in its motionless veerition" (its "magnificent seized swirl," in the Penguin edition).

20. This is the position taken by Bernadette A. M. Cailler in her *Proposition poétique: une lecture de l'oeuvre d'Aimé Césaire* (Sherbrooke, Quebec: Naaman, 1976), pp. 58–59.

21. Compare Cailler, *Proposition poétique*, pp. 61–63.

22. Samuel Ngugi, "Césaire's 'Return to My Native Land'," in *Standpoints on African Literature, A Critical Anthology*, ed. Chris L. Wanjala (Nairobi-Kampala-Dar-es-Salaam: East African Literature Bureau, 1973), p. 371.

6. Politics and Poetics

1. Aimé Césaire, *Lettre à Maurice Thorez* (Paris: Présence Africaine, 1956), pp. 14–15. The letter was not, as some commentators have alleged, a reaction to the Soviet Union's invasion of Hungary. The Hungarian uprising was in its early days when Césaire's letter first appeared, excerpted in *France-Observateur*, on 25 October. Hungarian Premier Hegedüs had called for Soviet intervention on 23 October; Césaire's letter is dated the 24th.

2. Marcien Towa, "Aimé Césaire, prophète de la révolution des peuples noirs," *Abbia* (Yaoundé, Cameroon), no. 21 (1969), 49.

3. "Césaire's revolt is not a simple intellectual revolt, still less a metaphysical one; but a political revolt that must result in the effective liberation of colonized people . . . Thus the colonization of which he

speaks takes in the Antilles as well as Asia and Africa . . . Henceforth transcending their narrow particularism, Antilleans and Africans are forging the same mystique and elaborating the soul of Negritude." B. Kotchy-N'Guessan, "Césaire et la colonisation," *Université d'Abidjan, Annales,* Série D: Lettres 5 (1972), 193.

4. Quoted by Thomas A. Hale in his *Les Ecrits d'Aimé Césaire, bibliographie commentée,* a special issue of *Etudes littéraires* (Montréal) 14, no. 3–4 (October 1978), 262 (my translation).

5. But one of the party's leading intellectuals, Roger Garaudy, did criticize the "negative" influence of surrealism on Césaire in his review of *Les Armes miraculeuses,* published in the communist daily *L'Humanité* on 24 August 1946.

6. See Hale, *Les Ecrits d'Aimé Césaire,* pp. 266–270.

7. Césaire's "Commémoration du Centenaire de l'abolition de l'esclavage" was delivered at the Sorbonne on 27 April; G. Monnerville and L. S. Senghor spoke on the same occasion. Césaire's speech is included in his *Oeuvre historique et politique,* third and final volume of the *Oeuvres complètes* (Fort-de-France—Paris: Désormeaux, 1976), pp. 403–415.

8. *Discours sur le colonialisme,* in *Oeuvre historique et politique,* p. 359. My translation.

9. Présence Africaine published an English-language version of Placide Tempels's *Bantu Philosophy* in 1959. The first edition in French dates from the forties and was published in the then Belgian Congo.

10. The allusion in the *Discourse* to Jaspers is particularly oblique and untranslatable—"intellectuels jaspineux"—who, along with other enemies of the people, have "emerged stinking from the flank of Nietzsche," (p. 379).

11. In "Culture et Colonisation," *Oeuvre historique et politique,* p. 451.

12. Mazisi Kunene, "Introduction," *Return to My Native Land* by Aimé Césaire, trans. John Berger and Anna Bostock (Harmondsworth, England: Penguin Books, 1969), p. 22.

13. Lilyan Kesteloot, "Entretien avec Césaire," in her *Aimé Césaire l'homme et l'oeuvre* with B. Kotchy (Paris: Présence Africaine, 1973), p. 228.

14. René Depestre in *Présence Africaine* (n.s.), no. 4 (October-November 1955), 36. Reprinted from *Les Lettres françaises,* no. 573, for 16–23 June 1955.

15. Aimé Césaire, "Réponse à Depestre poète haïtien (Eléments d'un art poétique)," *Présence Africaine* (n.s.), no. 1–2 (April-July 1955), 113. The poem has been reprinted twice with different titles and two different texts: as "Lettre brésilienne" in Kesteloot and Kotchy, *Aimé Césaire,*

l'homme et l'oeuvre, pp. 109–111, and as "Le Verbe marronner" in *Noria,* the last section of *Poèmes,* vol. I of Césaire's *Oeuvres complètes* (Fort-de-France: Désormeaux, 1976), pp. 299–301. The line naming Aragon was retained in the version given Kesteloot and Kotchy but was dropped from the *Oeuvres complètes.* The subtitle was dropped from both versions.

16. René Depestre, "Réponse à Aimé Césaire (Introduction à un art poétique haïtien)," *Présence Africaine* (n.s.), no. 4 (October-November 1955), 45.

17. See Miklós Szabolcsi, "Avant-garde, Neo-avant garde, Modernism: Questions and Suggestions," *New Literary History* 3, no. 1 (Autumn 1971), 67–70. Szabolcsi describes the *Tel Quel* group while himself remaining well within the bounds of Marxist orthodoxy. Compare Fredric Jameson's reading of Wayne C. Booth's *Rhetoric of Fiction,* in *Marxism and Form* (Princeton: Princeton University Press, 1971), pp. 355–359. Jameson's position can be gauged by his observation that "It is very often precisely from a relatively old-fashioned, anticontemporary, even reactionary viewpoint (see Yvor Winters and, indeed, Edmund Burke himself) that the most penetrating analyses of the actual are made" (*Marxism and Form,* p. 199).

18. *Le Ier Congrès international des écrivains et artistes noirs. Présence Africaine.* No. spécial 8–9–10 (June-November 1956). A short resume in English of the contributions of Richard Wright, John A. Davis, Davidson Nicol, and Colin Legum, as well as an interpretation of "Culture and Colonization," can be found in the short monograph by Susan Frutkin, *Aimé Césaire, Black between Worlds* (Miami: Center for Advanced International Studies, University of Miami, 1973), pp. 32–34.

19. Aimé Césaire, "Culture et Colonisation," *Oeuvre historique et politique,* p. 435.

20. J[ohn] A. Davis in the special number of *Présence Africaine* for June-November 1956, p. 214.

21. For Senghor's position at the same date see the excellent study by J. L. Hymans, *Léopold Sédar Senghor: an intellectual biography* (Edinburgh: for the University Press, 1971), chapter 27, pp. 153–154. As regards Césaire, however, it was no longer true in 1956 that in Hymans's words, "For those who formulated *négritude,* the cultural awakening was an end in itself" (p. 154).

7. Beheaded Sun

1. Jacqueline Sieger, "Entretien avec Aimé Césaire," *Afrique,* no. 5 (October 1961), 65.

2. André Breton, "AUTOMATIQUE (écriture)," *Dictionnaire abrégé du surréalisme,* in Paul Eluard, *Oeuvres complètes,* vol. I (Paris: Gallimard, 1968), p. 725.

3. Michael Riffaterre, "Semantic Incompatibilities in Automatic Writing," in *About French Poetry from Dada to "Tel Quel," Text and Theory,* ed. Mary Ann Caws (Detroit: Wayne State University Press, 1974), p. 225.

4. Laurent Jenny, "La Surréalité et ses signes narratifs," *Poétique,* no. 16 (1973), 499–520.

5. Aimé Césaire, "Le Coup de couteau du soleil dans le dos des villes surprises," *Soleil cou-coupé* (1948; rpt. Nendeln, Liechtenstein: Kraus Reprint, 1970), pp. 31–32.

6. In fact several traditions seem to exist independently of one another. A. Métraux published a religious image of St. James the Great that was identified with Ogun in Haiti. S. Bramly relates that in the macumba cult he studied in Brazil, St. George serves the same function. And Césaire himself in the poem "Lettre de Bahia-de-tous-les-saints" assimilated Ogun to St. George. See *Noria* in *Oeuvres complètes,* vol. I (Fort-de-France: Désormeaux, 1976), p. 294.

7. Bernadette A. M. Cailler, *Proposition poétique: une lecture de l'oeuvre d'Aimé Césaire* (Sherbrooke, Quebec: Naaman, 1976), p. 62.

8. Aimé Césaire, "Tornado," *Cadastre,* tr. Emile Snyder and Sanford Upson (New York: The Third Press, 1973), p. 36. The lines within brackets were not retained in *Cadastre;* they are given in my own translation. The French text is quoted in the Kraus Reprint edition (see n.5 above), p. 48.

9. Hannah Arendt, "The Poet Bertolt Brecht," in *Brecht, a Collection of Critical Essays,* ed. Peter Demetz (Englewood Cliffs, N.J.: Prentice-Hall, 1962), p. 45.

10. Aimé Césaire, "Lynch I" *Soleil cou-coupé,* Kraus Reprint, p. 9.

11. The French text reads "une entrée en matière," which would ordinarily be translated as "an introduction." The context requires a literal translation.

12. Michel Benamou located the castration complex as central to the agonistic tragedy of *And the Dogs Were Silent,* adding that the title *Soleil cou coupé (Beheaded Sun)* should be read in the same light. See his article, "Demiurgic Imagery in Césaire's Theatre," *Présence africaine,* no. 93 (1975), 168. My reading of "The Sun's Knife-Stab" confirms and extends Benamou's suggestion.

13. Bruno Jobin reached similar conclusions concerning Césaire's posture of self-sacrifice and mutilation in his article " 'Cadastre', lecture transcendante," *Etudes littéraires* 6, no. 1 (April 1973), 73–80. Our approaches are complementary in that Jobin treated a thematic com-

plex throughout the text of *Cadastre,* whereas I have sought to elucidate the function of the same elements within individual poems.

14. Bernadette Cailler, *Proposition poétique,* p. 118. See also Keith Walker, "Pour un bestiaire de Césaire," chapter 4 of his *La Cohésion poétique de l'oeuvre césairienne* (Tübingen-Paris: G. Narr-J.-M. Place, 1979), pp. 97–118.

15. Aimé Césaire, "Prophétie," *Les Armes miraculeuses* (Paris: Gallimard, 1970), p. 36. Also in *Poésie,* vol. I of his *Oeuvres complètes,* pp. 106–107.

16. M. a M. Ngal, *Aimé Césaire: un homme à la recherche d'une patrie* (Dakar-Abidjan: Nouvelles Editions Africaines, 1975), pp. 182–183.

17. Francis Huxley, *The Invisibles—Voodoo Gods in Haiti* (New York: McGraw-Hill, 1966), p. 239.

18. The word *Guinée* in Martinican Creole serves also to designate African varieties of plants. This usage is evident in the fourth line of the passage quoted from "Ode to Guinea."

19. See Alfred Métraux, *Le Vaudou haïtien* (Paris: Gallimard, 1958), pp. 88–89, 319; and Serge Bramly, *Macumba* (New York: Avon, 1979), pp. 203–210.

8. *Lost Body*

1. Other artistic details concerning the production of this boxed volume are as follows: thirty-five folios in quarto; typography ("Erasme Corps 20") by Pierre Bouchet; engravings printed by Roger Lacourière; a "tête de nègre" frontispiece; an engraving on the title page of each poem, frequently enclosing the printed title. The spine of the box reads "Editions Fragrance / Paris—1949[.]" This error in dating accounts for the occasional reference to *Corps perdu* as dating from 1949, although the *achevé d'imprimer* was 3 June 1950. One of Picasso's thirty-two engravings was executed as a watermark in handmade Montval paper. The two copies I consulted are in the Spencer Collection of the New York Public Library and in the Houghton Library of Harvard University.

2. Emile Snyder, "Introduction," *Cadastre: poems* [by] Aimé Césaire, trans. Emile Snyder and Sanford Upson (New York: The Third Press, 1973), pp. xi–xviii. Every other text—prose or poetry—mentioned in the introduction is dated. *Beheaded Sun* and *Disembodied* (Snyder and Upson's translation of *Corps perdu)* are not mentioned as individual collections. Nor do readers of the collection in English have any way of knowing that the poem "Longitude" was dropped from the

later edition of *Corps perdu* in *Cadastre*. The collection was kept at ten poems by the division of one poem into two, a process Césaire has employed elsewhere as well. The original text of "Présence" was divided so as to furnish the single strophe entitled "Présence" since 1961 and the longer poem entitled "Who Then, Who Then" ("Qui donc, qui donc"). A strophe of eleven lines in the original text of "Présence" was dropped entirely.

The reliability of the text of the *Cadastre* edition has been called into question by the publication in 1976 of the collected *Poèmes* in the *Oeuvres complètes*. A comparison of the editions of 1950, 1961, and 1976 shows that in *Cadastre* an uncharacteristic use of punctuation occurs in some poems of *Lost Body*. Unlike the editions of 1950 or 1976, in the text of *Cadastre* there is a proliferation of commas both within and at the ends of lines in "Your Portrait" ("Ton Portrait") and "Origins" ("Naissances"). In "Lost Body" the anomalous punctuation consists of the introduction of periods and of capital letters following them. In "Origins" the presentation of the text is so patently absurd—in the first strophe five one-word lines in succession end with commas—that one must entertain the hypothesis that Césaire did not review the proofs prior to publication. (The reader of English can gauge the results visually in the bilingual Third Press edition of *Cadastre*, which carefully follows the 1961 Paris edition.) In the text established for the *Oeuvres complètes* these peculiarities disappear. In the case of "Your Portrait" and "Origins" the improvement is immediately visible. Lines have been laid out in such a way as to suggest a scansion dependent on rhythmic and interpretive units rather than narrowly conceived grammatical units. In poetry of this type the punctuation one encounters exceptionally in *Cadastre* is distracting and potentially troublesome.

In all other respects the text of the 1961 edition was closer to being definitive than that of *Miraculous Weapons* in 1970. The only substantive change in the text of *Lost Body* between 1961 and 1976 can be found in the poem "Ahead of the Pack" ("De forlonge"), where one word has been changed (*ah* to *han*) in two instances for phonemic and visual consistency. Otherwise modifications of lines have been made for a better strophic division or simply to improve scansion of the text.

Quotation of the Snyder-Upson translation, occasionally with bracketed modifications, is indicated in the notes. All other translations are my own, with reference made to the *Poèmes*, vol. 1 of his *Oeuvres complètes* (Fort-de-France: Désormeaux, 1976).

3. In the *Oeuvres complètes* edition of 1976 *Corps perdu* had as its first poem "Jugement de la lumière," which had previously been the last poem of *Soleil cou coupé*. The fact that only the title page of *Corps*

perdu separated the two poems leads me to suspect an error in the composition of the volume of *Poèmes*.

4. The translation is from Snyder-Upson, p. 100, the French from *Poèmes*, p. 268.

5. M. a M. Ngal, *Aimé Césaire: un homme à la recherche d'une patrie* (Dakar-Abidjan: Nouvelles Editions Africaines, 1975), p. 126.

6. Stanley Burnshaw, "The Body Makes the Minde," *The Seamless Web* (New York: George Braziller, 1970), pp. 10–46. See also Roger Shattuck, "How to Rescue Literature," *The New York Review of Books* 27, no. 6 (April 17, 1980), especially 31–35.

.7. Snyder-Upson translation, p. 100. The term *throb* unfortunately has nothing of the suggestive onomatopoeia of *vibre* in the original. It can be preferred to the heavier English equivalent *vibrate* for rhythmic purposes only.

8. Graham Dunstan Martin, trans. and ed., Paul Valéry, *Le Cimetière marin* (Austin: University of Texas Press, 1971), p. 58.

9. Aimé Césaire, "L'Homme de culture et ses responsabilités," *Présence africaine*, numéro spécial: *IIe Congrès des écrivains et artistes noirs (Rome: 26 mars-1er avril 1959)*, vol. I, *L'Unité des cultures négroafricaines*, no. 24–25 (February–May 1959), 121.

10. Jacqueline Sieger, "Entretien avec Aimé Césaire," *Afrique*, no. 5 (October 1961), 66. My emphasis.

11. Lilyan Kesteloot, quoted by Jahnheinz Jahn in *Neo-African Literature* (New York: Grove Press, 1968), p. 263.

12. Ezekiel Mphahlele, in Jahn, *Neo-African Literature*, p. 263. The quotation is from Jahn's personal tape recording of Mphahlele's comments.

13. Yvan Labejof, "Autour d'une mise en scène de 'Et les chiens se taisaient,' " in Lilyan Kesteloot and Barthélemy Kotchy, *Aimé Césaire, l'homme et l'oeuvre* (Paris: Présence africaine, 1973), p. 154.

14. In 1950 it occupied the fifth position, after "Mot," "Présence," "Longitude," "Elégie-Equation." In 1961 "De forlonge," previously entitled "Au large," was placed ahead of "Corps perdu." In 1976 the only modification of this order was the surprising appearance of "Jugement de la lumière" at the beginning of the collection.

15. I follow the text of the *Oeuvres complètes*, vol. 1, *Poèmes*, pp. 277–278, for the numbering of lines. In *Cadastre* the seventh line ran too far into the right-hand margin and the last word, *cannibale*, was carried over to the next line. Formally, however, it is evident that this is not to be taken as a separate line. Between lines 12 and 13 the *Oeuvres complètes* edition includes the single word *sale* where *Cadastre* had *point sale*. In neither case does this constitute a separate line for the same reason given above.

16. Pierre Guiraud, *Langage et Versification d'après l'oeuvre de Paul Valéry* (Paris: Klincksieck, 1953), especially chapters 3 and 4. The International Phonetic Alphabet symbols have been used in the text for phonetic transcription.

17. Léandre Bergeron, *Le Son et le sens dans quelques poèmes de Paul Valéry* (Aix-en-Provence: Editions Ophrys, 1964), p. 17. Bergeron is somewhat more ready to assign a range of expressive values to individual sounds than is Guiraud, but his research is also based on more physical evidence. A companion volume to this study presents the acoustical charts realized from readings of three poems in Valéry's collection *Charmes*. It would be extremely useful to have corresponding data for some of Césaire's poems, preferably poems of different types.

18. Kesteloot and Kotchy, *Aimé Césaire*, p. 21.

19. Keith Louis Walker, *La Cohésion poétique de l'oeuvre césairienne* (Tübingen: Gunter Narr; Paris: J.-M. Place, 1979), p. 68.

20. Aliko Songolo, "Césaire's Surrealism and the Quest for Africa," *Ba Shiru* (Fall 1976), 35, 36. Songolo has coined the neologism *phenicism* to cover all the avatars of heroic death and rebirth in Césaire's work.

21. "Dit d'errance," in *Oeuvres complètes,* vol. I, p. 285. All references to poems in this chapter are to this edition unless otherwise indicated. English version in Snyder-Upson edition, p. 134.

22. In preparing the scansion of this poem I have counted the mute *e* as a syllable where it reinforces a metrical pattern that already exists in the strophe. In all other cases I do not count it, following most modern French usage in this regard. The plus sign after the figure numbering the syllables in a measure indicates that, while the measure (and the line) approximates the norm for a regular octosyllabic, decasyllabic, or alexandrine line, it does not strictly respect that norm. There is admittedly some interpretation involved even in the question of scanning Césaire's poems. Compare Césaire's use of a percussive rhythm in a text dealing with mutilation and dispossession in *A Season in the Congo,* I, 6 (trans. Ralph Manheim for Grove Press, 1968, p. 19):

Moi, sire, je pense aux oubliés.

Nous sommes ceux que l'on déposséda, que l'on frappa,

que l'on mutila; ceux que l'on tutoyait, ceux à qui l'on

crachait au visage. Boys cuisine, boys-chambres, boys,

comme vous dites, lavadères, nous fûmes un peuple de boys . . .

> As for me, Sire, my thoughts are for those who have been
> forgotten.
> We are the people who have been dispossessed, beaten,
> mutilated; the people whom the conquerors treated as inferiors,
> in whose faces they spat. A people of kitchen boys, house boys,
> laundry boys, in short, a people of boys. . . .

This is one of the texts performed by Yvan Labejof on 29 June 1979 in
Trois Ilets, Martinique. It is quite remarkable for the concentration of
stressed syllables, which in the fourth line cited intensify to an unrelieved pitch, an emotional outpouring of resentment. The use of rhythm
in this dramatic scene is entirely different from what Césaire was doing
in the poem "Song of Wandering" ("Dit d'errance").

23. Compare Césaire's query "et pourtant que te reste-t-il du temps
ancien" with Apollinaire's declaration in "Zone"—"A la fin tu es las
de ce monde ancien"—or again, in his "Le Pont Mirabeau," the admirable "Faut-il qu'il m'en souvienne . . ."

9. The Three Voices of *Shackles*

1. In the publicity statement printed on the back cover of the original
edition Césaire wrote—or otherwise provided the editors with information—as follows: "These poems were written at times sufficiently far
apart for their symbols, welling up day by day, to reveal several geo-
logical strata of the same man." Aimé Césaire, *Ferrements* (Paris: Seuil,
1960), back cover. References in the text are to *Poèmes*, vol. 1 of
Oeuvres complètes (Fort-de-France: Désormeaux, 1976).

2. Lilyan Kesteloot, "Première Lecture de quelques poèmes," in L.
Kesteloot and Barthélemy Kotchy, *Aimé Césaire, l'homme et l'oeuvre*
(Paris: Présence africaine, 1973), pp. 58–59. Whereas Kesteloot merely
provides the narrative sequence of the Afro-Antillean tale, Bernadette
Cailler, in her *Proposition poétique: une lecture de l'oeuvre d'Aimé Césaire* (Sherbrooke, Quebec: Naaman, 1976), pp. 87–89, gives a concise
but sensitive analysis of the poem, including indications of rhythmic,
phonemic, syntactic, and intertextual structures. It is among the best
analyses in her book.

3. Aimé Césaire did not undertake to collect Creole tales in Martinique himself. But his daughter Ina is a Creole linguist and folklorist;
see Joëlle Laurent and Ina Césaire, trans. and eds., *Contes de mort et de
vie aux Antilles* (Paris: Nubia, 1976), and Ina Césaire, "L'idéologie de la
débrouillardise dans les contes antillais," *Espace Créole*, no. 3 (1978),
41–48. Césaire has not participated directly in manifestations of popular culture in Martinique, but his son Jean Paul is currently the guiding

spirit behind a promising municipal arts program in Fort-de-France, which presented a stunning folkloric ballet during the AATF meeting in June 1979. The divergent orientation of the two generations could scarcely be more graphically demonstrated than by the examples within Aimé Césaire's own family.

4. The next poem in the collection, "Perseus Multiplying Myself a Hundredfold" ("Me centuplant Persée"), reiterates the same structures, this time centering on another mythological hero, Perseus, slayer of the Gorgon.

5. Aeschylus, "Prometheus Bound," trans. David Grene, in *Aeschylus I* (New York: Modern Library, 1942), pp. 242–243.

6. Aliko Songolo, "*Cadastre* et *Ferrements* de Césaire: une nouvelle poétique pour une nouvelle politique," *L'Esprit Créateur* 17, no. 2 (Summer 1977), 154.

7. See chapter 7, the section entitled "To Africa."

8. Lilyan Kesteloot, *Aimé Césaire* (Paris: Seghers, 1962), p. 93.

9. Henri Brunschwig, *L'Avènement de l'Afrique noire du XIXe siècle à nos jours* (Paris: A. Colin, 1963), p. 195.

10. The poems in question are: "Salut à la Guinée," "Le Temps de la liberté," "Afrique," "Pour saluer le Tiers Monde," "Indivisible," and "Petite Chanson pour traverser une grande rivière," which I interpret as belonging to songs of combat and of praise; and "Statue de Lafcadio Hearn," "Tombeau de Paul Eluard," "Mémorial de Louis Delgrès," "A la mémoire d'un syndicaliste noir," "Sur l'état de l'Union," and "En vérité," all of which belong to a third voice. "Hors des jours étrangers" provides a good test of the importance of the elegiac voice in *Shackles*.

11. Jacqueline Sieger, "Entretien avec Aimé Césaire," *Afrique*, no. 5 (October 1961), 65.

12. Aimé Césaire, "La Pensée politique de Sékou Touré," *Présence Africaine*, no. 29 (December 1959–January 1960), 71–72.

13. "Salut à la Guinée," in *Poèmes*, p. 147. One aspect of the geography is somewhat fanciful. The sea is addressed as "You[,] gulf," which would be fine except that the Gulf of Guinea is hundreds of miles to the south and east of the Republic of Guinea, which juts into the Atlantic on Africa's westernmost coast.

14. I use the term *epic theater* advisedly for, although there are parallels to be made with Brechtian techniques, especially in *A Season in the Congo*, Césaire's theater differs markedly from Brecht's in many respects.

15. In June 1979 Césaire announced that he was preparing a new play. Volume 2 of *Modernism and Negritude: the Theater of Aimé Césaire*, currently in progress, will incorporate any new work for the theater.

16. A. James Arnold, "Césaire and Shakespeare: Two Tempests," *Comparative Literature* 30, no. 3 (Summer 1978), 236–248.

17. Aimé Césaire, *Une Tempête (d'après "La Tempête" de Shakespeare): adaptation pour un théâtre nègre* (Paris: Seuil, 1969), p. 87.

18. Frederick Ivor Case, "Le Théâtre d'Aimé Césaire," *La Revue romane* 10, no. 1 (1975), 15.

19. Georges [M. a M.] Ngal, "Le Théâtre d'Aimé Césaire, une dramaturgie de la décolonisation," *Revue des Sciences humaines* (n.s.) no. 140 (October-December 1970), 636.

20. In the same collection the title "Elegy" (originally "Elégie-Equation") is applied ironically to a poem that combines the surrealist epiphany with an eschatological vision. Despite the title it falls outside consideration of Césaire's elegiac voice.

21. Aimé Césaire, *Toussaint Louverture: la Révolution française et le problème colonial,* 2nd ed. (Paris: Présence Africaine, 1962), pp. 290–293.

22. *Poèmes,* p. 194. The translation is meant to be literal and to indicate only the syntactic convolution of the *que . . . ne* constructions.

23. Thomas A. Hale, *Aimé Césaire: His Literary and Political Writings with a Bio-Bibliography* (Ann Arbor: University Microfilms, 1974), pp. 115–116.

24. The *balisier* is a bananalike tree that is significant in Césaire's imagery. In 1958 he took its red flower, its "heart," as the symbol of his own political party. This poem, however, appears to have been written before Césaire's break with the communists.

25. Aimé Césaire, "Discours prononcé en l'honneur de la visite de L. S. Senghor," *Oeuvre historique et politique,* vol. III of *Oeuvres complètes,* p. 543.

Epilogue. Negritude at Forty-Five

1. Aimé Césaire, "La Martinique telle qu'elle est," from the tape recording graciously provided to me by Mrs. Emma D. McNairy of Clearwater, Florida. The French text as Césaire delivered it on 25 June 1979 read, at this point, "le grand ethnographe allemand, qui a tellement influencé Senghor et moi, Frobenius . . ." In the published text of the address Césaire's avowal of Frobenius' influence disappeared and he became "the great German ethnologist and philosopher Frobenius . . ." See *The French Review* 53, no. 2 (December 1979), 185.

2. Césaire's reply as I transcribed it in my notes at the convention. J. L. Dupres gave a different version in his article "Conférence d'Aimé Césaire au congrès francophone d'Amérique," part 2, *France-Antilles* (Fort-de-France), (28 juin 1979), p. 3: "We came in contact with various

philosophies. In the end we must take our bearings and make judgments . . . One has to choose that part of world culture that conforms to Martinican reality."

3. "Un schéma dynamique, catalyseur des aspirations d'un peuple et préfigurateur de l'avenir, précisément parce que susceptible de mobiliser l'énergie émotionnelle de la collectivité," in *French Review* (December 1979), p. 187.

Index